LEA'S COMMUNICATION SERIES
Jennings Bryant/Dolf Zillmann, General Editors

Selected titles in Mass Communication (Alan Rubin, Advisory Editor) include:

Bryant/Zillmann • Media Effects: Advances in Theory and Research

Harris • A Cognitive Psychology of Mass Communication, Second Edition

Lang • Measuring Psychological Responses to Media Messages

Moore • Mass Communication Law and Ethics

Van Evra • Television and Child Development

Zillmann/Bryant/Huston • Media, Children, and the Family: Social Scientific, Psychodynamic, and Clinical Perspectives

For a complete list of other titles in LEA's Communication Series, please contact Lawrence Erlbaum Associates, Publishers.

TELEVISION AND CHILDREN
Program Evaluation, Comprehension, and Impact

Brian R. Clifford
University of East London

Barie Gunter
Jill McAleer
Independent Television Commission

 LAWRENCE ERLBAUM ASSOCIATES, PUBLISHERS
1995   Hillsdale, New Jersey   Hove, UK

Lawrence Erlbaum Associates, Inc., Publishers
365 Broadway
Hillsdale, New Jersey 07642

Cover design by Mairav Salomon-Dekel

Library of Congress Cataloging-in-Publication Data

Clifford, Brian R.
    Television and children: program evaluation, comprehension, and
impact / Brian R. Clifford, Barrie Gunter, Jill McAller.
        p.   cm. — (LEA's communication series)
    Includes bibliographical references and indexes.
    ISBN 0-8058-1682-8 (acid-free paper). — ISBN 0-8058-1683-6 (pbk.
: acid-free paper)
    1. Television and children. 2. Television programs for children—
Evaluation. 3. Child psychology. I. Gunter, Barrie.
II. McAleer, Jill L., 1944–   . III. Title. IV. Series.
HQ784. T4C55 1995
302.23′45′083—dc20   94-24129
                                                                CIP

Books published by Lawrence Erlbaum Associates are printed
on acid-free paper, and their bindings are chosen for strength
and durability.

Printed in the United States of America
10 9 8 7 6 5 4 3 2 1

Contents

Preface   **vii**

Chapter 1   Introduction   **1**

Chapter 2   The Research   **22**

Chapter 3   Children's Evaluation and Comprehension
of Drama Programs   **38**

Chapter 4   Impact of Drama Programs on Children's
Knowledge, Beliefs, and Attitudes   **60**

Chapter 5   Science Programs With Single Themes:
Evaluation, Comprehension, and Cognitive Impact   **90**

Chapter 6   Multitopic Science Magazine Shows:
Evaluation, Comprehension, and Cognitive Impact   **129**

Chapter 7   Children's Perceptions of and Learning
From TV, Entertainment (Quiz) Programs   **165**

Chapter 8   Interpreting the Cognitive Impact
of Television   **200**

References   **228**

Author Index   **240**

Subject Index   **245**

Preface

Television plays an important — perhaps even a significant — part in the lives of the vast majority of the population. It is used for many different purposes, by different people, at different times, in different places. It is an easy medium, not only in the sense of being readily available but also in the sense of requiring minimal engagement and interaction. It is also readily responsive to human needs. Thus, viewers can be stimulated or relaxed by it; they can be entertained or horrified by it; they can be educated or intrigued by it; and they can be isolated or "networked" by it. All this at a touch of a button.

That television is a desirable medium is testified to by the presence of one or more sets in more than 98% of households in the United States and the United Kingdom; the presence of a videorecorder in more than 70% of these households; and the great number of hours viewed per day by their owners and their offspring. And yet there seems to be a duplicity of thought concerning this desired and appreciated medium. When one looks at the metaphors employed to describe the functions and operations of television, and adults' interaction with it, they are predominantly pejorative — "the one-eyed monster," "the uninvited guest," "the plug-in drug," "the boob-tube," "the electronic baby sitter," "the goggle box," "the idiot box," "the hypnotist," and "the Trojan horse." Thus, although adults seem to like television, as shown by their behavior activity, they seem to fear it cognitively, as shown by their linguistic behavior. But this apparent duplicity is resolved by noting the asymmetric application of their fears. This is shown by Winn (1977/1985), one of the earliest and most vociferous critics of television. Her barbs were reserved for children and television, not adults and television. In some way, the latter were not so threatened, not so endangered by the plug-in drug. Why should this be?

Although there are many reasons for adults' concern over television and children—some deep and hidden, others more open to debate—one major argument is that young recipients are poorly equipped to handle the onslaught of this ubiquitous and attractive medium, with its highly constructed and realistic content, presented in an easily absorbable way. Although children are known to be eager learners from any and all media, it is held that they lack the skills and abilities to "read" the adult television messages being given out because of their limited knowledge of their physical and social world, and because of the presence of only embryonic learning and processing mechanisms.

As a result of both these internal lacks and the surfeit of external, seductive, stimulation by a powerful technological medium, many people argue that children should be viewed as a special audience where television is concerned. This special status relates to both the technology and formal features of television and to its content. Because of one or the other, or both, of these dimensions of television, the "TV prigs" as Fowles (1992) called them, argue that children's brains are rotted; they are made violent; avarice is cultivated; they are politically desensitized; and turned away from wholesome educational pursuits such as reading and health-producing physical activity. In short, they are cultivated into a soporific passivity, characterized by the death of both a critical faculty and the impulse to probe, question, and think. In the place of these desired qualities, a desire for endless novely, change, excitement, trivia, and titillation is cultivated.

And yet there are contrary views about the potentiality and actuality of children's interaction with the television medium. Thus, Hodge and Tripp (1986) argued that television is not a time-out from thinking but rather that it produces grist for the mills of thought and innumerable opportunities for cognitive growth. The "wastelands" of television culture can, according to Wirth (1988) be "cultivated." According to others, television offers children a "window on the world," magical or otherwise, through which they can develop fresh perspectives on life, explore new possibilities, anticipate as-yet-unmet social problems, be provided with impetus for self-reflection, and enjoy educative and emotional uplifting and stimulation of imagination.

Now, as with most things human, the reality is immensely complex. Both the perspectives discussed here on the child's interaction with television have degrees of truth. Television can inform, educate, enlighten, enthuse, challenge, and inspire. It can also deaden, misinform, mislead, and waylay children. As with most things technological, in and of itself, television is neither intrinsically benign nor malign—it is how it is used and abused. But here the advancement of reasoned argument grinds to a halt because views abound on whether television is an abused, and thus an abusing, technology, or is being used wisely and thus forms a potentially important tool in the development of children, and society more generally. The problem is that these views tend to take the form of assertions and opinions, anecdotally grounded, rather than being based on informed reflections. This is unfortunate and inexcusable because research on children and television has developed hugely in the last three decades, and is available for public consumption. Having said this, however, it must be admitted that this research is still fragmented; being characterized by very different foci, different methodologies, different theoretical orientations and explanatory models, not to mention conflicting findings.

This book is intended to be an empirical contribution to this ongoing debate concerning children and their relationship with television. It is hoped that our contribution lies in the scope of the study undertaken, in terms of the types of program we sought to explore, the age range of the children that we investigated, the weight we gave to demographic and background differences in our viewers, the comprehensiveness of the outcome measures of viewing we looked at, and the desire to focus on the cognitive, rather than the behavioral, impact of television programs.

In terms of the scope of the study's investigation of programs, we wished to explore children's reactions to drama, informational, and entertainment content. Within drama, we focused specifically on police drama, and within that, we looked at two programs that had both similarities and differences in their content and presentational formats. Within informational programs, we focused on several science series that, again, exhibited both similarities and differences. Of major concern was whether magazine-style programs, in which several topics were covered in the same program, had more impact and were evaluated more positively, than science programs that focused on only one topic. In one study we compared two science programs from prime-time television, whereas in another, we compared and contrasted the impact of three programs, again drawn from prime-time television, but in one case made specifically for a child audience, whereas in the other cases the programs had been made for a more general and adult audience. The third area of programming we investigated involved quiz shows, which we believe is an interesting choice, because, at one level, they exhibit, in manifest form, the chief function of television — entertainment, whereas at another level they trade on information retrieval abilities and skills. Now while informing and educating viewers has always been an aim of at least public-service broadcasting, television's positive information role has often been doubted. To see if children could learn from quiz shows, while supposedly being only "amused to death" seemed to us to be worthwhile and potentially informative.

In all cases, the programs used in the various studies were taken from general television programming and did not involve programs specifically created under an "educational television" rubric. The aim of the broad sampling of genres, and programs within genres, was to afford us generalizability of findings. In the literature it is frequently the case that a huge edifice of assertion is predicated on a few minutes of one program within one genre. We were determined to avoid this pitfall.

In terms of the age range of the children we looked at, we were aware that most research had involved very young children, usually under the age of 7, and that the 8 to middle teens age-group had been largely ignored. This is understandable but regrettable. It is understandable because cognitive growth is most rapid and perceptible before the age of 7 and then supposedly remains quiescent until about 11–12 years of age. It is regrettable, however, because between the ages of 8 and 15 two major cognitive developmental stages are achieved, if Piagetian theory is to be believed. Even if one does not accept stage-developmental accounts of cognitive growth, then the acquisition of information-processing skills should be continuing apace throughout this period. In addition, there can be little doubt that social and intellectual schemas are also accumulating as a result of the child's ever-widening social and educational experiences in this period and this accumulation should have implications for how children choose to watch television, what they value in terms of particular programs, and, in turn, the impact that specific programs will have on them.

In addition to an interest in children's present cognitive functioning, as a function of their current attained age, we were also interested in finding out how different background experiences and learning impacted on program evaluation, perception, and comprehension. Children of different ages have, by definition, different life experiences merely by having transacted with the world for different lengths of time. Within the same age group different children will have accrued different experiences by virtue of being different individuals. A pretheoretical assumption we made was that children are active processors of television, and a large part of that "active processing" is predicated upon the experiences, values, knowledge, opinions, attitudes, and motivations that a child brings to the viewing situation. Throughout our experimentation, therefore, we were always on the look out to see if and how demographic and background experiences helped predict the findings we obtained on impact, comprehension, and evaluation of the programs we presented them with. These demographic and background factors involved such things as gender, language facility, amount of television viewed, reading habits, personal or family experiences of issues being presented, and both relevant and tangential school-based study. Of specific interest was the degree to which a child's general knowledge of the area under investigation predicted information acquisition, attitude, and opinion stabilization or change, and knowledge growth. To the extent that such preexisting knowledge predicted current knowledge acquisition, we would have evidence for the proposition that what a child takes from television depends very much on what he or she brings to it: a key tenant of the "active" school of thought concerning the interaction of children with television.

A great many of the studies in the literature are characterized by the use of only one or two outcome measures. Frequently, only one memory or one attitude dimension is looked at, depending on the focus of the study. At the outset we decided that several measures of impact should be employed. Thus, whether we were looking at police drama, science information, or quiz shows we always sought to elicit attitudinal, evaluation, and appreciation measures, as well as recall and comprehension performance. Frequently, these measures were looked at in a before-after way. In addition to looking at these various measures individually, we also looked at them interactively—that is, how liking, valuing, and/or appreciating a program acted to increase or decrease the child's learning from it. This "multivariate" approach to the question of television's impact upon children we regard as quite important.

The last aspect of this book that has a degree of novelty, or at least freshness, about it, is our focus on cognitive impact rather than behavioral impact. That is, we were interested primarily in what children thought about the issues raised by the programs we exposed them to, and how, and if, short-term changes could be effected by such exposure. In addition to what they thought about the issues raised, we were also interested in how the cognitive structures that fed into, informed, and shaped these cognitions, values, appraisals, and opinions were augmented or consolidated, again short-term, by program exposure. In other words, we wished to explore the psychological aspects rather than the behavioral aspects of the child's interaction with television. This is an area of research that requires development because it acknowledges the fact that any effects that television have must be mediated by what the child viewer makes of the content being conveyed; whether they believe it, whether they view the message as credible, sensible, relevant, and realistic; and whether it agrees, or clashes nonsensically, with what they already know about the social and physical world. Children do not absorb uncritically what television offers; they filter such offerings through appraisals, evaluations, and appreciations of what they know and feel about such offerings. This must never be overlooked.

It was with this view of the child–television interaction that we—a psychologist, a media researcher, and an educationalist—embarked on our exploration. We found the results interesting, thought-provoking, and not always as we would have anticipated. We hope that our readers also experience some of these novel insights in a battle zone that is destined to endure and even intensify as the nature and amount of telecommunications technology escalates and become even more attractive to children. There is no doubt that television is here to stay; there is no doubt that children will continue to be attracted to it. The one doubt that does remain is what impact it has on children. This book is designed to put in place one piece of the mosaic that, when finally completed, will serve to remove this remaining doubt.

Brian R. Clifford
Barrie Gunter
Jill McAleer

1 Introduction

This book explores children's ability to understand and learn from television programs. The success and fulfillment that people enjoy in their adult lives can be greatly determined by the nature of their intellectual and emotional development during childhood. This development is shaped by children's early life experiences. These include direct experiences deriving from their interactions with other people and indirect or vicarious experiences obtained through various mediated sources. Today, the latter are dominated by the mass media, the most prevalent and prominent of which is television. But how do children experience television? How much do they understand of what they watch? Are their perceptions of the world significantly shaped or altered by the programs they watch? Are some programs more influential than others as sources of learning and socialization?

Given the reach that television now has, most children in modern and many developing societies are exposed to it almost from the time they are born. It is important therefore that we understand the different ways in which it might affect them. There is evidence to suggest, for instance, that infants in households with television demonstrate their first awareness of it as young as 6 months (Hollenbeck & Slaby, 1979), although it is more generally accepted that proper viewing begins in earnest between 2½ and 3 years of age (Huston & Wright, 1983; Schramm, Lyle, & Parker, 1961). Certainly, the frequency with which young children have been observed to glance at the television set increases markedly at this age (Levin & Anderson, 1976). As they grow older, children may devote 2, 3, or even more hours a day to watching television, and in so doing are exposed to a vast range of material that may entertain them, inform or educate them, or involve them in a variety of other ways.

1

A great deal has been researched and written about the effects television supposedly can have on the way children behave (e.g., Bryant & Anderson, 1983; Comstock, Chaffee, Katzman, McCombs, & Roberts, 1978; Meyer, 1983). Much more attention has been focused on possible negative effects than on any positive outcomes of watching television. Whereas due care and attention needs to be given to the showing of any programs that might be unsuitable for young viewers, there is much to be said for the benefits of television for children when it is used sensibly (Davies, 1989; Gunter & McAleer, 1990). It is not the purpose of this book, however, to dwell on behavioral effects issues. We are concerned principally with the information children absorb from programs. The effects under the microscope here were cognitive rather than behavioral, and were to be measured in terms of changes in children's knowledge or beliefs, and associated attitudes, which might be contingent upon exposure to different types of television material.

The informational content of television varies considerably from one program type to the next. Moreover, content differences cannot always be meaningfully considered in isolation. Programs can be discriminated along a number of dimensions. Content is one factor; others include presentation style or format and intended audience. For the purposes of the research on which we report, we distinguished between three broad strands of programming—drama, factual, and entertainment. Within two of these strands, a further subdivision was made into children's and adults' factual and entertainment programs.

We were interested in what could be called, broadly, *informational* influences, thus we selected programs that contained testable informational content. With factual programs it goes without saying that they contained the sort of material we were looking for. The programs examined within this realm dealt with science topics. With drama, the programs selected here too, contained informational material about which children could be tested. The type of drama in focus was represented by two fictional police series. Finally, in the sphere of entertainment we chose to examine quiz shows. These satisfied the essential criterion of being not simply "entertaining" but also comprising games and quizzes in which contestants were asked general knowledge questions. These, we reasoned, represented material from which viewers could conceivably "learn."

Past research has indicated that television can have a variety of influences on children—just like many other sources of communication with which they interact, be it with parents, peers, teachers, or other media. However, the nature of those influences is often misconceived or oversimplified. Thus, although the effects of television can be either positive or negative, the important point to grasp is that they are rarely simple or direct. Television-related effects, when they happen, can occur at a number of levels—influencing knowledge, beliefs, attitudes, moods, and behavior. In addition, a key consideration in the evaluation of television's impact is the role played by a variety of mediating factors. These include the character and background of children, the nature of their past and present viewing experiences, and the development of certain important cognitive skills and attitudinal sets toward television that affect the ways they respond to programs.

Television-related effects, when they occur, may exhibit a chainlike set of reaction processes. A direct link from television to behavior, for instance, can often be difficult to isolate. Instead, television's influence may begin by imparting information to children who then absorb it into existing knowledge systems. Here it may add to or confirm what the child already knows. It may operate to reinforce or modify beliefs or attitudes. Then, in turn, it may produce a behavioral intention or motivational set to behave either in a generalized or highly specific fashion, the latter often depending also on appropriate eliciting cues being present in the environment (Berkowitz, 1984). The starting point, however, is most often the communication of information.

The way in which television information is absorbed and then stored by children is affected by what they already know or believe or feel (see W. Collins, 1984). In developmental psychology, enrichment theory posits that prior experiences and expectations can play a major role in interpreting current sensory input (Bruner, 1957; Vernon, 1955). Contrasting with this view is differentiation theory that conceptualizes each sensory stimulus as an information-rich input from which distinctive features are extracted by receivers (Gibson, 1969; Gibson & Levin, 1975). Television has been thought to act as a secondary socializer in children's lives. It can provide unique knowledge or provide information that can be compared with other sources, or acts to reinforce current values, beliefs, and behavior (Corder-Bolz, 1980). Although children's early learning from television may affect their perceptions of real life, they presently come to interpret what they see on television in the context of real-world experiences (Dorr, 1983). It is essential then, when examining the impact of television programs on children, to have some idea about what they have brought with them to the viewing situation. This means ascertaining what they already know or believe or feel about the kinds of issues or topics being presented in or covered by a program they are currently watching, before they start watching it.

CHILDREN AS "ACTIVE" VIEWERS

The emergence of cognitive models of mass communication's effects has also placed emphasis on children's understanding of television (Bryant & Rockwell, 1991). A primary component of many cognitive models is the notion of *schema*. This has been defined by one writer as "a network of interrelated elements that defines a concept for some individual" (Crockett, 1988, p. 33). Two principal functions of schema are to order new information and to facilitate inferences to be drawn from incomplete information (Taylor & Crocker, 1981). With well-developed schema, even if an individual misses some of the information content of a media message, the gaps can be filled in by inferring the full meaning.

Cognitive approaches to understanding audience responses to mass media contents assume a more active role on the part of the individual. Thus, television viewers may be assumed consciously to construct and order the informational content of programs. There is also a belief on the part of some cognitive theorists that conscious processes are paralleled by unconscious processes (Haskell, 1987). There may be occasions when a viewer needs to switch on consciously to a program and actively apply a set of known rules in order to make sense of it. On other occasions, cognitive processing may occur that is outside the control of the individual (Bargh, 1988). Much television viewing is likely to be goal-directed and intentional, but there are elements of programs such as particular production features, repetitive story lines, and so on, that do not require the constant conscious attention of the viewer and may therefore be processed automatically.

One of the basic premises of our perspective then is that what children get out of television critically depends on what they bring to it. Children are not passive receivers, rather they are active selectors. Furthermore, they actively select what to watch in order to satisfy particular and varied needs and moods, and they place their own meanings on program content. Historically, a great deal of emphasis has been placed by researchers on examining television's effects on children. A number of recent research efforts have drawn attention to the young viewer as a determiner of what is watched, why, and how (E. Palmer & MacNeil, 1991). Researchers have identified various uses and gratifications that can be derived from watching television (Palmgreen & Rayburn, 1985). These include watching to obtain information, to be diverted from everyday problems and worries, to strengthen social contact with others, or in contrast, as an alternative source of companionship in the absence of social contacts, to avoid having to do other things, to fill time, and to ignore others in the household (see Dominick, 1987). Television can also play a role in defining the viewer's sense of personal identity (J. Fiske, 1982) and can provide a source of learning about personal and social problems (Faber, Brown, & McLeod, 1986). Although the motives for watching television may vary with the type of program, as well as across different types of viewers, most children and adolescents use the medium in the service of satisfying some need or other (Rubin, 1985).

Age and experience are important ingredients in this process. With increasing age and viewing experience, children develop a better under-standing of television's content, and become progressively more able to make fine distinctions between programs and more sophisticated and critical judgments about them (W. A. Collins, 1979; Cullingford, 1984; Hagen, 1967). This is based on their learning of the syntax and semantic codes used by the medium, together with autonomously evolving cognitive structures that make interpretation, inferential reasoning, and comprehen-sion of life events—whether real or mediated by television—more refined and adultlike (E. Palmer & MacNeil, 1991; Rubin, 1986).

Young viewers' reactions to television programs are increasingly shaped by these aspects of their television "literacy" as well as by knowledge they may already have that relates to the content of a program, derived from other information sources (Dorr, Graves, & Phelps, 1980). Programs themselves have different functions for viewers and can be differentiated into various types. As children grow older, they become better able to distinguish one type of program from another and have different expect-ancies of program genres (Dorr, 1983). Some programs are designed, principally, to inform or to educate, whereas others are made to entertain. Most programs, however, have latent as well as manifest functions and both types of function can play a significant part in attracting the audience.

Entertainment-oriented programs such as drama series and serials are expected to amuse and excite, but they may also have the capacity to cultivate awareness and impressions of aspects of life that are unknown and unfamiliar to the child. The effects of television drama often act via viewers' involvement with familiar television characters (Hoffner & Cantor, 1991). Such programs can influence knowledge, beliefs, attitudes, and values; provide illustrations of how people might behave in different contexts; and offer insights into how to deal with personal and social problems. Programs with a fictional narrative often contain elements of truth or images of "reality" that can be absorbed, retained, and utilized at a later date by young viewers, particularly when they meet similar or analogous situations themselves in real life.

Some mass communications researchers have emphasized this mode of television influence upon young viewers (see Wober & Gunter, 1988). The dramatic content of television is regarded as having a potentially powerful shaping effect on children's perceptions of the world around them. The world of television drama and entertainment is identified as providing biased and stereotyped depictions of reality, which can distort the beliefs of individuals who are heavy viewers who attach credence to the things they see in programs (Gerbner, Gross, Morgan, & Signorielli, 1980, 1986). Through the mechanisms of *mainstreaming* and *resonance* false perceptions of reality are cultivated and acted upon (Gerbner et al., 1986). Mainstreaming refers to a phenomenon whereby differences in beliefs among individuals from different subcultures or demographic classes are much less pronounced among heavy viewers of television than among light viewers. Resonance refers to special cases in which television's depictions of social reality are consonant with a typical segment of the general population's actual or perceived reality. Thus, television further reinforces particular social beliefs that are already prominent. It is argued, in turn, that the more television children watch, and the more they therefore live in the mainstream of the television world, the more their impressions of social reality will be distorted or reinforced in the directions of television depictions.

In consequence, it is held that faulty perceptions are cultivated concerning such aspects of life as gender, family, and occupational roles; the characteristics of demographic groups such as the aged and ethnic minorities; the work done by various professions such as doctors, lawyers, and the police; and the prevalence of crime. This concept of a single, unitary, all-pervasive world view, cultivated by television, is regarded by some writers, however, as oversimplistic (Wober & Gunter, 1988). When taking into account the fact that no two individuals see the same thing identically and that what a person sees or believes is the end point of a history of developing interaction between self and society, objective and subjective reality, and direct and vicarious experience, then the analysis is driven to the individual-viewer level in seeking clarification of the impact of television upon children.

From a cognitive perspective, the effects of mass media in regard to shaping viewers' perceptions of social reality have been framed in terms of a construct accessibility model. *Accessibility* refers here to the readiness with which a construct in memory can be utilized in processing incoming information (Sanbonmatsu & Fazio, 1991). Regular activation of a construct increases the ease with which it can be accessed. Generalizing this cognitive theory to mass communications, this means that social concepts, objects, and phenomena that are repeatedly depicted or portrayed by the mass media may be primed so as to become more prominent in the memories of media consumers. The process of priming itself does not represent a change in the degree of association between two phenomena, nor is it a change in belief about the frequency of events or objects (and thus is not the same as a cultivation effect). Priming does not represent an attitudinal set to respond to events in a particular fashion, nor is it an expectancy value about social events or social situations. Instead, priming is a cognitive process that is continuously occurring in response to ongoing social experiences, whether mass mediated or direct. Each social experience may produce or reactivate existing constructs in memory that represent a coherent body of information about some entity (Higgins & King, 1981). Constructs may contain information about individuals, groups, objects, events, and situations. They may represent knowledge about different topics, codes of conduct or personal plans, perceptions, beliefs, and feelings.

A television portrayal can prime a construct about that entity in a viewer's store of world knowledge, rendering that construct more accessible and therefore more likely to be "top of the mind" in terms of beliefs about that entity. If that construct rather than others about the same category of objects is repeatedly primed by television it will become more accessible than their constructs in the same family and the one most likely to influence viewers' judgments about the object in question.

In this book we examine the extent to which children's knowledge, beliefs, and attitudes concerning different aspects of the real world can be shaped in a general fashion or in a more focused way by the content of television programs they watch. We do this, however, by establishing the baseline state of their knowledge, beliefs, and attitudes on topics with which specific programs are concerned and then measure any change in those concepts after program exposure. In this way, the influence of television is itself conceived to be delimited and mediated by what children already know, believe, and feel. In addition, children's level of comprehension and retention of program content needs to be addressed because the influence that television has is dependent on the information that children take from it. If they fail to absorb its content to any great extent, it is unlikely that we can expect television to effect significant changes in children's knowledge, beliefs, or attitudes.

CHILDREN'S COMPREHENSION OF TELEVISION

Researchers have devoted increasing amounts of attention to children's understanding of television. There is still a great deal we do not know, however, about the way children cognitively process programs. Broadcasters produce and transmit programs to mass audiences often unaware of the fact that to place children, especially those who have not yet reached their teens, on an equal footing with older viewers ignores significant differences in cognitive information-processing abilities that exist across even fairly narrow age bands (Liebert, Sprafkin, & Davidson, 1982). Children's abilities to comprehend programs develop through their primary and secondary school years. When very young, children's understanding and perception of programs is not simply at a lower level than that of older children, it is qualitatively different.

One model of children and comprehension assumes that, when very young, children are cognitively immature with egocentric, stimulus-bound conceptions of the world (see E. Palmer & MacNeil, 1991). Preschoolers' understanding of television, for example, is very limited. One study found that fewer than 50% of preschoolers understood more than half the material they viewed, even though it had been judged by adults to be age appropriate (Friedlander, Wetstone, & Scott, 1974).

DEVELOPMENTAL DIFFERENCES

Age is related to children's comprehension of television in a variety of ways. Very young children, for instance, have difficulty integrating and remembering much of what they see in a program. Up to age 8, children do not follow a plot well at all, even in programs made specifically for their age group (e.g., Calvert & Watkins, 1979; W. Collins, 1983; Friedlander et al., 1974).

Age differences in comprehension are not simply a function of age per se, however, but are associated with the growth of cognitive skills and increasing familiarity with the medium. Research throughout the 1970s and 1980s indicated that young children do not understand causal sequences in televised drama plots very well and experience difficulty following aspects of story lines that are not made explicit (W. Collins, 1981). Although children before the age of 8 can retain surface details, actions, and settings, they cannot understand or draw inferences about plots or subplots (W. Collins, 1970). These strategic skills only come with maturation, growing world knowledge, and learning how to "read" television and its symbol systems.

Young children's inability to associate events with antecedent and consequent events affects their overall understanding of a program and contributes to the poor recall often observed in young viewers (Hayes & Kelly, 1984). Even at age 7 or 8, children exhibit poor perception, organization, and comprehension of information in television programs (W. Collins, 1975). Up to this age, only about 50% of the implicit information in a drama program is comprehended, and 66% of the essential information. By age 11–12, this has risen to 70% and 85%, respectively. Most significantly, an interruption technique, whereby an ongoing film is stopped and the children are asked "What will happen next?", completely nonpluses children under the age of 8. Only about 30% can correctly guess the following sequence of events; by age 12, 70% can.

With age and television-viewing experience, children learn to encode central information better, and to filter out extraneous, nonessential material (Cullingford, 1984; Hagen, 1967). This is accompanied and perhaps precipitated by a shift from attention to unusual sights and sounds to attention to the plot itself (J. C. Wright & Huston, 1983). With this developing skill at following plot structure the ability to make inferences about characters and especially the reasons and motivations for their behavior also develops (Collins & Westby, 1981). Comprehending television involves grasping the relationships between characters and scenes that, although related, are separated in time. Each of these skills involves conceptual and knowledge skills that young children simply may not possess.

Children are much less capable of organizing essential program information effectively when younger than age 7 or 8, and do not, at that tender age, appear to grasp the social lessons that are a part of some programs (Christenson & Roberts, 1983). Rubin (1986) also noted that the behavior of these young children is closely tied to immediate perception, and their judgments are based on what they can see. Older children have developed cognitive skills that enable them to make inferences beyond what is immediately perceptible. These children are able to understand subtle plot shifts and to infer connections between events in a program that are not overtly depicted on screen.

According to Collins, this development with age is predicated upon (a) knowledge of the exposition of forms—the general structure of stories (see J. Anderson, 1990); (b) knowledge of the world; and (c) knowledge of the structure of television and its particular conventions. Here, then, we have a happy coincidence: If television is giving out subtle messages about the world then the young child may often be unable to understand them. In contrast, although the older child may be able to apprehend television's messages, by this stage of his or her development, world knowledge or a more informed view about television forms could have developed sufficiently to act as a sounding board against which to assess the "reality" or "acceptability" of the message being sent.

In this book our research with children explored their varying abilities cognitively to process television drama narratives, particularly in association with age. Comparisons were made between children ages 8–9 years, 10–11 years, 12–13 years, and 14–15 years in terms of their memory and comprehension of the story content of two television police drama episodes.

TELEVISION AND THE GROWTH OF BELIEFS AND PERCEPTIONS

In this discussion we indicated that there were presumptive reasons for believing that children can potentially learn from not simply factual and informational programs on broadcast television, but also from drama and entertainment programs. The remainder of this chapter outlines some findings that illustrate the kinds of learning opportunities that television offers in programs that are classed as drama entertainment-oriented as well as informationally oriented.

Learning From TV Drama

It is in the field of drama programming that the critics of television locate their worst fears concerning the negative influences of television. Televised dramatic portrayals are believed to be a source of social misperceptions, faulty beliefs, and distorted world views. Such programming is deemed regularly to project stereotyped and erroneous messages about, for example, gender roles, different races, and the elderly; about the distribution of different occupations and professions in society; and, potentially the most worrying of all, false beliefs about the prevalence of violence and crime in today's world (C. Wright, 1986). It is felt that frequent viewing of television crime drama, for example, which purportedly contains a great deal of violence (however defined), is connected with exaggerated public perceptions of the incidence of crime and how it is policed and controlled (see Gerbner & Gross, 1976; Gerbner et al., 1980, 1982, 1986).

The question to be addressed in this domain, however, as in all others, is whether, when compared against other social forces and in the context of the way people use and react to programs, the influence of television on the viewer's perceptions and beliefs about such societal matters is strong, weak, or nonexistent. This question is addressed in the research presented in this book by focusing on the influence of television on young people's beliefs and perceptions concerning crime and police work.

Criticism of the media in their coverage or portrayal of crime (and here both factual and fictional presentations have often been treated in an undifferentiated fashion) implies four assumptions that may or may not be true. First, there is an inherent distortion in media portrayals of crime and its resolution. Second, television is an important if not the most important source of information about crime. Third, viewers absorb this media information uncritically and, thus, finally, develop beliefs and perceptions about law enforcement and crime that are essentially false with respect to reality.

We have already had occasion to refer to the cultivation theory of Gerbner et al. (e.g., 1980, 1986), which is the dominant theory in this domain of television's influence on social beliefs and perceptions. Interestingly enough, this on-going empirical study of the media's impact began by looking at the relationship between television viewing and the public's belief about crime. This work purported to show that both adult and child samples of "heavy" television viewers over estimated the prevalence of crime in society compared to the estimates offered by "light" viewers. The conclusion was drawn that imbibing a diet of crime-based programs, replete with violence, criminal acts, and their immediate resolutions, progressively built up a model of reality that could be referred to as a *television reality* that was more extreme, and thus false, with respect to *social reality*, and further, that these false perceptions and beliefs had important and dire consequences at both the personal and the societal level.

But what, really, is the evidence for this view? Several steps are required to prove empirically that the observed correlation is in fact causative. Let us begin with the incidence of crime and crime prevention in television drama.

In terms of the first link in the supposed causal chain between television content and viewer's beliefs about the real world, reported research evidence has indicated that the incidence, nature, and type of crimes on television do tend to be very different from those in real life (Cassata, Skill, & Boadu, 1979; Dominick, 1973; Gerbner et al., 1977; Gerbner, Gross, Jackson-Beeck, Jeffries-Fox, & Signorielli, 1978; Gerbner, Gross, Signorielli, Morgan, & Jackson-Beeck, 1979; Katzman, 1972; Sutherland & Siniawsky, 1982).

There are differences between program types in respect of the nature of crime portrayals. A major and noticeable difference between prime-time crime drama and soaps is the delay in "closing the case." Resolutions traditionally occur in the space of one episode in police dramas but in soaps the case can drag on for months or even years (Cassata et al., 1979). This comparison of crime portrayal in drama and soaps, incidentally, gives the lie to the treatment of all crime portrayals as uniform and undifferentiated. However, as with police dramas, soaps are also held to misrepresent the facts and to present a mismatch between TV reality and social reality in terms of who perpetrates what crime, who suffers from it, and the frequency of various crimes and the nature and speed of their resolution.

Invoking the construct accessibility model (Sanbonmatsu & Fazio, 1991), one might expect those more frequently occurring types of crime depiction to produce stronger "priming" and therefore to be more accessible in viewers' memories. Depending on whether or not alternative real-world constructs are more heavily primed, one would hypothesize that repeated television-world constructs would achieve prominence in the minds of viewers, especially among heavy viewers.

What then of the evidence that heavy and light viewers respond differentially when questioned about real-life crime and police? Gerbner et al. (1977, 1979) compared the responses of heavy and light adolescent viewers to questions concerning: (a) the proportion of all men who have jobs in law enforcement and crime detection, (b) the percentage of all crimes that are violent crimes (murder, rape, robbery, and aggravated assault), (c) the relative incidence of fatal violence between strangers compared to relatives or acquaintances, and (d) their perceived likelihood of themselves being involved in some kind of violence.

Their answers were always to be a choice between a TV reality and a social reality estimate. In all cases, heavy viewers gave greater endorsement to the TV reality answer. Gerbner et al. (1979) also found heavy viewing adolescents gave television-based estimates to questions concerning the activity of police—such as, that they used force and violence at the scene of a crime; that they drew their guns frequently; and that, if they were shooting at someone, they would hit a running man more often than they would miss him.

These findings appear convincing until it is realized that young people's knowledge of real crime figures tends, in fact, to be hazy. A more basic question is whether young people can distinguish between fictional portrayals of police and the real thing. It seems they can; television and real police are not generally perceived in the same way. Several studies have established among adults that viewers differentiate between fictional and factual depictions on television and that this perceptual distinction serves as an important mediator of television's cultivation effects (Elliott & Slater, 1980; Slater & Elliott, 1982; Tannenbaum, 1979).

Even young viewers, however, can make important distinctions between real and fantasy content on television. Rarick, Townsend, and Boyd (1973) showed that both delinquent and nondelinquent U.S. adolescents held heterogenous views of real police but essentially homogeneous views of television police. On the whole, all respondents felt that television police were idealized dramatizations, different from the real thing. Thus, previous experience served to differentiate the perceptions of real police, but did not blur the distinction between TV police and the real thing.

What is missed by the original cultivation approach is the fact that gross estimates of heavy and light viewing leaves out of account both the fact that any one viewer may view a wide spectrum of programs and program types, thus diluting the impact of any one program, and that any two people classified as heavy or light may watch very different types of programs (Wober & Gunter, 1988). Thus, a deeper level of analysis is needed to address issues concerned with the content of programs actually seen, and the information absorbed and the messages learned from television. Children are known both to perceive and to process fantasy and reality content in different ways (van der Voort, 1986) and to extract different meanings from television according to the label they attach and the type of program they are watching (see also Hodge & Tripp, 1986; P. Palmer, 1986).

These conceptual and theoretical doubts about cultivation theory leave a void in the area of understanding the relationship between television and the growth of social beliefs and perceptions. As we have already seen, the construct accessibility model offers an alternative cognitive-based framework for television effects analysis. The notion that constant exposure to an object either in the real world or on television can prime memory construct representations of it provides a possible mode of explanation for the supposedly distorting effects television portrayals may have on viewers' social beliefs. Exposure to an object not only primes memory representations of that object, but also primes constructs such as attitudes and beliefs that are closely associated with that object. This spread of priming activation across attitudes or attitudinally relevant information can moderate the interpretation and influence of new information (Houston & Fazio, 1987). This could explain assumed generalization of television-world beliefs, shaped by repeated exposure to stereotyped television portrayals, to perceptions of the real world. However, such cognitive effects may depend on the perceived relevance of television-world events to the real world, a factor not clearly elaborated in the construct accessibility model.

What remains to be done is to establish a model of influence that does justice to all the known facts. From this discussion it should be clear that a more sophisticated model is required than that offered by cultivation analysis. As Gunter (1987a) indicated, this is likely to involve research at no less than four levels. First, the possibility will have to be considered that the relationship between levels of exposure to television and perception and belief about crime and law enforcement may be mediated by a program specificity effect. That is, television's influence may depend not so much on the total amount of television viewed as on how much informationally relevant programs are watched (e.g., Weaver & Wakshlag, 1986).

Second, the influence of specific television content may depend on how viewers perceive and interpret the content of programs (e.g., Pingree, 1983; Teevan & Hartnagel, 1976). Unless viewers view programs as realistic and reflecting real life then their content is likely to have little impact (e.g., Potter, 1986). In assessing their perceptions of television content, van der Voort (1986) reported that children have their own scales for deciding on, for example, the seriousness of incidents of violence. Their opinions about televised violence did not invariably concur with researchers' a priori classifications of violence on TV.

Third, conceptual distinctions will have to be drawn between different frames of reference that may be operating, when making judgments about crime, which are based on the viewer's different levels of real-world experience. Tyler (1980, 1984; Tyler & Cook, 1984) distinguished between societal-level judgments that refer to general beliefs about the frequency of crimes in the community at large, and personal-level judgments that have to do with perceived personal vulnerability to crime and one's own estimate of being victimized. These latter two levels of judgment are not related to media experiences, but rather to direct personal experience with crime.

Fourth, at both the personal and societal level of judgment, the perceived likelihood of other- or self-involvement in crime are situation-specific and may not be the same from one setting to the next (e.g., Tamborini, Zillmann, & Bryant, 1984).

As far as this book is concerned, this increased complexity in the understanding of the influence of television on perceptions and beliefs is to be welcomed. However, yet another layer has to be imposed because of our subject matter — children. Consideration of television's influence as it relates to children involves awareness of cognitive growth as a major influence in the power of television to shape perceptions, beliefs, and attitudes.

Cognitive Growth and the Mediation
of Television's Influence

As mentioned previously, as children grow older they sharpen their powers of discrimination along many dimensions. As young viewers become more discriminating about television programs are they less likely to be influenced by their content? The answer seems to be yes.

Teevan and Hartnagel (1976) investigated the possible effects of watching violence on 12- to 18-year-old adolescents' perceptions of crime and their reactions to such perceived crime. Usefully, these researchers distinguished between objectively defined content violence and children-defined violent episodes (i.e., objective vs. subjective violence, and thus, perhaps, salience). A further question addressed was whether, if violence was perceived, was it seen by the children as an effective means of achieving goals or of overcoming problems.

There was little relationship between the reported amount of viewing of programs objectively defined as violent and either the children's perception of crime or their reaction to it. However, programs that were watched by the children and that they themselves defined as violent were related to both beliefs about crime in the wider society and the children's fear of crime. Thus, here we have children of different ages discriminating between different types of violence and evidence that such discriminations have implications for what children take away from these differently perceived programs.

In the same vein, van der Voort (1986) investigated the relationship between a program's perceived realism and its capacity to absorb children. He looked at programs such as "The Incredible Hulk" and "Dick Turpin" (both classed as adventure series) and "Starsky and Hutch" and "Charlie's Angels" (crime drama). In a sample of 314 Dutch children, van der Voort found that realistic programs were watched with more involvement, more emotion, and less detachment, and that crime drama programs were those rated most realistic. Here, then, children are shown to be capable of discriminating between program types. Thus, not all portrayals of crime, violence, and law enforcement are perceived as being alike, nor are they all accepted as accurate reflections of reality. These discriminations are then seen to have behavioral consequences in how a program is processed.

Potter (1986) tried to bring order to the role of perceived program realism by suggesting that some viewers treat television as a "magic window," that is that television's content is perceived to be an accurate representation of real life, and should thus be closely encoded. Others, he argued, treat television as a mode of instruction. By this he meant that certain viewers believe that television content is capable of expanding or augmenting personal experience. In this sense, television can provide moral or social solutions or possible coping strategies for application in real life. Potter characterized a third type of perceived realism that focuses on characters and situations in programs — what he called *identity*. Once again, depending on the closeness of the perceived television portrayal to people and situations known in real life, learning and coping is felt by the viewer to be possible.

Potter concluded that a viewer's perception of social reality (e.g., estimates of real-world crime) will critically depend on how he or she perceives the reality of the television programs they have chosen to watch.

However, over and above discriminations of violence, discriminations between program types, and different perceptions of television reality — which all develop with age — there is an even more fundamental consideration: the extent to which the young viewer truly understands what the story line of a drama is all about. This is a question of cognitive growth.

Learning from television is critically dependent on the way individuals watch and are able to comprehend the content. We have already mentioned studies that show that the amount of recall of plot action, events, consequences, and implications increase with age (e.g., W. Collins 1982), as does the ability to keep track of the order and relationship between events in a plot that may be separated in time (e.g., W. Collins, 1973, 1979).

Working with children ages 10–12, Pingree (1983) showed that this ability to follow a television story line may have important implications for the influence of drama programs on young viewers' beliefs about the real world. Pingree presented children with an edited television program and then divided the children up on the basis of their ability to follow the story line and to relate one part of the story to another. Prior to this, she had taken note of both the children's amount of television viewing and their social reality beliefs. Although greater amounts of reported television viewing were associated with exaggerated perceptions of crime and violence in society, there were important differences between children who were good and bad at following a program story line. Children who were good at following the story line exhibited weaker associations between their reported viewing and their social beliefs than did children who were poor at program comprehension. Additionally, children who were good at program understanding held a more integrated and coherent outlook on the world than did poor comprehenders.

Pingree concluded that young viewers who are better able to follow television story lines are probably more active viewers, possibly thinking more about the content and comparing it with other available sources of information. Alternatively, such children may be more discriminating and knowledgeable about television itself, and may simply choose not to believe fictional representations (e.g., Gunter, 1987a). Whatever the correct interpretation of this specific finding, all the studies serve to indicate that age (as a shorthand way of referring to cognitive and social development) is a critical determiner of whether television messages will be attended to, understood, absorbed, and become part of that person's world view.

Television and Knowledge Growth

Although children can absorb knowledge incidently from watching television programs designed principally to entertain, to what extent do they acquire information from programs also broadcast in prime-time schedules that are factual and designed to impart knowledge? Part of the research in this book examines children's learning from science programs. How effective are such television factual broadcasts? Do children learn from them?

From the earliest days of the medium, television has been accused of impeding the development in children of both the ability to learn and the motivation so to do. Is this the case? Two classic studies carried out with children during the early days of television in Britain and the United States examined among other things the role of television in shaping children's knowledge and beliefs. The U.S. study by Schramm et al. (1961) was published in *Television in the Lives of our Children*. The British work was done by Himmelweit, Oppenheim, and Vince (1958) and was reported in *Television and the Child*.

With regard to television's effects on knowledge, both found only limited effects. Schramm and his colleagues concluded that most effects involved knowledge about entertainment. An expected increase in children's vocabulary did not occur except for names and phrases referring to entertainment figures and products. Himmelweit et al., however, found increases in knowledge about geography, science, sports, music, handicrafts, and household chores, but none for English literature, history, nature or rural studies, art and architecture, current affairs, or religion. Both sets of authors concurred that the positive effects of watching television upon knowledge were confined to less intellectually able children whose access to and ability to use alternative sources of information was limited, and Schramm's group concluded that the more intelligent might suffer in terms of knowledge from a great deal of television viewing because of the greater intellectual value of displaced activities. According to Comstock (1989), these outcomes lead to several conclusions:

- Television viewing is most likely to increase knowledge about what it specializes in — entertainment.
- Television's contribution, if any, to scholastic achievement is thereby likely to be limited.
- Effects are limited not only by what is broadcast but by what is viewed.

- When television diverts attention from, or displaces engaging in, more informative and stimulating activities, the effects of viewing on knowledge may be negative.

As recent qualitative research has clearly shown, children are indeed knowledgeable about television (Gunter, McAleer, & Clifford, 1991). Even before they have reached their teens, many youngsters are able to articulate clearly and at length about the contents and characters of mainstream television dramas, the formats and presenters of television factual programs, and explain in detail the way different game shows are played.

There is, in addition, evidence that children and teenagers can acquire and retain information disseminated by popular television programs when their formats are designed to edify. This was made clear two decades ago by the evaluation of the "CBS National Citizenship Tests" by Alpert and Leidy (1970). This series was intended to teach its audience facts about U.S. government institutions. For a program covering Constitutional rights and obligations, three comparable groups of about 1,000 teenagers were tested representing a preprogram sample, a postprogram nonviewer sample, and a postprogram viewer sample.

Six months later, a national sample of 9,000 teenagers divided into viewers and nonviewers was again tested. The tests covered topics included and not included in the program, and both factual knowledge and beliefs or attitudes.

There were no shifts in knowledge or beliefs concerning matters not covered by the television program among either viewers or nonviewers. However, for covered material there were definite gains recorded among viewers for both knowledge and beliefs. These gains appeared to persist after the passage of 6 months. One of the reasons, therefore, why commercial television viewing may seem to have such limited effects on the knowledge of young people may be due to the preponderance of entertainment programming in which it specializes: It may, simply, not have enough "information programs" with sufficient "pulling" power for youngsters.

A similar, apparently conflicting, story is also found with learning from news programs. There have been a number of studies of the use of television news by children and teenagers (e.g., Comstock et al., 1978) and they indicate that:

- A large majority of children and teenagers believe they get most of their information about public events from television, ranking it far above teachers, parents, peers, or other media.
- Exposure to news programs increases factual knowledge, as does exposure to newspapers and other print media, but children and

teenagers are far more likely to see news than to read news, so television is the primary information provider.
- Children and teenagers typically are not much exposed to the news by any means.
- Exposure to news programs is increased when parents have a high interest in the topics currently being covered or when parents strongly encourage their offspring to express their opinions about events and issues.
- The opinions of children and teenagers correlate positively with the perceived opinions of parents and not with those of favored newspeople, indicating that although television may supply information, parents influence opinions.
- Learning from news increases when information is repeated and when a story has a high emotional content.

Children claim to watch television because it provides both factual knowledge and personal and social knowledge (e.g., Greenberg, 1976; Katz & Foulkes, 1962; Rubin, 1977). Evidence exists that learning in both these domains is associated with television viewing. However, television is not always an easy medium to learn from and it is often difficult to predict when learning will take place (Salomon, 1983a). Gunter (1987) reported that children often have poor recall of broadcast news material despite the fact that such programs are not fast-paced, and are specifically designed to communicate information. Such, however, is also the case with adults (Berry & Clifford, 1985; Berry, Gunter, & Clifford, 1982; Gunter, Berry, & Clifford, 1981, 1982; Gunter, Clifford, & Berry, 1980).

Nonetheless, television has been shown to play a role in the political cultivation of children (e.g., Chaffee, McLeod, & Wackman, 1973). Evidence on factual television's information effects derives from a mixture of survey and laboratory-based research. Various surveys of children have indicated degrees of association between areas of public affairs knowledge and reported exposure to relevant content on television. Laboratory studies have demonstrated the varying effectiveness of television programs with factual content in imparting their information content to young viewers under controlled viewing conditions. Furnham and Gunter (1983) showed that political knowledge in the United Kingdom is directly related to children's interest in news and current affairs. In the United States, Dominick (1972) showed that more than 50% of a child sample stated that their knowledge concerning the president and vice president came from television, and Atkin and Gantz (1978) demonstrated that, over a 1-year period, political knowledge growth in 5- to 10-year-olds was predicted by reported news viewing. In the United Kingdom, Furnham and Gunter (1983) showed that heavy viewing of television was a weak, but still relatively important, variable relating to political knowledge, in a sample of 16- to 18-year-olds.

In terms of current affairs, a series of studies have looked at the role of television in communicating information about the "troubles" in Northern Ireland. Cairns, Hunter, and Herring (1980) showed that knowledge about the IRA among children was greatest in an Irish sample, less apparent in a Scottish sample that received news broadcasts concerning Ireland, and least well-developed in a Scottish sample that did not receive such television coverage. With Irish samples only, Cairns (1984) replicated this "television effect," but another study (Cairns, 1982, cited in Cairns, 1984) found the effect only with 11-year-olds, not with 8-year-olds.

Research on children's learning of factual content from television has taken place under artificial viewing conditions in which specific variables can be systematically manipulated and controlled. Such studies have not simply measured whether learning occurs, but what factors mediate retention of factual program content. Much of this work has focused on the impact of television news on children's learning about public affairs. Other research has derived from investigations of television's usefulness as a formal educational medium.

In line with the argument advanced earlier that children are active rather than passive viewers, and with the assertion that it is often difficult to predict what and when children will learn from television, a study by Drew and Reeves (1980) is interesting.

They presented 8- to 13-year-olds with a news item surrounded by either other news items or cartoons, and sought recall of details of the critical news item. They found that perceiving the news item as intending to inform, liking it, and believing it, all related positively to learning (and recalling) its content. An intriguing and as yet unexplained finding was that older children did better when the news item was surrounded by cartoons, whereas younger children did better when the item was surrounded by other news items!

The research discussed here strongly suggests that the influence of television is mediated through young viewers' intentions and cognitive skills level. It is possible that different viewing (and learning) strategies will be employed depending on the viewer's motivations. Salomon (1983b) asked 12-year-olds if they could learn better from television than from print. The children averred that they could learn more easily from television because it was an easy medium, whereas print learning required effort and intelligence on the part of the reader. If failure to learn was obtained, children ascribed this to stupidity in the case of television but difficulty of the medium in the case of print. In an objective test of learning of a common text, presented either on television or in print, Salomon found no difference in recall of detail but greater evidence of inference-making in the print condition.

Salomon (1983b) ran another study with 90 12-year-olds divided into high and low ability groups and found that perception of television as an easy medium led to less effort being expended in the television condition and as a consequence less learning took place. If the children's cognitive set was altered by emphasizing that the program "was for fun" versus "was for learning from" then although this made no difference to the learning from print, it did for television, especially for the high ability groups. Thus, whether television has a learning influence or not very much resides with the viewer, not the television. In this book we examine how well children are able to learn from television science programs. Memory and comprehension of program content were investigated in relation to attitudinal orientations toward each program. As we see, certain attitudinal sets emerged that were significant predictors of learning.

Much research has been conducted into the harm television can do to the development of creative, analytic, imaginative, and linguistic abilities. Most of the research is interpretationally complex, particularly with regard to the question of direction of causality. One basic argument has been that television trains children to passively sit and watch (e.g., Singer, 1980) because the fast pacing of television formats prevents the luxury of time to assimilate, reflect, imagine, and create in one's own mind, and thus dulls thinking and intellectual ability.

Elsewhere, however, Salomon (1981, 1983a) considered the role of mental processing in regard to television by way of his concept of the amount of invested mental effort required while viewing. Different media may carry with them different learned expectations among people about how easy or difficult it is to learn from them. Compared to print, for example, television is generally regarded as a medium requiring little mental effort. It is this attitudinal set toward television that may in part underlie frequently observed poor memory and comprehension of television content; change this "mental set" and we may change the outcomes of television viewing for young viewers.

In this book, we are not be concerned with the systematic or controlled manipulation of mental set among young television viewers. We do nevertheless observe that level of involvement is both reflected in and an antecedent of factual learning from television programs. Such learning could take place from entertainment-orientated programs as well as from factual programs.

Television plays a large part in children's lives and it may be that it displaces certain activities that may have greater intrinsic worth (Williams, 1986). On the other hand, there is evidence that the programs children watch are varied and actively processed rather than passively received (see Bryant & Zillmann, 1991). Research has shown that children can discriminate between program types that are superficially similar, and that they perceive aspects of program content in ways different from that customarily identified by objective, adult-imposed, content analysis. It is also known that personal experience is brought to bear upon judgments of realism concerning television content and that such experience and judgment can impact on any potential influences that television may have on attitudes, beliefs, and perceptions.

Perhaps the most important questions addressed in the television influence debate relate to the role that the viewer has in that influence process. A simplistic model of influence that assumes that exposure to television is both necessary and sufficient to explain and predict the views people hold regarding societal issues is rejected. New applications to understanding mass media effects of cognitive models may provide conceptually better explanations of television's influences on children's knowledge and perceptions of the world. Within this framework it is important also to look at different types of programs being viewed by children and how these programs were cognitively processed before difficult issue of the potential and actual power of television can be assessed. This level of analysis is particularly important in order to begin to understand more fully why children learn and don't learn from informational and factual programs on popular television. It is with these perceptions of the issue that the research we report in the rest of this book is concerned. And it is to that research we now turn.

2 The Research

Understanding children's involvement with and response to television is a complex area of study. Although the subject of children and television has been the focus of public debate that in turn has both spawned and been fueled by research by psychologists, sociologists, educationalists, and communications specialists, there is still a great deal of disagreement over the impact that television has on the lives of young people. This volume attempts to provide answers to some of the most pressing questions about television's influences on children and to add usefully to the published research literature by describing a new program of investigation that uses more than one research technique to shed light on how children respond to selected categories of television material.

The research sets out to measure the comprehension, evaluation, and effects of television programs at a perceptual or cognitive level using a classic experimental psychological design. The research measured young viewers' immediate responses to programs and the subsequent cognitive impact that particular viewing experiences had on them. The key variables under investigation were knowledge, beliefs, and attitudes relating to selected subject matters. Effects on these variables of television programs whose contents either dealt directly with or were closely related to the subject matter in question were the psychological phenomena being measured. The classic design involved pretesting participants, in this case children ages between 8 and 15 years, for existing knowledge, beliefs, and attitudes on the critical subject areas, then showing them a program whose contents deal with the same subject, and finally testing participants once again for their reactions to the program and for any changes in knowledge, beliefs, or attitudes. For comparison purposes, some children were tested twice but were shown no program at all.

As a preparatory stage, prior to setting up the experiments, qualitative research was conducted in which children were interviewed in small groups of six and were invited to talk in their own words among same-age peers about programs they watch. Different children participated in the focus groups and experimental studies. This initial research enabled us to study the ability of children to articulate opinions about programs in their own words and to get an idea about the language and terms young viewers of different ages used when referring to their viewing experiences. This was important in knowing how best to design the dependent measures to be pursued in the subsequent experiments in which larger numbers of children would be tested for their comprehension of programs shown to them and questioned on two occasions about their beliefs and attitudes on topics relating to the contents of various programs.

METHODOLOGY

The project began in the spring of 1988 and was funded by the Independent Broadcasting Authority (IBA) for a period of 2 years. It was separated into two distinct research phases: the first qualitative, the second quantitative. The qualitative phase consisted of a series of group discussions with children on a wide range of television genres. Information obtained from the qualitative work then fed into the quantitative phase that concentrated on children's responses to three specific program areas—police drama, science, and quizzes—and was concerned with their attitudes, beliefs, knowledge, recall, and comprehension of program material.

THE QUALITATIVE PHASE

The Samples

A number of primary and secondary schools in one of the outer London boroughs (local government areas) were approached, of whom 13 primaries and 11 secondaries agreed to participate. This particular borough had a wide ethnic and social mix, which was one of the reasons for its selection. Additional schools were recruited during the quantitative phase.

Groups of children were provided by the different schools in accordance with age and gender quotas specified by the authors. The only additional requirement in this qualitative phase was that the children selected should be willing to talk in a group and were unlikely to be inhibited by the presence of a tape recorder. Very occasionally, a child turned out to be reluctant to participate fully and sometimes a particularly outgoing child would tend to dominate a group. Both of these situations were more likely to occur with the younger children. However, the great majority of children were delightfully responsive and only too keen to chat in depth about the programs they watched and did not watch.

Although it is acknowledged that using groups in a school environment does not replicate a real-world viewing situation, it seemed to be the most practical way of obtaining large enough samples for the subsequent experiments and analyses to be meaningful. The aim of the discussions was to provide insight into children's knowledge of, attitudes to, and appreciation of different program areas; the resulting information to be used as a basis for designing experiments for the second phase of the project.

There were 336 children interviewed on a number of different program types, details of which are provided in Table 2.1.

Program Samples

Television ratings compiled for the U.K. television industry by the Broadcasters' Audience Research Board (BARB) and supplied by the IBA, were examined and a wide range of programs were analyzed in terms of content

TABLE 2.1
Numbers of Children Interviewed About Each Program

| | Ages | | | | | | | |
| | Primary Children | | | | Secondary Children | | | |
Program Areas	7–8	8–9	9–10	10–11	11–12	12–13	13–14	14–15
Drama series	6	6	6	6	6	6	–	6
Soap operas	6	–	6	–	6	6	12	–
Situation comedy	–	–	6	6	6	12	6	–
Quiz/game shows	–	6	–	6	6	12	6	–
Entertainment*	6	6	6	6	12	12	–	–
Sport	–	–	6	6	6	6	6	6
Science/Info*	6	6	6	6	6	18	18	6
News	–	–	–	–	6	6	6	12

Note. There were equal numbers of males and females per age group for each program area.

*More children were recruited for certain program strands such as Entertainment and Science/Information so that a full range of programs could be discussed. Other genres (e.g., News, Sports, and Situation Comedy) were not deemed to be of sufficient interest to the younger children to warrant any lengthy discussion. In addition, many of the oldest age range were involved in end-of-year examinations (prior to General Certificate of Secondary Education [GCSE]) and some schools were reluctant to let us have access to these particular year groups.

and format in order to establish their potential usefulness for experimentation. As a result of this exercise, program excerpts were selected from programs known to be widely viewed by children in the age range studied by this research, and recorded so as to provide a focus for the subsequent group discussions.

Group Discussions

The children were interviewed in groups of six (with an even gender split within each group) by an experienced interviewer who was also a qualified teacher and therefore was used to talking to children. Each group ran for approximately 1 hour and was audiotaped throughout. In order to put the children at ease quickly, they were interviewed within friendship groups and the opening questions always concentrated on their general use of television in the home. These were questions to which the youngsters easily "knew" the answer and did not require them to express any opinion of their own, something it was felt they might have been reluctant to do initially. These "icebreaker" questions elicited information on the kinds of viewing equipment to which each child had access, that is, the number of video recorders and TV sets in their own household and where they were situated. The children were also questioned on the number of hours they watched television and which member of their household had "control" of the set.

A few sample statistics serve to give the flavor of the children with whom this research was conducted. The majority of pupils in the sample viewed for approximately 4 hours a day, slightly higher than the national average of 3–3.5 hours a day (see Gunter & McAleer, 1990). Approximately 92% had more than one television in the household and a further 57% claimed to have a personal set in their bedroom. This latter finding tended to apply more to boys than girls. Surprisingly, many of the girls did not seem to mind if brothers had access to their own set while they went without. However, most children tended to watch television with their family and only resorted to solitary bedroom viewing late at night or when there was something specific that they alone wanted to watch. In all, 95% of the sample claimed to have a videocassette recorder (VCR) in the home; this exceeded the national average, at the time of this research, of 73% for households with children (Svennevig, 1989). Parents were seen as the most likely members of the household to exercise control over the set in terms of which program the family should watch. Only 11% of the sample said that they decided the viewing schedule for the evening as opposed to other members of the household and of these, girls were more likely to claim to exercise this form of control than boys.

The discussions then moved on to address specific program strands. Each group was questioned on their likes and dislikes of a particular television genre as well as their likelihood of watching and why. After eliciting these general responses to specific categories, the children were shown several clips from a range of relevant programs representing the genre under discussion and were encouraged to talk about these in more detail. Each discussion was designed to be as open-ended as possible in order to probe individual comments in detail. However, a semistructured format was still imposed in that certain key questions were asked in each interview so as to enable comparisons to be made among each of the different age groups.

The audiotapes were then transcribed, with general themes, and recurring features occurring across tapes being abstracted and highlighted. This enabled patterns of response or commonalities to be identified in order to feed into the second, quantitative phase of the research.

A summary of the children's qualitative responses to the three program areas studied in the second phase, which is the main focus of this book, are alluded to in chapter 3. Subsequent chapters then deal with results of the experimental studies. A full account of the qualitative research including several further program areas examined in the qualitative phase has been reported in detail elsewhere (Gunter et al., 1991).

THE QUANTITATIVE PHASE

From the transcripts of the qualitative phase, three main television genres were selected for experimentation. Specific programs representing these genres were selected and then analyzed in depth in order that program content and format as well as children's responses to them could provide the basis for designing a set of questionnaires to be used as pre- and posttest measures.

The genres selected were drama, information, and entertainment; within these broad categories, it was decided to concentrate on children's responses to and understanding of police drama series, science-based information programs, and television quiz shows, respectively.

Police drama series and science programs offered narrative and pictorial content about which factual and inferential questions could be asked. Under the entertainment heading, TV quiz shows represented a type of lighthearted programming that also contained factual information, derived from the general knowledge questions put to contestants in these shows.

EXPERIMENT 1: POLICE DRAMA

From children's responses, and due to its regular high position in the ratings, the ITV police drama series "The Bill" was chosen as the main material for testing. "Juliet Bravo" was then selected for comparison as this particular program had produced a mixture of both positive and negative responses from children in the qualitative phase in terms of preference and realism. A further requirement that influenced program selection was the 9 p.m. "watershed." As the project aimed to explore children's understanding of programs that they were most likely to watch at home, a conscious decision was made not to show them anything they might not normally be allowed to watch. It was also felt that program length was an important factor. Too long a program, particularly when being viewed in a group situation, could create problems of inattention. In addition, there was a limit as to how long schools would let us have access to whole classes of children at any one time.

Both "The Bill" and "Juliet Bravo" had certain elements in common at the time of this research; that is, the setting in each case was a local police station, female officers were portrayed in positions of authority, and there was a tendency for an even spread of both major and minor incidents to be featured each week. There were also opposing elements. "Juliet Bravo" was set in a northern country market town, appeared to have no plainclothes (undercover) or ethnic minority officers attached to the station and the narrative tended to unfold in a leisurely fashion. In contrast, "The Bill" was set in a run-down area of inner London with a large number of station staff that included both plainclothes and ethnic minority officers. It also offered a much faster moving narrative. This contrast of opposites and similarities provided a wealth of material for testing purposes.

At the time of the project, both series were being screened in a regular weekly slot during peak family viewing time. It was acknowledged that some of the children might have already seen the episodes selected as test material so this factor was allowed for in the questionnaires and then used as a possible explanatory variable within the analysis.

The selected program episodes had similar themes in that they dealt with missing children who were subsequently found as a result of action by leading female characters, who both took on key roles within the narrative. "The Bill" dealt with the problem of a surrogate mother's refusal to hand the baby over to the biological father, who then kidnapped it in desperation. The plot was further complicated by the fact that the surrogacy had been undertaken illegally, a fact that the mother attempted to conceal from the police thus hindering their investigation.

"Juliet Bravo" concentrated on a teenage runaway who had fled from home having discovered that her school teacher was having an affair with her father. The plot was complicated by the fact that the wife knew of the affair but had not said anything; a feature that she also attempted to keep from the police. She had also encouraged her daughter to develop a close relationship with the teacher. The distraught teenager, having felt betrayed by all of the adult world and convinced that she was a laughing stock at school (now that the affair had become public knowledge), eventually attempted suicide, despite police struggles to find her in time.

Both programs then, dealt with adult themes within a family program but with no explicit sex or violence. It was anticipated that a full comprehension of the narrative would require detailed concentration and that previous experience would aid this comprehension process. We were, therefore, keen to discover the extent to which children were able to follow complex narratives dealing with topics that they were unlikely to have experienced in real life and how programs of this nature might influence their perceptions of real-life police.

Four different schools were used for Experiment 1, two secondary and two primary from which comparable groups in terms of age and gender were recruited; details of these are provided in Table 2.2. Because of the schools' socioeconomic mix, a certain number of children for whom English was a second language (ESL) and who were therefore less fluent were also included in the groups and their responses are considered in the analyses.

As a result of the program analyses and the qualitative phase, three questionnaires were designed, one as a prescreening test, the other two to be administered postscreening. At the prescreening stage, all children within their year groups were presented with a structured questionnaire consisting of both open-ended and precoded items. Precoded items either used a scaling measure or multiple choice format, the latter being a method that many children are familiar with from their work in school. The youngsters were given as much time as they needed to complete the questionnaire. The secondary pupils (age 11 +) were encouraged to work through the questionnaire on their own, although the researcher did offer guidance in terms of clarification if required. With the primary pupils, a slightly different method was adopted in that all of the questionnaire items were read out one by one, to enable the less able readers to cope with the content. Open-ended questions were also kept to a minimum as a further means of assisting the less able.

TABLE 2.2
Experiment 1: Police Drama—Sample Details

Age	"The Bill"		"Juliet Bravo"	
	Male	Female	Male	Female
10–11	12	13	18	12
11–12	13	10	12	10
13–14	13	10	14	10
15–16	12	10	10	10
Total	50	43	54	42

The prescreening questionnaire aimed to test:

1. the children's knowledge of police work in general (i.e., the different activities carried out by policemen as opposed to police-women, or plainclothes vs. uniformed police).
2. the children's beliefs about the quantity and types of crime most prevalent nowadays and the frequency with which they were solved, and
3. the children's attitudes toward real-life police—their characteristics and their role within society.

Demographic details (e.g., gender and age) as well as additional background information such as the child's previous experience with real-life police and their viewing profiles, that is the number of hours of television watched, and their awareness of police series, both factual and fictional, were collected at this stage.

The screening itself and the administration of the two postscreening questionnaires took place 7 days later. The same children within their year groups were presented with a full screening of the selected program, either "The Bill" or "Juliet Bravo" (although the advertisements had been edited out of "The Bill" beforehand). Their general behavior (i.e., the degree of attention paid to the screen at differing narrative points) during viewing was also observed. The children were then asked to complete a structured questionnaire immediately afterward. The questionnaires administered to the two different screening groups ("The Bill" or "Juliet Bravo") were identical in terms of format, but individual questions were altered as necessary to take into account the differences in content concerning character representations and narrative events in the two programs.

These questionnaires sought to examine:

1. the children's comprehension of the narratives taking account of both implicit and explicit plot information, causal reasons for character behavior and the sequencing of events;
2. the children's beliefs about the "realism" in terms of its portrayal of the police and events; and
3. the children's attitudes toward the program in terms of likes and dislikes and the degree to which they were able to identify with programs of this type.

The same children were then asked to complete an edited version (i.e., the open-ended questions were removed) of the prescreening questionnaire in order to measure any change in knowledge and beliefs after having seen the programs. Questionnaires belonging to children who were absent at either the pre- or postscreening stage were removed from the sample at this stage and were not included in the analyses.

Control Groups. In order to partial out changes in attitude and knowledge as a result of mere elapse of time as opposed to viewing program-relevant material, control groups similar in terms of number, age, and gender were also recruited. The children in these groups were presented with the same prescreening questionnaire as the experimental groups and were then given the edited version to complete 7 days later but were not subjected to a program screening beforehand, thus controlling for the effect of mere passage of time. The use of a 7-day interval between pre- and posttesting for both the experimental and control groups was seen as a means of minimizing pretesting sensitization effects. At the pretest stage, none of the children was told about the screening or the posttest questionnaire related to it. They also had no knowledge of the repeat test until they were presented with the questionnaire at the posttest phase.

Adult control groups were also recruited in order to compare responses to the narrative questionnaire administered at the posttest stage. Two groups of 10 adults (5 male and 5 female) were shown the test material, either "The Bill" or "Juliet Bravo" and were then asked to complete the narrative questionnaire to see if their responses were similar to those of the older experimental groups (ages 15–16) or whether they would achieve a higher level of recall and comprehension, thus indicating a continuing increase in television sophistication up to adulthood.

Detailed statistical analyses were carried out on all questionnaires from both the experimental and control groups, the results of which are reported in full in chapters 3 and 4. Chapter 3 focuses on children's evaluative responses to each program, attitudes toward different aspects of these police dramas, and their comprehension of narrative plot details. Chapter 4 examines the extent to which these programs produced any immediate, postviewing shifts in knowledge, beliefs, or opinions relating to the police, police work, and crime.

EXPERIMENT 2: SCIENCE I

Two separate experiments were carried out to investigate learning from science programming. The differences between these two experiments related to the nature of the programs selected for experimentation. In the first experiment, two contrasting programs were selected as test material, both of which concentrated on one topic only for the duration of the program. Programs selected for the second experiment adopted more of a magazine format and presented a selection of items that bore little relationship to each other.

The two programs selected for the first science experiment, based on children's responses in the group discussions, were "Body Matters" and "Erasmus Microman." The former, which is classified as adult programming, had produced a favorable response from children in terms of liking, whereas the latter, in spite of having been created specifically for the younger age range, was deemed by them to be less interesting.

Both series had one main feature in common in that they concentrated on one topic in detail each week and offered insight into the topic's basic characteristics from a range of perspectives. In the two programs selected as test material from each of the series, "Body Matters" offered an in-depth study of the way the human skeleton was structured, "Erasmus Microman" investigated Michael Faraday's attempts to produce electricity. However, there were significant differences in the way in which the information was presented within the two programs.

"Body Matters" had three presenters (all qualified doctors) and was studio-based with a live audience who were encouraged actively to participate in order to demonstrate specific concepts. Large-scale working models of parts of the body were produced to enable the viewer to appreciate their individual functions. A wide range of detailed information was presented at a fast pace, often containing an incongruous or humorous element designed to attract and hold the viewer's attention. The program was aimed at a family audience and was screened at a peak viewing time of 7 p.m.

"Erasmus Microman" was slower paced, offering a distinct didactic style. Each week the viewer was invited to go back in time to meet a renowned scientist from history and see how he or she conducted his or her initial experiments. The journey back in time was made on screen by two children (both actors) accompanied by Erasmus Microman, a "professor" type character from whom the program gets its name. The original experiments were demonstrated on screen and the two child actors were encouraged to hypothesize and test out some basic theories for themselves, thus participating in "active" learning within a prestructured environment, currently deemed to be an appropriate way of teaching science to young children by U.K. educationalists.

Two questionnaires were devised, to be administered at the pre- and postscreening stages. Two comparative groups of children in terms of age and gender, were recruited from four different schools, two secondary and two primary. Details of the group compositions are presented in Table 2.3.

At the prescreening stage all children were presented with an open-ended general knowledge questionnaire that sought to measure the extent of their prior knowledge on a range of disciplines (e.g., history, geography, science, and current affairs). Embedded within this questionnaire were specific

TABLE 2.3
Experiment 2: Science Program I—Sample Details

Age	"Body Matters"		"Erasmus Microman"		Total
	Males	Females	Males	Females	
8–9	14	14	14	13	55
14–15	14	13	14	15	56
Total	28	27	28	28	111

items relating to the test material. A longer version of the questionnaire was piloted beforehand with a small group of children whose ages ranged from 8 to 14 to enable inappropriate items to be eliminated from the final version. The difficulty levels ranged from very easy to quite hard and it was assumed from the pilot test that the poor ability members of the younger age range (8–9) would only be able to answer approximately 20% of the questions, whereas the more able members were expected to score up to 80% according to their intellectual ability. Approximately 25% of the questions were derived from the program material, which were then duplicated at the posttest stage in order to measure knowledge growth as a direct result of exposure to relevant program material. This pretest questionnaire also provided a general achievement measure allowing assumptions to be made about children's overall background knowledge that could then be fed into the analyses as an additional possible explanatory variable.

As with the drama experiment, children were tested within their peer groups and were given as much time as they required to complete the questionnaire. Each item was read aloud for the younger pupils and because of the open-ended format, assistance was given as and when necessary with spelling and writing down the answers, although for the majority of items a one-word answer was all that was required and all children were told not to worry about correct spelling.

The program screenings and administration of the posttest questionnaires took place 7 days later so as to minimize the effects of pretest sensitization. The same children were presented with a full screening of either "Body Matters" or "Erasmus Microman" and were then asked to complete the questionnaire immediately after the screening. The two questionnaires administered to the two different screening groups were altered as necessary to take account of the differences in format and information offered by the two programs.

These questionnaires, containing a mixture of precoded (scaling or multiple-choice) and open-ended items (including those from the pretest questionnaire) sought to examine the following:

1. the children's comprehension of the information presented by the television text;

2. the children's recall of information and the extent of knowledge growth as identified by comparison of common questions at the pre- and postscreening stages;
3. the children's own belief as to the likelihood of being able to learn from televised information programs; and
4. the children's attitudes toward the program content and form of presentation in terms of likes and dislikes.

Demographic data such as age, gender, and whether English was their first or second language as well as amount of TV viewing and program preferences were also obtained at the posttest stage.

Information was also collected on the extent to which children had studied the program's topic in school previously and whether they read newspapers or magazines regularly (another source of general knowledge information). General viewing behavior in terms of the degree of attention paid to the screen was also observed and noted. Full details of the results from this experiment are reported in chapter 5.

EXPERIMENT 3: SCIENCE II

The methodology used for the second science experiment was similar to that used for the first in that children were presented with the same pretest questionnaire structure as in Science I but with the program-related questions obviously changed, and then subjected to a program screening and posttest questionnaire 7 days later. The postscreening questionnaire was also similar in format to that used in the previous experiment, but individual items were altered as necessary to take account of differences in style and information offered within the programs. However, in this second science experiment there were differences in the format of the test material, in the number of science programs shown, and two additional age groups were included in the sample.

The three programs selected for testing were "Owl TV," "Know How," and "Tomorrow's World." "Owl TV" was a children's nature program that had just begun its first series at the time of testing and was aimed at the infant/junior age range (6–10 years). "Know How" was a science program aimed at slightly older children (9–15 years) whose presenter, Johnny Ball, had been well liked by the discussion groups in the qualitative phase. "Tomorrow's World" was a long-established adult science program that investigated new technology and (according to the ratings) had been popular with the viewing public in general for many years. All three programs had one main feature in common (i.e., they adopted a magazine format and offered a variety of brief items on a range of topics). However, as the number of items varied within programs, both "Owl TV" and "Tomorrow's World" were edited down to only four items so as to provide appropriate comparisons with "Know How." There were still, however, sufficient variations in content, style, and speed of presentation in all three programs, to provide a suitable range of material for testing purposes.

"Owl TV" offered information on wallabies and their young, elephants, sea creatures, and dinosaurs, introducing new concepts, such as "symbiotic" relationships and causal reasons for dinosaurs becoming extinct, in a simplistic fashion. "Know How" was presented at a very fast pace, attempting to explain sophisticated concepts such as suspension, teleportation, gravity, and video-disc manufacture as graphically as possible. "Tomorrow's World" offered insight into methods of reconditioning damaged records, new kinds of running shoes that reduce bone damage, the repair of nerve cells, and plastic car manufacture.

The posttest questionnaire was split into sections to reflect the different items in the programs; the questions themselves sought to measure the extent to which children had understood the concepts involved as well as the recallability of specific features.

Sample details are shown in Table 2.4. There were 290 children who took part in this experiment. Of these participants, 150 were males and 140 were females. The children were spread across four age groups: 8–9 years ($n = 74$), 10–11 years ($n = 77$), 12–13 years ($n = 73$), and 14–15 years ($n = 66$). The sample was heterogeneous in terms of language facility, with 162 children having English as their first language and 128 children having English as their second language.

As with the previous experiments, the questionnaire was read aloud to the younger age groups and assistance was given where necessary in terms of spelling and writing in the answers to open-ended questions. Similar demographic information and other relevant background data was collected as in the previous experiment. The results of this experiment are reported in chapter 6.

TABLE 2.4
Experiment 3: Science Program II — Sample Details

Age	"Owl TV"		"Know How"		"Tomorrow's World"		Total
	Male	Female	Male	Female	Male	Female	
8–9	12	12	14	12	12	12	74
10–11	13	12	13	13	13	13	77
12–13	12	12	13	11	13	12	73
14–15	12	10	11	11	12	10	66
Total	49	46	51	47	50	47	290

EXPERIMENT 4: QUIZ SHOWS

Television quiz shows were chosen as a relevant representative of entertainment programs as it had become evident from the group discussions that quiz shows were popular with all age ranges mainly because of the opportunities they offered for audience participation and because children, like adults, appear to enjoy seeing people competing for prizes. These programs also offered informational content in the form of general knowledge questions that contestants were required to answer in playing the games. Taking account of both our children's responses to the content and format of quiz shows and BARB viewing figures for individual programs, three quiz shows, "Blockbusters," "Every Second Counts," and "Knock Knock" were selected as test material. All of these were generally popular, although age appeared to be an important variable when determining the extent of popularity. Older children were more scornful of "Knock Knock" in terms of content and prizes. All three shows had one thing in common in that they required contestants to answer a selection of general knowledge questions but there were marked differences in presentation, types of contestants, and the difficulty level of the questions.

In "Blockbusters," the contestants tended to be GCSE 'A'-level students (ages 16–18 and extremely able in terms of intellectual ability) who competed against each other to answer a wide range of fairly difficult general knowledge questions presented to them in a "traditional" quiz style. That is, the presenter read the question or clue and the contestants competed against each other (either singly or in pairs) to be the first to offer the right answer. A high degree of general knowledge was essential to achieve success. There was a good range of prizes offered for the successful contestant or contestants.

"Every Second Counts" was hosted by Paul Daniels (a popular TV magician and comedian). It was aimed at a family audience and was more relaxed and informal in style. The contestants tended to be married couples who competed against each other in their pairs by answering general knowledge questions to which they were offered two possible answers, thereby increasing the element of luck and precluding the need for a high level of general knowledge. Each correct answer gained the contestants so many seconds of time. The winners, who were the couple who accumulated the most time, went on to compete for the star prize at the end of the show in a round in which they competed against the clock, using up the seconds of time they had won in the first part of the program. As with "Blockbusters," there was a good range of expensive prizes offered.

"Knock Knock" was more like a "game" show in format in that there was a lot of physical activity and rushing around the studio. Child contestants (ages 11–14) still had to answer general knowledge questions but these tended to be at a fairly simple level. Therefore, speed of answering seemed to be the main method of achieving success. Each stage of the "game" had quite complex scoring and rules that added to the visual excitement, but the final prizes, although appropriate for the age group involved were of much lower value than those offered in the other two test programs.

All three programs were analysed in depth and formed the basis for both the pre- and posttest questionnaires that were then administered to three comparative groups in terms of age and gender from five different schools in the outer London area. The composition of the groups are detailed in the Table 2.5.

As with the science experiments, general knowledge questions were devised to act as a pretest of knowledge level for each of the programs. Each questionnaire was similar in terms of style, but the content of the questions varied in accordance with the program being tested. Difficulty levels ranged from "very easy" to "quite hard," with approximately 50% of the questions derived from the test material. It was anticipated that few children would be able to score much more than 80%. Questions were presented in both an open-ended and multiple-choice format and subjects were also asked about the extent to which they viewed different quiz programs and their participation in other forms of general knowledge testing such as crossword puzzles, board games, and so on.

The postscreening tests were carried out 7 days later. The same children, within their year group, were presented with a full screening of the selected programs, either "Blockbusters," "Knock Knock," or "Every Second Counts," and were then asked to complete a structured questionnaire immediately afterward. The questionnaires administered to the three different screening groups were altered as necessary to take account of the differences in program style and information but certain items and structure remained the same between groups.

These posttest questionnaires sought to examine the following:

1. the children's recall of information (e.g., social background of contestants/scores achieved) and comprehension of the "rules of the game" as presented by the television text;

TABLE 2.5
Experiment 4: Quiz Shows—Sample Details

Age	"Knock Knock"		"Blockbusters"		"Every Second Counts"		Total
	Male	Female	Male	Female	Male	Female	
9–10	14	12	14	12	14	12	78
11–12	13	12	13	12	14	11	75
13–14	11	11	13	10	12	11	68
Total	38	35	40	34	40	34	221

2. the children's recall of information and the extent of knowledge growth as identified by comparison of common questions in the pre- and postscreening stages;
3. the children's own reasons as to why they watch quiz shows; and
4. the children's attitudes toward the programs in terms of likes and dislikes relating to various program attributes.

As with the previous experiments, assistance was given where necessary in completing the questionnaires and demographic details were obtained as before. The way in which the children watched the programs in terms of attention paid to the screen and the extent of participation in the question-and-answer sequences was also observed. The results of the questionnaire analyses are reported in chapter 7.

This research, then, focused on both what children watched and why, and the functional significance of programs to them. It explored children's general opinions about programs and probed their ability to articulate, in their own words, what they thought and felt about drama, factual, and light entertainment program strands. It then moved on to consider young viewers' direct responses to specific programs, their ability to comprehend and remember program content, and the impact of that content on relevant areas of knowledge and belief. Both an open-ended and controlled experimental perspective was used to facilitate freedom to expression on the part of children and to produce quantitative data relating to their comprehension of what they watch, and the cognitive-level impact programs may have on them. Before turning to the quantitative analyses of the experiments, however, it may prove informative to consider the points arising from the group discussions in the qualitative phase that fed into the later experimental work. These points are the basis of the following chapter.

3 Children's Evaluations and Comprehension of Drama Programs

The observation that children appear to watch and follow television programs with ease can readily give rise to the misconception that television's impact is equally effortless. Appearances, however, can be deceptive. Learning from television requires more effort than is often realized (Salomon, 1979, 1983b). What are important to the effective learning and remembering of programs include the ability to understand program content, familiarity with the genre, and relevant background experience and knowledge against which material presented in programs can be judged (Gunter, 1988).

As children grow up, their understanding of their own environment and the world at large improves. Children attempt to integrate new experiences into their existing framework of knowledge in order to make sense of them. This process applies when children watch television programs. They compare what they see on television with what they "know" from their own experience elsewhere and form their own impressions of the veracity of the contents of programs (Gunter & McAleer, 1990).

With increasing age children's evaluative responses to television change in nature, reflecting the development of new tastes in viewing as well as maturation of abilities to follow programs and to question the truthfulness of their contents (Cullingford, 1984).

In this chapter we are principally concerned with how children respond to television drama programs. The example of drama we have chosen is the police genre, through which we explored young viewers' understanding in two ways. The first technique involved an assessment of children's perceptions of police drama episodes. At this level of "subjective" understanding we were able to find out to what extent children believed or were convinced by the people and events they saw in the programs shown to them. The second technique involved testing the children for their recall of events in the program's story line. This represented a measure of "objective" understanding that reflected the ability of children to remember and correctly piece together elements from the drama.

As we have seen already in chapter 1, there is more to learning from television than simply deciding whether the things shown in programs are acceptable or comparable with existing knowledge. For some children, relevant background knowledge does not exist. For these young viewers, and even for those who do have some relevant background experience, the comprehension of programs is a skill in its own right that develops throughout early and middle childhood (Salomon, 1979).

Children learn about television as well as from it. What they know about television influences how much they take from it. Children at age 7 or 8 remember much less from televised narrative dramas than they do at age 10, and improve by yet another significant margin by the time they reach 12 years of age (Newcomb & Collins, 1979).

During their early years as viewers, children remember what they have seen in television drama differently from the way adult viewers will recall the same material. At age 8 or 9, research has shown that children will retain relatively little central plot content from a typical drama program (W. Collins, Wellman, Keniston, & Westby, 1978). Comprehension improves steadily as children grow older, eventually reaching adult levels by age 13 or 14 (W. Collins, 1979, 1983; Leifer & Roberts, 1972; Newcomb & Collins, 1979). By this stage, children may remember 90% or more of central plot information.

Because much of television's programming shows people interacting with one another, verbally and overtly, children's comprehension of television has been linked to their ability to understand character depictions (Babrow, O'Keefe, Swanson, Meyers, & Murphy, 1988). Children's ability to make attributions and organize their impressions about others, rather than depending on observable characteristics, improves as they grow older (Wartella & Anderson, 1977). Children's general experience in dealing with other people, then, plays a significant part in enhancing their understanding of television material.

With age and increased understanding of programs, both because of growing general experience and experience specifically with television itself, children appear able to follow programs with more information. Younger children benefit in their comprehension from redundancy in information, repetition of content, and anything that emphasizes the central plot or theme. Older children can dip in and out of a program and still put the pieces together to form a coherent whole (Hagen, 1967; Maccoby & Hagen,

1965). They can also separate the central content from the more incidental plot elements and subplots with greater effectiveness (W. Collins, 1975). This means that older children can readily ignore nonessential material, whereas young children are less able to do so (Christenson & Roberts, 1983). Children change with age in what they consider to be essential plot content and younger children may even be distracted from the central program theme by having their attention attracted toward nonessential, but perhaps for them more interesting, imagery (Cullingford, 1984).

Children's comprehension of television increases steadily with age and may reach a point where older children take quite different information from television than do younger children (W. Collins et al., 1978). Older children are able cognitively to process more program content and do so with greater efficiency. With increased age, it is not simply a case of children's tastes and interests changing, their mode of understanding television exhibits important qualitative shifts. With more advanced cognitive skills, children are able to grasp deeper meanings from television programs as they grow up (Rubin, 1986). The grammar of television becomes more accessible to them enabling a higher level of conceptual thinking to be brought to bear on any programs they watch (Rice, Huston, & Wright, 1986).

Children's inferential abilities develop with age with the result that they are not tied to what is overtly portrayed. They become able to "read between the lines," to see what is not shown and infer plot elements and relationships between characters that have not explicitly been mentioned in any of the narrative (W. Collins, 1970, 1983; W. Collins et al., 1978).

The growing cognitive abilities of the child enable the young viewer to cope with longer programs. Anderson and Collins (1988) reported that children under the age of 5 can understand and draw inferences from short programs, but they have difficulty with and frequently fail to follow full-length dramatic programs. Anderson and Collins suggested that children's improved comprehension of longer programs with age, however, is due more to their increased experience with the media and to their growing general knowledge of the world than to shifts in their ability to discern central content or to make inferences. With their less well-developed cognitive systems, children's program preferences and modes of responding to programs are different from those of adult viewers. They can recall program events and make some inferential judgments by age 9, but their style of thinking about programs is quite different from that of adults.

The view adopted here, then, is that the cognitive processes and constructs used by children to interpret and understand television programs are different from those used by adults. These alter with cognitive development and lead to different modes of understanding television and its content. But understanding and ability to remember televised events generally improves with age. Even among adults variations in performance can also be found to be associated with noncognitive variables such as socioeconomic class, ethnic group, varying degrees of experience with television, or with types of programs, and with background knowledge and experience (Dorr, 1980).

In this chapter, we report a study of children's subjective and objective understanding of televised dramatic narrative fiction. Young viewers were shown episodes from two television dramas, both taken from British-made police series, and were first asked to provide information about their perceptions and opinions concerning each program's content and, second, were tested for their recall and comprehension of plot elements. The latter were tested in respect of explicit and implicit story elements. Differences in comprehension were looked at in connection with the age, gender, mother tongue (i.e., English first language or other), viewing experiences, and relevant background knowledge and experiences of the children.

METHOD

The study comprised three stages: pretest, program exposure, posttest. During the pretest, the children were given a questionnaire that probed their knowledge and beliefs about the police and police work, their attitudes toward the police, personal contact with police, personal experience with crime, and television viewing patterns. Further demographic information concerning their age, gender, and whether English was their first language was also obtained. During the posttest, they were given an edited version of this instrument and a test of their comprehension of program content.

Specific episodes of two popular U.K. police dramas were selected as test material, "The Bill" and "Juliet Bravo." At the time of the research, both series had (as detailed in chapter 2) been on television for at least 2 years, shown at peak viewing times on ITV and BBC1 respectively. Qualitative research had yielded a mixture of both positive and negative opinions from children about both series (see Gunter et al., 1991). Each episode was analyzed in depth to determine the areas of content and format to be investigated. Although information on the content and format has been detailed in chapter 2 the two series have a number of important differences and similarities that need to be made clear. "The Bill" is set in an urban environment, has a relatively fast-moving narrative, and features approximately an equal number of plainclothes and uniformed police. "Juliet Bravo" is set in a rural location, has a relatively slow narrative pace, with high concentration on the role of the uniformed police officers. Both programs are similar insofar as they feature women in authority positions, and in the case of the test episode used in this study, both plots concerned missing children. The episode of "The Bill" featured a baby snatched from a surrogate mother by the putative father, whereas the "Juliet Bravo" episode featured an attempted suicide by a runaway teenager distraught at the discovery of her father's affair with one of her school teachers. Both cases were solved by the main "authority" female figures.

In devising a test of understanding of each episode, questions were produced that probed explicit and implicit comprehension of the program's dramatic narrative. Explicit comprehension addressed the ability of children to recall precise factual details concerning events that had occurred in the program. Implicit comprehension required children to make links between events in the story that were not overtly depicted or acted out.

Two comparable groups of children (in terms of age and gender) were recruited from schools in the outer London area. These consisted of 58 males and 41 females who were shown an episode of "The Bill" and 54 males and 38 females who were shown an episode of "Juliet Bravo," with ages ranging from 9 to 16 years. A third comparative group comprising 41 males and 41 females was recruited for control purposes (i.e., testing for stability of attitudes and beliefs over time, in the absence of exposure to the programs).

PROCEDURE

Seven days prior to being shown the relevant television programs, the two test groups were invited to complete a prescreening questionnaire as a means of determining their existing knowledge, beliefs, and attitudes toward the police and the role of the police in the community.

A week later, each school was revisited and the children viewed one of the test programs. Afterward, they completed two further questionnaires. The first sought to measure children's comprehension of the narrative, as well as their perceptions of the way in which the drama reflected police characterization and roles within the "real" world. The second questionnaire was an edited version of the prescreening questionnaire and sought to measure any change in knowledge and beliefs after having viewed the test programs. The control group completed a pre- and postscreening questionnaire within a similar 7-day period, but were not exposed to any program material, nor therefore did they complete a comprehension questionnaire. The results concerning shifts in knowledge, beliefs, and attitudes from pretest to posttest, contingent on viewing the test episodes, are presented and discussed in the next chapter. This chapter focuses on children's direct evaluative responses to and comprehension of the test programs.

SUBJECTIVE UNDERSTANDING

Children's evaluations of police dramas on television were assessed with a set of 30 attitude statements. Some of these statements concerned televised police series in general, whereas others related specifically to the two test programs. All these judgments were invoked as a means of measuring children's subjective understanding of television drama programs. This level of understanding is concerned mainly with young viewers' abilities to discern how realistic and involving were the contents of the televised dramatic narratives shown to them. Research elsewhere has shown that distinctions between fantasy and reality can play an influential mediating role in shaping the nature and strength of children's attitudinal and behavioral responses to television (Feshbach & Singer, 1971; Hearold, 1986).

There is also an important developmental dimension to the issue of children's subjective understanding of television. Older children can more readily draw distinctions between fantasy and reality in programs than younger ones. Between the ages of 8 and 10, children seem to pass through a critical period of development in their understanding of television; before this period young viewers have difficulty making refined judgments about television content (Eron, Huesmann, Brice, Fischer, & Mermelstein, 1983).

As well as learning to make finer distinctions between different kinds of television program, along a reality–fantasy continuum, children also come, with age, to perceive more clearly the qualitative differences between televised behavior and real-world events (Hodge & Tripp, 1986). The evaluation of television content in this way is believed by some writers to represent an important antecedent judgment that determines whether or not information acquired from television is incorporated as credible social reality knowledge (Rubin, Perse, & Taylor, 1988). Unrealistic television content may be discounted as irrelevant to judgments made about the real world.

Realism in a program can play another important role. Earlier research had addressed the significance of the perceived reality of television by asking either child or adult samples whether the people shown on television are like those encountered in real life, whether places shown are like real places, and whether the problems and behavior of television people resemble those viewers are likely to encounter themselves (Greenberg & Reeves, 1976; Reeves & Lometti, 1979). Greater perceived realism can evoke more powerful emotional responses and involvement on the part of the children (van der Voort, 1986). It has been observed that with increased realism, viewers begin to take into account a wider range of format features and content attributes when evaluating television violence (Gunter, 1985a). Subjective classification of a program or elements of it as being more realistic may therefore result in greater involvement and one might also predict that more is taken from the program in consequence.

General Attitudes

The first way we sought to uncover the evaluations that the children made of the police dramas they were shown involved presenting an eight-statement questionnaire that purportedly contained statements made about police drama programs in general. We asked the children to *strongly agree* (1), *slightly agree* (2), *neither agree nor disagree* (3), *slightly disagree* (4), or *strongly disagree* (5) with these statements. We then went on to break these agreement patterns down by both demographics and extent of real-life police contact to see if there were any clearly discernible trends. The opinions examined here were concerned with children's degree of involvement with dramatic characters, perceptions of the morality of characters, lessons that could be learned from the program and reality of the people who were featured.

The overall picture for the children's general opinions about police drama programs on television is summarized in Table 3.1, which shows the percentages of children who indicated that they *agreed slightly* or *strongly* with each statement. At least 7 of 10 of the children across both test-episode groups indicated that these types of programs portray good and bad in people, show realistic people, and can help viewers understand other people's problems. A majority of the children further reported feeling a

TABLE 3.1
General Opinions About Police Drama on Television

	Age Groups				
	All %	*9–10* %	*11–12* %	*13–14* %	*15–16* %
Both the good and the bad side of people are shown in this type of program	75	75	83	72	65
The people in these programs seem like real people	73	82	83	48	70
Programs like this make you think	70	85	72	56	57
This type of program helps you understand other people's problems	70	86	67	55	64
This type of program shows everyday problems as they really are	69	76	74	48	75
Programs like this make you feel how other people feel	64	75	65	45	64
Programs like this make you think of things that might happen to you	59	67	64	45	56
You can imagine yourself being one of the characters	44	66	39	23	46

degree of empathy with the people portrayed in such programs, whereas a substantial minority also claimed to be able to imagine themselves as being one of the characters.

There were a number of age-related differences in attitudes about police drama on television. Generally, older children were less likely to endorse impressions of realism in such programs, they were less likely to feel that police dramas provided special insights into people's problems and feelings, and were less inclined to agree that these programs could make you think about problems and events. After the age of 10, there was a substantial drop in the extent to which the children agreed that they could imagine being one of the characters in a televised police drama, although the increase in 15- to 16-year-olds may be indicating a different "reading" of the programs from that of the 13- to 14-year-olds.

Program-Specific Attitudes

We continued our examination of children's perceptions of televised police drama by looking at their opinions regarding particular aspects of the two test programs. The children were presented with a 22-item questionnaire that consisted of statements relating to specific elements within the program they had just seen ("The Bill" or "Juliet Bravo"), and were again asked to circle a number between 1 and 5 that represented *strongly agree* (1), *slightly agree* (2), *neither agree nor disagree* (3), *slightly disagree* (4), or *strongly disagree* with these statements. These statements related to the perceived realism of the television programs, the stereotypes of plainclothes versus uniformed branch, and men and women police officers, and to presentation features of the program.

Reality Perceptions. The perceived reality of television programming is known to be a powerful mediating variable that can influence the strength and nature of children's responses to what they see on the small screen (Atkin, 1983; Feshbach, 1976; Sawin, 1981; Snow, 1974). The perceived realism of a program can affect the degree of emotional arousal or upset it can cause viewers (Green, 1975; Ross & Condry, 1985). Children, however, do not all react to realistic program content in a uniform fashion. Children's differential emotional responses to real versus fictional television is significantly determined by the child's level of cognitive development (Cantor & Wilson, 1984; Hoffner & Cantor, 1985; Sparks & Cantor, 1986; Wilson, Hoffner, & Cantor, 1987).

Children appear to draw distinctions between realistic and less realistic television content via a number of different types of judgment. They may invoke knowledge about television production; utilize form cues such as whether the characters are human or animated; or use knowledge of the real world gained through direct experience (Dorr, 1983). Young viewers may also ask fairly pointed questions about television depictions. For example, they may begin by questioning if an object or event portrayed in a program exists in the real world. If they are not sure about this, they may question whether it is possible that it might exist for real. Finally, is it at all plausible that such an object or event would really happen (Morison, McCarthy, & Gardner, 1979)? In the current study, a number of questions were put to children about the realism of the police dramas they were invited to watch.

Broadly, the children were able to make a clear statement about the distance from real life of each police drama episode they watched. They agreed that "The Bill" was like a real-life police station more often than that portrayed in "Juliet Bravo." This was most clearly seen in the oldest age group (15- to 16-year-olds; see Table 3.2). An interesting deviation from this pattern was for girls, who were more likely to believe "Juliet Bravo" was more lifelike.

The children basically believed that the crimes shown on the drama programs tend to be those that occupy the police mostly in real life. Conversely, they did not agree that the television portrayals were more exciting than actuality. The only notable exception to this was the youngest age group who viewed "The Bill." This group believed the level of excitement presented in the drama was greater than the real-life experiences of the real police.

Again, our respondents disagreed that the dramas made police work look easy. They felt that the difficulty experienced by TV police exhibited in the programs reflected the difficulty found by police in solving crime in real life. Again, the only deviation from this pattern was among the youngest groups under both program conditions. This may indicate failure to comprehend certain of the subtle stresses and strains presented in the television drama, and a focusing on the actions and apparent solutions.

A slightly strange finding concerns the pattern of agreement with the proposition that the police in drama programs solve crimes more often than do the police in real life. Here, the younger viewers appeared to have the correct perception and the older children to be incorrect (i.e., the latter believed that the rate at which TV crimes are solved reflect the solution rate in real life). There is little doubt that both "Juliet Bravo" and "The Bill" depict the solution of crimes much more frequently than they are solved in real life. However, a feature of both programs is that in certain episodes crimes are left unsolved. This atypical kind of ending may be gaining salience for the older children and may thus be forming the basis of their judgments. Real crimes are rarely solved; the television programs have unsolved crime endings; thus the two are in harmony, thus we cannot agree that the television programs misrepresent reality, thus low agreement with the proposition that asserts that they do.

Apart from the youngest group of children, in respect of "The Bill," only a minority of children agreed that the distribution of ages in the two dramas

TABLE 3.2
Perceptions of Realism of Two Police Drama Programs: Age Differences

		Age			
		9–10	11–12	13–14	15–16
	TV Show	%	%	%	%
The crimes in "The Bill"/					
"Juliet Bravo" are the same					
as those that happen in	"TB"	74	86	65	86
real police situations	"JB"	76	72	68	42
"The Bill"/"Juliet Bravo" show					
you police stations as they	"TB"	65	64	62	86
really are	"JB"	72	64	62	86
"The Bill"/"Juliet Bravo" seems					
more real than other police	"TB"	70	82	54	86
programs	"JB"	59	44	11	5
The police in "The Bill"/					
"Juliet Bravo" solve crimes					
more often than the real	"TB"	61	61	31	46
police	"JB"	66	48	47	47
"The Bill"/"Juliet Bravo"					
makes police work seem	"TB"	78	43	23	46
easy	"JB"	62	32	42	42
The police in "The Bill"/					
"Juliet Bravo" do more					
exciting things than the	"TB"	74	39	46	35
police in real life	"JB"	48	52	32	21
Most of the police in					
"The Bill"/"Juliet Bravo"					
are younger than	"TB"	61	39	23	19
the police in real life	"JB"	35	24	11	5
The police in "The Bill"/					
"Juliet Bravo" have to work	"TB"	48	32	12	0
harder than real police	"JB"	21	36	21	0
"The Bill"/"Juliet Bravo"					
is too violent to be	"TB"	30	14	8	0
realistic	"JB"	10	28	11	5

Note. "TB" = "The Bill"
       "JB" = "Juliet Bravo"

reflected the distribution of ages in the police force generally. This may be a function of the contact or lack of it that the children have with police. Once again, the often frenetic activity shown on television was held faithfully to reflect the frenetic activity of police stations in real life. This must be seen as a false perception on the part of the children. The children clearly did not believe that the level of violence shown in "The Bill" and "Juliet Bravo" overstated the violence prevalent in real-life police work. All age groups seemed to perceive real police work as concerned with violence, and to be underrepresented in these particular police drama portrayals.

Given that most of the 22 statements presented in this part of the study were concerned with realism, it is reasonable to assume that real-life contact with the police could be a factor influencing the nature of children's perceptions of the two police dramas. We thus went on to see if having had some degree of contact with the police produced different patterns of agreement to those produced by children who had no or low contact (see Table 3.3).

The one discrepant group in agreeing that the police officers in the police dramas "solve crimes more often than in real life" were children who watched "The Bill" and had low real-life contact with the police. Contact was measured according to the extent to which the children reported that they had ever been to a police station or the police had visited a school, or they or their families had been victims of criminal activity. They believed that fewer crimes were solved in real life and this must be taken to be the correct perception. Children whose families had been victims had a slightly better grasp of the reality than those who had neither been victims nor knew of anyone who had been victimized. Those who had little contact or no victimization agreed much more strongly that television police drama over represented young police officers compared to real life.

Contact and/or victimization produced a mixture of agreement patterns in terms of the statement concerning "work rate." The children who

TABLE 3.3
Perceived Realism of TV Police Drama and Real-Life Experience

		Real-Life Contact With Police		Real-Life Victim	
	TV Shows	High %	Low %	High %	Low %
"The Bill"					
Police (in the program)					
solve crimes more	"TB"	40	71	53	48
often than real police	"JB"	56	50	56	52
Most of the police in the					
program are younger	"TB"	31	45	19	44
than police in real life	"JB"	25	16	15	28
Police in the program have					
to work much harder than	"TB"	24	23	25	22
real-life police	"JB"	29	11	4	28
There are too many WPCs in					
the program for it to be	"TB"	19	13	6	24
like real life	"JB"	23	7	11	17
The program is too violent	"TB"	12	16	6	18
for it to be realistic	"JB"	17	11	7	17

Note. "TB" = "The Bill"
"JB" = "Juliet Bravo"
WPC = Woman police constables

watched "Juliet Bravo" and had high contact with the police agreed much more (the true perception) with the proposition than those children who watched "The Bill." Again, in terms of victimization, "The Bill" viewers showed little difference as a function of victimization, but for those children who viewed "Juliet Bravo," a much greater proportion agreed with the proposition that television police work much harder than real police if they had no history or experience of victimization, than those who did have such experience.

Stereotypes of Police.   We next looked at stereotypes of the police as they possibly existed in the minds of our respondents. Stereotyping influences of police portrayals on television upon which particular attention were placed upon those relating to perceptions of gender-type behaviors. Did children hold different beliefs about male and female members of the police force? Did they perceive differences in the way male and female police offers were portrayed in the police drama episodes they watched? Children have previously been found to perceive television characters in terms of the gender-typed dimensions of strength (males) and attractiveness (females) (Reeves & Greenberg, 1977; Reeves & Miller, 1978). Boys and girls are known to prefer programs featuring characters of their own gender and to pay closer attention to scenes dominated by same gender characters (Sprafkin & Liebert, 1978). This chapter restricts itself to findings that concern children's perceptions of police characters in the two television drama episodes. Chapter 4 explores changes in perceptions contingent upon watching these police drama programs.

The pattern of agreement to propositions addressing these issues is presented in Tables 3.4 and 3.5. The interesting response patterns here were those concerning whether positions of authority correlate with ability in the case of women police constables (WPCs), whether WPCs being in charge was seen as atypical, and whether the sheer number of WPCs in the program was perceived to be close to real life.

There was little agreement that positions of authority meant higher ability in the case of WPCs. This lack of agreement held for all age groups and both genders. However, within this overall low level of agreement "Juliet Bravo" viewers agreed more strongly, as did girls overall, with the proposition.

In only two cases did the majority of children agree that having a woman police officer in charge was unusual—the oldest age group who watched "The Bill," and the second youngest group in the same condition. Collapsing over both program groups there was little difference in agreement with this proposition as between males and females. Clearly, the children did not consider the number of WPCs in either "The Bill" or "Juliet Bravo" to be unlike real life.

TABLE 3.4
Stereotypes of Police

Statements	TV Shows	All %	Male %	Female %
The male and female officers always get on	"TB"	50	55	56
well together in "TB"/"JB"	"JB"	72	72	71
In "TB"/"JB" the women police officers often have to do different	"TB"	66	66	66
things than the men	"JB"	56	56	55
In "TB"/"JB" the woman inspector must be a better officer than	"TB"	29	33	24
the man	"JB"	42	39	45
Having a woman police officer in charge of	"TB"	43	41	44
men is unusual	"JB"	32	37	26
There are too many WPCs in "TB"/"JB" for it	"TB"	17	21	12
to be like real life	"JB"	14	20	8

Note. "TB" = "The Bill"
"JB" = "Juliet Bravo"

Presentation Features.   Another aspect of the television dramas presented, over and above content, in which we were interested, was format. Were the two programs differentially evaluated in terms of acting, speed of action, and textual matters? Our findings showed that there was just a slight suggestion that some of the dialogue in both television dramas was a little over the heads of our respondents, especially the younger ones.

A clearly appreciable difference occurred for the two television programs presented in terms of the quality of acting. "The Bill" was much superior according to the children surveyed here. This perception was held by all age groups and by both males and females. Somewhat surprisingly, "Juliet Bravo" was seen as too fast-paced by the two youngest groups, whereas "The Bill" generally was not, although the 11- to 12-year-olds did experience some difficulties. With age, the action on "Juliet Bravo" seemed to become more agreeable (see Table 3.6).

OBJECTIVE UNDERSTANDING

In addition to the assessment of children's subjective understanding, operationalized in terms of their evaluative responses to the two police drama episodes, the second focus of this study was on their ability to follow

TABLE 3.5
Stereotypes of Police: Age Differences

Statements	TV Shows	9–10 %	10–11 %	13–14 %	15–16 %
The male and female officers always get on well together in "TB"/"JB"	"TB"	61	61	58	41
	"JB"	79	76	74	53
In "TB"/"JB" the women police officers often have to do different things than the men	"TB"	61	75	65	59
	"JB"	52	52	68	53
In "TB"/"JB" the woman inspector must be a better officer than the man	"TB"	44	29	23	23
	"JB"	52	52	32	21
Having a woman police officer in charge of men is unusual	"TB"	30	57	27	55
	"JB"	38	28	32	32
There are too many WPCs in "TB"/"JB" for it to be like real life	"TB"	30	14	4	23
	"JB"	10	28	5	16

Note. "TB" = "The Bill"
"JB" = "Juliet Bravo"

TABLE 3.6
Presentation Features

Statements	TV Shows	9–10 %	11–12 %	13–14 %	15–16 %	%
You cannot always understand what they are talking about in "TB"/"JB"	"TB"	43	61	57	23	32
	"JB"	41	55	44	42	21
"TB"/"JB" has good acting in it	"TB"	83	91	82	69	86
	"JB"	25	28	36	21	11
"TB"/"JB" is often too fast	"TB"	40	26	54	31	46
	"JB"	66	86	76	42	37

Note. "TB" = "The Bill"
"JB" = "Juliet Bravo"

and remember details from each program. Children's objective comprehension of each program was assessed in two ways. One series of questions explored their understanding and memory of actual events, overtly shown in the program, and another set examined their ability to infer from the story line relationships between events that had not necessarily been acted out. The mean scores for overall, implicit, and explicit comprehension of each program are presented in Tables 3.7, 3.8, and 3.9, with scores broken down further by age group, gender, and fluency in English (Table 3.7); contact with real-life police and personal experience of victimization (Table 3.8); and knowledge about real-life police (Table 3.9).

One-way analyses of variance were computed to assess differences in levels of comprehension of the two police drama episodes as a function of each of these variables. These analyses revealed significant age effects on total comprehension ["The Bill": $F(3,95) = 21.6$, $p < .001$]; and on implicit comprehension ["The Bill": $F(3,95) = 21.1$, $p < .001$; "Juliet Bravo": $F(3,88) = 4.3$, $p < .001$].

There was one significant gender effect that was in respect of explicit comprehension among children who watched "The Bill" [$F(1,97) = 4.6$, $p < .03$]. Girls registered better comprehension than boys. There were no significant effects associated with fluency in English.

Reported contact with the real police had one significant effect on comprehension. Among children who watched "Juliet Bravo," low reported contact with the police was linked to better implicit comprehension than high reported contact [$F(1,90) = 4.9$, $p < 0.03$].

TABLE 3.7

Comprehension Scores for Two Police Drama Episodes as a Function of Age, Gender, and Fluency in English

	"The Bill"			"Juliet Bravo"		
	Implicit Comp.	Explicit Comp.	Total Comp.	Implicit Comp.	Explicit Comp.	Total Comp.
All	10.7	7.3	18.0	10.9	7.6	18.5
Age Groups						
9–10	9.2	7.7	17.0	11.0	7.4	18.4
11–12	10.1	6.5	16.7	10.0	6.4	16.4
13–14	10.2	6.7	16.9	12.1	8.5	20.6
15–16	13.7	8.5	22.2	10.7	8.5	19.3
Gender						
Male	10.9	7.0	17.8	11.0	7.5	18.5
Female	10.5	7.8	18.3	10.8	7.7	18.5
Fluency in English						
English as second language	9.7	6.8	16.6	10.9	7.1	18.5
English as first language	10.9	7.4	18.2	10.9	7.8	18.7

Note. Maximum scores possible:
Implicit comprehension = 16
Explicit comprehension = 10
Total comprehension = 26

Whether or not children reported having been a victim of crime had a significant effect on implicit comprehension among "The Bill" group [$F(1,97) = 5.7$, $p < 0.02$]. Children who claimed to have been victimized had higher implicit comprehension scores. This factor also appeared to have a significant effect on total comprehension [$F(1,90) = 8.2$, $p < 0.005$] among the "Juliet Bravo" group. Once again, children who reported experience of crime victimization had higher scores (see Table 3.8).

There were several factors looked at in this experiment that seemed to have little if any effects. None of the viewing variables — total TV viewing — had any significant effects on comprehension levels. Neither having seen the test episode before nor reported regularity of watching either TV series made any difference to comprehension levels.

Knowledge about the difference between the role of uniformed versus plainclothes police officers was related to comprehension of the test episodes. Our assessment of children's knowledge about the differences between the roles of uniform versus plainclothes police and male versus female police officers was made by having them choose which of several activities were done by the various types of police officers. These responses, from which we computed knowledge scores, are shown in Tables 3.9 and 3.10. A high knowledge score was linked with significantly better total comprehension ["The Bill": $F(1, 97) = 3.4$, $p < 0.05$; "Juliet Bravo": $F(1, 90) = 13.5$, $p < .001$]; explicit comprehension ["Juliet Bravo": $F(1, 90) = 17.0$, $p < 0.001$] and implicit comprehension ["The Bill": $F(1, 97) = 7.25$, $p < 0.008$]. (See Table 3.11.)

TABLE 3.8

Comprehension Scores for Two Police Drama Episodes as a Function of Contact with Real Police and Being a Victim of Crime

	"The Bill"			"Juliet Bravo"		
	Implicit Comp.	Explicit Comp.	Total Comp.	Implicit Comp.	Explicit Comp.	Total Comp.
Contact With Real Police						
Low	11.1	7.4	18.5	11.3	7.6	18.9
High	10.1	7.1	17.1	10.4	7.6	18.0
Been a Victim of Crime						
Yes	11.5	7.3	18.8	11.3	8.6	19.9
No	10.3	7.3	17.6	10.7	.2	17.9

Note. Maximum scores possible:
Implicit comprehension = 16
Explicit comprehension = 10
Total comprehension = 26

TABLE 3.9
Correct Knowledge of Uniform and Plainclothes Police Officers' Tasks, by
Program Viewed

	"The Bill" %	"Juliet Bravo" %
Directs traffic; sorts out traffic jams	93	86
Meets with informers	56	44
Writes reports back at the station	64	74
Investigates big crimes	59	58
Walks the beat	83	77
Patrols in cars	52	41
Investigates small crimes	73	67
Answers inquiries at station	19	32
Does undercover work	74	74
Responds to emergency calls	73	63
Interviews suspects	51	56
Helps with crowd control	85	80
Advises on home security	50	55
Visits schools to give advice	79	86
Gives evidence in court	64	67
Gives orders to other police	21	32

TABLE 3.10
Correct Knowledge of Men and Women Police Officers' Tasks, by Program
Viewed

	"The Bill" %	"Juliet Bravo" %
Responds to emergency calls	72	60
Investigates house burglary	66	64
Tracks down a murderer	37	34
Directs traffic	68	65
Assists with crowd control	35	23
Interview a rape victim	71	64
Deals with drunk/fast drivers	54	42
Interviews a suspect	58	75
Searches for missing child	79	68
Helps with serious accident or disaster	73	80
Investigates bank robberies	43	57
Comforts people	65	59
Writes reports/answers phones at station	65	64
Does undercover work	44	51
Meets with informers	50	54
Gives orders to other police	35	45

TABLE 3.11
Comprehension Scores for Two Police Drama Episodes as a Function of
Knowledge About Real Police

	"The Bill"			"Juliet Bravo"		
	Implicit Comp.	*Explicit Comp.*	*Total Comp.*	*Implicit Comp.*	*Explicit Comp.*	*Total Comp.*
Duties of Plainclothes Police Versus Uniform Police						
Low	10.0	7.3	17.3	10.6	.8	17.4
High	11.4	7.3	18.7	11.3	8.5	19.8
Duties of Male Versus Female Officers						
Low	10.5	7.3	17.7	11.0	7.4	18.4
High	11.3	7.4	18.7	10.7	8.1	18.8

Note. Maximum scores possible:
Implicit comprehension = 16
Explicit comprehension = 10
Total comprehension = 26

DISCUSSION

This chapter has reported an experimental study that explored children's subjective and objective comprehension of two television drama narratives. The measures used examined children's perceptions of those aspects of the real world dealt with by the programs and their ability to remember details from each program.

Subjective Understanding

Children's impressions of each program, including their perceptions of the realism of settings, characters, and events, provided the indicators of their subjective understanding. The poll began by obtaining a few impressions about police dramas in general. This revealed that although a majority of children tended to perceive a degree of realism in the character portrayals and problems featured in contemporary TV dramas of this sort, these views became less widespread with increasing age. A similar pattern emerged in respect of impressions that such programs can teach valuable social lessons, make viewers think, and can evoke empathic feelings. In other words, although contemporary police dramas were seen by many children as a source of information as well as of entertainment, the extent to which children get involved in these programs lessens as they enter their teenage years.

On focusing children's attention on features of specific program episodes they have just watched, finer distinctions in opinions and subjective understanding emerged. For a start, there were marked differences in perceptions of the two contemporary police drama episodes used here in terms of particular aspects of realism. Children have previously been observed to invoke qualitatively different kinds of program evaluations in judging the realism of dramatic television content (Dorr, 1983; Morison et al., 1979). Although production format cues have been found to play a prominent part in establishing the reality of television content among children (M. Brown, Skeen, & Osborn, 1979; Quarforth, 1979; Skeen, Brown, & Osborn, 1982), these were not prominent in the present study. Nevertheless, the children did draw a number of distinct reality judgments about the two police drama episodes.

Where there were consistencies across the two programs in aspects of the way they were evaluated, both programs were judged to be more realistic in certain respects than in others. For example, the types of crimes portrayed in both programs were believed by most children to be like those with which real police have to deal. However, far fewer children generally believed that these TV police led more exciting lives than real-life police, and fewer still believed that these police worked harder than real police.

Complicating the picture still further, increased age was not invariably associated with a decrease in reality perceptions. Although belief in what was shown in the two programs became less widespread with age for certain elements of each program, there were other aspects of each drama for which older children held more widespread reality perceptions. Research elsewhere has shown that even though children become increasingly sensitive to production formats as they grow older (Leary, Wright, & Huston, 1985), this trend is more pronounced for some types of program than for others. With crime drama programs featuring violent content, perceived realism declines with age (Greenberg & Reeves, 1976; Huesmann, Lagerspetz, & Eron, 1984). Other program types have been observed to yield no marked shifts in children's reality perceptions as they become older (Dorr, 1983; Wright, Kunkel, Pinon, & Huston, 1987). For some program types (e.g., family comedies) perceived realism has even been found to increase with age (Dorr, Kovaric, Doubleday, Sims, & Seidner, 1985). These findings reveal how important it is to explore children's reality perceptions in respect of specific aspects of actual programs. Although broad distinctions across program genres in terms of their relative realism can provide some indication of how children respond to television, such simplistic measures fail to reveal deeper and more complex perceptual distinctions that children make about program content.

Objective Understanding

Evidence emerged that children aged 9 to 16 were able to follow the story line of episodes from two British-made police drama series, although this objective comprehension was significantly better among older teenagers than among younger teenagers and preteens. This confirmed earlier research findings showing an age-related progression in program comprehension (W. A. Collins, 1979; Cullingford, 1984).

Generally, the children's comprehension and memory of the content of the two police dramas achieved a respectable level. The overall level of comprehension for "The Bill" was 69.2% correct and for "Juliet Bravo," 71.2% correct. The children surveyed in this study showed that they could understand both explicitly presented material and inferential material implied in story lines. This level of understanding was consistent across various measures of retention and comprehension. There was little evidence, overall, for the view expressed by Sheppard (1990) that the greatest part of adult-oriented television viewed by children (necessarily) goes over their heads.

Stating the results in this way, however, grossly oversimplifies a number of important differences that occurred in respect of the age–comprehension relationship between different programs. Research conducted among U.S. children has shown marked increases in memory and comprehension of information from television dramatic narrative as a function of age. Accurate retention of essential plot information was observed to improve from 66% at age 7 to 8 to 92% at age 13 to 14 (W. Collins et al., 1978). Among those children in the current study who were shown an episode from "The Bill," for example, 15- to 16-year-olds achieved a significantly higher total comprehension score than younger children. There was, however, very little difference in terms of total comprehension of plot features of this episode between 9–10s, 11–12s, and 13–14s. In total, 15–16s scored about 86% correct responses compared with an average over the remaining age groups of 65%. These results are consistent with those of W. Collins (1975) and W. Collins et al. (1978), who observed similar shifts in comprehension levels between preteenage and early teenage viewers.

Turning to "Juliet Bravo" viewers, the highest comprehension score occurred among 13- to 14-year-olds, who scored marginally higher than the 15- to 16-year-olds. In a similar age reversal, 9–10s scored better in total comprehension than did 11–12s. Over all age groups, the children gave correct responses to comprehension questions 71% of the time (compared with 69% for "The Bill" group).

There were further variations in linkages between comprehension and age in respect of different types of comprehension. Two types were examined in this study, namely explicit comprehension (of events and happenings explicitly shown in the programs) and implicit comprehension that required children to draw inferences between events and happenings. There was little to choose between children who watched either "The Bill" or "Juliet Bravo" in their performance on explicit or implicit comprehension. However, over the children in these two groups in general, explicit comprehension (75%) was greater than implicit comprehension (68%). What emerges from these results then, is that the children were able to understand and recall a substantial proportion of the plot content from these two police drama episodes, and that this was true of all the age groups studied for implicit as well as explicit features of the programs.

Gender effects were not at all prevalent. In fact there was only one main effect of gender in all the analyses conducted: this was for comprehension of explicit material among "The Bill" group. In this case, females performed better than males. The language ability of the children (i.e., whether English was their first or second language) proved to be nonsignificantly related to comprehension of police drama.

Previous research had shown that young viewers' degree of contact with the police in real life did not make much difference to the perceptions they held of police portrayals on television (Rarick et al., 1973). Nevertheless, this variable was examined again in the current research in connection with comprehension of fictional television police drama narratives. Although contact with the police is in fact a rare occurrence, such contact could be expected to "open the eyes" of the children to the reality of policing. If this is so then real-life contact should serve as a counterpoint to the "false reality" that many people claim television affords of such groups as the police. However, in terms of comprehension of story lines, contact had a variable effect. It did not appear as a significant factor in relation to comprehension of "The Bill," but it did with "Juliet Bravo." Its relationship here was, however, limited to implicit comprehension, with low contact with the police being associated with better comprehension.

Another aspect of contact with the police that we looked at concerned whether the respondent had been a victim of a crime or knew of someone who had been a victim. This type of contact seems to have been more nascent. This factor was significantly related to both total comprehension and explicit comprehension among the "Juliet Bravo" group, with children who had experience of crime victimisation producing higher scores. In "The Bill," there was a relationship of police contact with implicit comprehension only, with, once again, children who claimed to have had experience of victimization scoring more highly.

Prior viewing was a very weak predictor of comprehension. Thus, the measures of amount of TV viewing, having seen episode before, factual TV crime program viewing, U.K. and U.S. police drama viewing, and weight of viewing test program all failed to exhibit significant relationships with program comprehension.

In contrast with the prior-viewing habits just cited, background knowledge concerning the respective roles of CID and uniformed police was related to comprehension to a certain extent. Thus, for "The Bill," but not for "Juliet Bravo," high knowledge in this domain appeared as significantly related to total comprehension and implicit comprehension, with high knowledge children obtaining higher scores.

In summary then, comprehension of televised police drama is best seen as mainly a function of the age of the child, with his or her gender, language fluency, or previous viewing experience in terms of either the amount or nature of such television programming viewed being largely noncontributory. Previous experience and world knowledge, however, conceptualized as either developed knowledge or exposure to victimization, can be seen as a weakly contributory consideration.

4 Impact of Drama Programs on Children's Knowledge, Beliefs, and Attitudes

In chapter 3, results were presented concerning children's abilities to comprehend and remember the narrative story content of dramatic television programs from the police genre. Children's opinions about different aspects of these programs were also examined. In this chapter we turn our attention to the impact that police drama episodes might have on children's perceptions of the police and the work that they do. Such potential effects of television police drama episodes are explored in the context of previous empirical work in this field.

An influential theory proposed in the mid-1970s by Gerbner and his colleagues at the Annenberg School of Communications, University of Pennsylvania, offered an alternative perspective to popular cause–effect models of television's impact on its audience. The new model argued that television's influence could not be understood by any research perspective that failed to give adequate representation to the complexity of the world of television drama with its integrated system of characters, events, actions, and relationships (Gerbner & Gross, 1976; Gerbner et al., 1977, 1978).

According to Gerbner, viewers learn information from dramatic television material that is then incorporated into their conceptions of social reality. Through analysis of relationships between individuals' reported television viewing habits, particularly the amount of time they spend watching, and their perceptions of their social and cultural environment, it was felt possible to reveal television's contribution to the attitudes, beliefs, and values people hold with respect to the world in which they live.

PERCEPTIONS OF POLICE AND CRIME

The earliest empirical test of cultivation theory focused on relationships between television viewing and the public's beliefs about crime. During the second half of the 1970s, Gerbner and his colleagues reported a series of studies among U.S. samples in which they presented evidence for links between claimed amounts of television viewing and perceptions of the prevalence of crime and violence in society, degrees of personal fear or being involved in crime, and mistrust of other people and authorities. These relationships were found among adult and child samples (Gerbner et al., 1977, 1978).

Gerbner's thesis and findings have not been universally accepted. One alternative view postulates that the effect of viewing television programs featuring crime-related themes could be the opposite to that indicated by the Gerbner group. According to this view there is little reason to expect that people will view material that produces aversive states such as fear, but because crime programs on television invariably feature the triumph of justice — in crime drama the bad guys are usually caught and punished in the end — individuals who watch these programs may be finding comfort and reassurance through them (Zillmann, 1980).

Support for this position has been provided by Gunter and Wober (1983) who found a positive relationship between beliefs in a just world and exposure to television crime drama programming. This finding conflicts with the contention that viewing crime drama cultivates fear and mistrust and leaves open the possibility that what is cultivated instead (or in addition at least) are perceptions of a just world. It also leaves open the possibility, however, that those who believe in a just world seek to support these beliefs by more frequent exposure to crime drama on television.

Although one might argue that most individuals would not normally choose to watch material that causes an extreme aversive response, there is no doubt that scary movies or TV programs hold inherent appeal for many people. The scariness has to be contained, however. Indeed, there is evidence to show that apprehensive individuals may turn to fictional content with crime or frightening themes, possibly as a means of psychologically coping with their real-world fears (Boyanowsky, 1977; Boyanowsky, Newtson, & Walster, 1974).

Recent research has indicated that, regardless of the direction of causality inferred from correlational links between television viewing and perceptions of crime, demonstration of the nature and significance of television's contribution to these anxieties and beliefs requires a more sophisticated model of influence than that put forward by Gerbner and his co-workers (Gunter, 1987b). Increasingly, recognition has been given to other elements that represent important mediating variables:

1. television viewing patterns;
2. perceptions and comprehension of television content;
3. judgments about different types of crime; and
4. personal experience with crime and police

Television Viewing Patterns

Much of the early research on the role of television in shaping public perceptions and attitudes regarding crime and law enforcement depended on nonspecific measures of television viewing. In general, viewing measures did not differentiate between exposure to different kinds of television content. However, relationships between levels of exposure to television and perceptions of crime may be program specific. In other words, any influence of television on beliefs about crime may depend not so much on the total amount of television viewed per se, but more significantly on how much informationally relevant programs (i.e., those with specific crime-related content) are watched (Weaver & Wakshlag, 1986).

Perceptions and Comprehension of TV Content

The influence of television may depend not simply on what is watched but on how viewers perceive and interpret the content of programs (Pingree, 1986; Teevan & Hartnagel, 1976). Research has shown that viewers can be highly discriminating when it comes to portrayals of violence, crime, and law enforcement on television (Gunter, 1985a, 1987b). Audiences are capable of making clear distinctions between how certain social entities (such as criminals or the police) are depicted on television and how they appear or are believed to be in real life. Such perceptually subtle distinctions may be drawn even by children (van der Voort, 1986).

Comparisons of what young people think about television police and real-life police have shown that the two versions are not generally perceived in the same way (Rarick et al., 1973). Even programs with crime or law enforcement themes may have little impact on beliefs about crime and law enforcement agencies in real life, if viewers are not prepared to recognize the content of such programs as offering an accurate representation of the real world (Potter, 1986).

As well as the perceived realism of programs on television that carry crime and law enforcement-related content, the impact of television on young viewers' beliefs about social reality may also be mediated by their ability to follow the story line of a television drama.

Learning from television may depend, among other things, on the way individuals watch and are able to comprehend programs. Research has shown that the ability to remember facts from television programs and to draw inferences that go beyond the explicit content in programs improve with age through early and middle childhood. We have already seen that findings indicate that children younger than 8 have difficulty keeping track of the order and relationships between events in a plot separated in time, but are able to follow them when they occur closer together (W. Collins, 1973, 1979).

In chapter 1 we highlighted a study with children ages between 10 and 12 years by Pingree (1983), who found that the ability to follow a television story line may have important implications for the influence of drama programs on young viewers' beliefs about the real world. Children answered questions about their viewing habits and beliefs about the prevalence of violence and criminal behavior. They also watched an edited television drama program and answered questions about it.

Although across the sample as a whole, greater reported amounts of television viewing by the children were associated with exaggerated perceptions of crime and violence in society, these associations were weaker among those children who exhibited especially good program comprehension. It also emerged that children who were good at program comprehension held a more integrated and coherent outlook on the world than did other youngsters.

Judgments About Different Types of Crime

Previous research has indicated that not all judgments about crime are equally susceptible to media influences. A distinction can be made, for instance, between different types of perceptions of crime and safety, and between different fear states (Gunter, 1987b). One broad conceptual distinction has been made between personal-level and societal-level judgments (Tyler & Cook, 1984). Another distinguishes between perceptions of crime in different situations (Weaver & Wakshlag, 1986). Evidence has emerged that shows that viewers discriminate between crime in different settings (e.g., in urban or rural locations) and that estimates of risk from crime in distant settings tend to be more extreme than those in respect of locations closer to home. Furthermore, television viewing patterns tend to be more closely related to perceptions of crime in distant than in near locations (Gunter, 1987b). Factual television material about crime has been found to exert a more profound influence on viewers' perceptions of crime than drama material. However, even this effect tends to occur for societal-level rather than personal-level judgments about crime (Tamborini et al., 1984).

Personal Experience With Crime

There is a body of research evidence indicating that individuals distinguish sources of information relevant to their perceptions of social reality on a number of levels: (a) direct, personal experiences; (b) experiences of others (i.e., relatives and friends); and (c) experiences presented through the mass media as either factual information (e.g., news programs) or fictional depictions (e.g., crime drama programs). It appears that social perceptions are most strongly influenced by the most direct form of experience available to the individual. Thus, actual, real-life experience tends to have the most powerful effect. When direct experience is lacking or highly ambiguous, however, the individual is then most susceptible to the suggestion of less direct (mass) mediated experience (Hawkins & Pingree, 1982; Zillmann, 1974).

There is increasing research evidence that real-life experiences of crime and law enforcement can make a difference to perceptions of teleportrayals of crime and may affect relationships between exposure to televised crime and perceptions of crime in the real world. Elliott and Slater (1980) investigated relationships between viewing of law enforcement programs and perceptions that various crime drama programs were realistic. These relationships were examined in three different groups of adolescents—(a) Group 1 had no direct experience with law enforcement agencies; (b) Group 2 had contact in a positive way through form classes in law enforcement or sponsorship through school supplied by such agencies; and (c) Group 3 had negative contact with law enforcement agencies because they had violated the law and been arrested, convicted, and either spent time in prison or had been put on probation.

It was found that adolescents with positive experiences with the police perceived crime drama programs (e.g., "Charlie's Angels," "Rockford Files," "Hawaii Five-O") in the least realistic terms. The negative direct experience group, on the other hand, saw four out of six crime programs as more realistic than either the limited or positive direct experience groups. The authors accepted, however, that their data could not determine for certain whether heavier viewing levels contributed to more perceived realism or whether such programs were watched because they were seen as realistic. Some sort of reciprocal relationship may be likely.

In a multiple regression analysis of data from this study, Slater and Elliott (1982) found a number of television and real experiential variables to be significantly related to perceptions of safety. Greater reported police drama viewing per se was linked with greater perceived safety, but perceiving greater realism in law enforcement programs was related to greater perceived danger. Understanding of law enforcement processes was positively associated with greater frequency of direct experiences with the police (regardless of their nature or outcome), but was negatively associated with greater perceived realism of crime programs. Direct experience with the police resulting in punishment for the individual concerned together with perceived program realism were positively related to acceptance of television portrayals of police behavior.

In extending research in this field, this chapter presents further results from the study introduced in chapter 3, which looked at the impact on children's perceptions and understanding of the police and police work of two television police dramas. This chapter seeks to examine the data further to discover the ways in which a televised dramatic narrative can act as a possible mediating influence in shaping children's social attitudes and beliefs about the police.

A Cognitive Model of TV Influence

Although the cultivation model has described relationships between patterns of television viewing and beliefs about social reality, is there a psychological explanation for why television portrayals may shape viewers' knowledge and beliefs about the real world? Cognitive psychology has yielded explanations in terms of information-processing models. The notion is that individuals store information about social entities in semantic memory where memory representations in terms of constructs reside. Events that follow repeated patterns are stored as schema, according to which individuals are able to anticipate how a behavioral episode will be played out on the basis of learned experience regarding that episode.

If an object or event is repeatedly experienced in the same way, even when seen on television, the construct representation of it in an individual's semantic memory becomes more accessible (Sanbonmatsu & Fazio, 1991). Thus, a particular pattern of attributes of an object and the accompanying beliefs that the individual holds about it can become "primed" by repetitive television depictions of it. Such priming may result either in changes to mental constructs and hence beliefs about an object, or it may consolidate a body of opinion about it where only a disparate or diverse set of perceptions currently exist.

METHOD

The details of how this study was conducted were described in chapter 2 and explained further in chapter 3. This chapter focuses on differences between pretest and posttest responses to the questionnaire that examined children's knowledge and beliefs about the police and police work, and their attitudes toward the police. Changes in children's knowledge and perceptions of the police were examined in relation to respondents' age, gender, fluency in English, reported personal experiences with the police and crime, and reported viewing habits. The mediating role of young viewers' comprehension of police drama narratives in affecting changes in knowledge and opinions was also explored. The performance of two experimental groups, exposed respectively to "The Bill" ($N = 58$ males and 41 females) and "Juliet Bravo" ($N = 54$ males and 38 females), was compared with that of a control group ($N = 41$ males and 41 females) of same-age children who, although tested twice at equivalent times, were not shown any television police drama material.

KNOWLEDGE ABOUT POLICE

Both before and after viewing the test programs, the children were asked a range of questions that dealt with their knowledge and understanding of the roles and duties of uniform and plainclothes police officers, and of male and female police officers. Specifically, all children were given a list of 16 types of things that the police may have to do. The same list was presented to them twice, on the first occasion 1 week before they watched a police drama episode and a second time shortly after seeing one of the two test episodes. First, the children were asked if they thought each of these things would be carried out only by uniformed police, only by plainclothes detectives, or by both equally, or by neither. Second, the children were asked if they thought the different activities were carried out by male police officers, female police officers, or both. Correct responses in each case were checked with local police officials.

This procedure was repeated 1 week later, immediately after the children had watched their selected police drama program. The listed items and overall patterns of response pre- and postviewing are shown in Tables 4.1 and 4.2. Respondents were given 2 points for each correct answer.

A series of two-way analyses of variance were then conducted on these data to find out if any significant shifts in knowledge had occurred contingent upon viewing the test programs and if such shifts were related systematically to demographic factors, reported viewing experience, and comprehension of test program content.

Mean scores are shown in Table 4.3. There were significant age effects for all groups ["The Bill": $F(3, 97) = 6.3$, $p < 0.001$; "Juliet Bravo: $F(3, 87) = 4.0$, $p < 0.01$; control: $F(3, 78) = 3.5$, $p < 0.02$]. Knowledge levels improved progressively with age. There were no significant shifts in knowledge as a function of exposure to the test episodes. Among the "Juliet Bravo" group only, however, there was a significant age-by-test interaction [$F(3, 87) = 4.5$, $p < 0.006$]. The odd result here indicated that the oldest and second-youngest age bands exhibited a downward shift in knowledge

TABLE 4.1
Perceived Duties of Uniformed and Plainclothes Police Officers
(Pretest Scores, With Posttest Scores in Parentheses)

	Uniformed Police Only %	Plainclothes Only %	Both %	Neither of These %
Directs traffic; sorts out traffic jams	91 (81)	3 (5)	5 (12)	3 (3)
Meets with informers	7 (9)	51 (54)	38 (34)	4 (3)
Writes reports back at the station	18 (28)	12 (10)	69 (62)	2 (1)
Walks the beat	80 (73)	5 (9)	12 (13)	3 (5)
Patrols in cars	47 (41)	6 (11)	45 (47)	2 (1)
Investigates small crimes	70 (68)	9 (12)	19 (18)	2 (3)
Answers inquiries at police station	58 (56)	10 (10)	25 (28)	7 (6)
Does undercover work	7 (4)	74 (72)	17 (22)	2 (2)
Responds to emergency calls	68 (63)	2 (5)	13 (18)	18 (14)
Interviews suspects	17 (18)	28 (19)	53 (63)	2 (95)
Helps with crowd control	83 (77)	3 (4)	13 (17)	2 (2)
Advises on home security	52 (56)	9 (12)	31 (30)	8 (3)
Visits schools to give advice	82 (76)	4 (9)	14 (14)	0.5 (1)
Gives evidence in court	18 (17)	13 (15)	67 (66)	3 (3)
Gives orders to other police	13 (16)	31 (17)	26 (52)	31 (15)
Investigates big crimes	4 (14)	59 (45)	36 (39)	2 (2)

after viewing the test episode, whereas the other age bands changed hardly at all.

There were no significant gender effects and no interaction effects involving gender of respondents. There were two effects related to fluency in English ["Juliet Bravo": $F(1, 89) = 4.6$, $p < 0.04$; control: $F(1, 80) = 4.8$, $p < 0.03$]. Both results signified that children with English as a first language did better than those with ESL.

Contact With Police

We next investigated whether real-life contact with police (e.g., having them visit the school) or having been a victim or having knowledge of someone who had been a victim of a criminal act, mediated the influence of exposure to a police drama. Mean scores are shown in Table 4.4.

There were no significant effects due to reported level of contact with real police and no interactions. There were two significant effects among the program exposure groups in respect of reported personal victimization in a crime ["The Bill": $F(1, 99) = 5.0, p < 0.03$; "Juliet Bravo": $F(1, 89) = 19.8$,

TABLE 4.2
Perceived Duties of Men and Women Police Officers
(Pretest Scores, With Posttest Scores in Parentheses)

	Mostly by Female Police Officers %	Mostly by Male Police Officers %	Both %	Neither of These %
Responds to emergency calls	19 (17)	7 (4)	67 (73)	7 (7)
Investigates house burglary	4 (5)	30 (26)	65 (69)	1 (0)
Tracks down a murderer	3 (4)	50 (39)	35 (51)	12 (7)
Directs traffic	7 (10)	25 (20)	67 (68)	2 (2)
Assists with crowd control	5 (4)	65 (63)	29 (34)	1 (0)
Interview a rape victim	68 (63)	8 (9)	23 (26)	1 (3)
Deals with drunk drivers	4 (2)	47 (49)	48 (50)	1 (0)
Interviews a suspect	6 (10)	22 (10)	66 (77)	6 (3)
Searches for missing child	13 (20)	10 (6)	74 (22)	3 (2)
Helps with serious accident or disaster	9 (10)	13 (18)	77 (69)	2 (3)
Investigates bank robberies	3 (2)	41 (37)	50 (55)	7 (7)
Comforts people when something bad has happened	63 (68)	4 (3)	30 (28)	3 (2)
Writes reports/answers phones at station	20 (16)	6 (6)	65 (72)	8 (5)
Does undercover work	1 (5)	25 (28)	47 (43)	28 (24)
Meets with informers	8 (12)	23 (25)	52 (46)	18 (17)
Gives orders to other police	4 (5)	17 (14)	40 (55)	40 (26)

$p < 0.001$]. Children who claimed to have been a victim of crime scored higher than did children who made no such claim. This effect did not occur among children in the control group.

Viewing Habit Effects

When we looked at knowledge shift as a function of previous viewing habits it was clear that these effects were marginal. The marginality can be seen in Table 4.5.

There was just one main effect on knowledge concerning the duties and roles of uniform and plainclothes police officers as a function of reported viewing of U.S. police drama programs [control: $F(1, 80) = 7.4$, $p < 0.008$]. Light viewers scored higher than heavy viewers. No aspect of previous or routine viewing of the test programs produced a significant effect on knowledge about police.

Episode Comprehension Effects

There were clear effects of test episode comprehension ability on knowledge scores for "The Bill" [$F(1, 97) = 14.5$, $p < 0.001$]; and for "Juliet Bravo"

TABLE 4.3

Shifts in Knowledge about Plainclothes versus Uniform Police as a Function
of Watching TV Police Drama Episodes, Broken Down by Age, Gender, and
Fluency in English

	Group 1 "The Bill"		Group 2 "Juliet Bravo"		Group 3 Control	
	Pretest	Posttest	Pretest	Posttest	Pretest	Posttest
All	25.9	26.0	25.9	25.5	26.2	26.2
Age Groups						
9–10	24.4	24.7	24.7	25.2	25.8	25.6
11–12	25.7	26.0	25.6	24.8	25.7	25.4
13–14	26.1	26.0	27.1	27.6	26.8	27.6
15–16	27.5	27.3	27.1	25.1	26.9	26.7
Gender						
Male	26.2	26.2	26.1	25.5	26.6	26.5
Female	25.6	25.6	25.7	25.6	25.8	25.9
Fluency in English						
English as Second Language	26.9	26.2	24.8	25.0	25.1	25.3
English as First Language	25.8	25.9	26.4	25.8	26.5	26.4

Maximum = 32

$[F(1, 89) = 13.9, p < 0.001]$. High comprehension scorers on test programs
scored better on knowledge than did low comprehension scorers. However,
high comprehension scorers were no more likely than low scorers to
improve their knowledge on exposure to an episode from a police drama
series (see Table 4.6).

Perceptions of Police Roles

The children were asked to indicate their impressions of the characteristics
of male and female police officers in terms of 15 evaluative scales. In each
case, the children were asked if they thought either policemen or policewomen were "a lot like these things"; "a little like these things"; "not very
much like this"; or "not at all like them." Once again these impressions were
elicited on two occasions, once before and then again after viewing the
episode of their presented police television drama series. The 15 items were:
"is helpful to people"; "is clever"; "likes to boss people around"; "is strong";
"is kind"; "tends to act tough with people"; "is brave"; "is good at taking
orders"; "is very fit"; "gets angry easily"; "is hardworking"; "never listens to
other people's points of view"; "is weak"; "enjoys fighting"; and "gets on
well with other police officers."

TABLE 4.4
Shifts in Knowledge about Plainclothes Versus Uniform Police as a Function
of Watching TV Police Drama Episodes, Broken Down by Contact With Real
Police and Victimization

	Group 1 "The Bill"		Group 2 "Juliet Bravo"		Group 3 Control	
	Pretest	Posttest	Pretest	Posttest	Pretest	Posttest
Contact With Real Police						
Low	26.3	26.0	25.9	25.6	26.1	26.2
High	25.2	25.9	25.9	25.5	26.2	26.2
Been or Knowing a Victim of Crime						
Yes	26.5	26.8	27.8	27.1	26.0	26.0
No	25.6	25.5	25.1	24.4	26.3	26.3

Maximum = 32

First, it is informative to consider which attributes were most widely
associated with men and women police officers, averaging over the percentages who endorsed each attribute in respect of either men or women police
officers for all groups. Although there were some variations in endorsement
of attributes between groups, there was a remarkable degree of similarity
overall. For male police officers the most endorsed attributes prior to viewing
the drama episodes were that they are "helpful to people" (94%), "get on well
with other police officers" (94%), "brave" (89%), "hardworking" (88%) and
"very fit" (88%). The least often endorsed attributes were that male police
officers "enjoy fighting" (26%) or that they are "weak" (17%).

Female police officers were primarily seen as being "helpful to people"
(100%), "kind" (96%), "getting on well with other police officers" (97%),
"hardworking" (92%), "good at taking orders" (92%), and "clever" (91%).
Attributes not generally associated with female police officers included that
they "get angry easily" (27%), "like to boss people around" (25%), "never
listened to other people's points of view" (24%), or that they "enjoy
fighting" (11%).

There were a few differences in children's impressions of the characters of
men and women police officers. Prior to viewing the test programs male
police officers were seen a good deal more often than female police officers
as "strong" (81% vs. 63%), "tending to act tough with people" (59% vs.
35%), "getting angry easily" (46% vs. 36%), "never listening to other
people's point of view" (34% vs. 24%), "like bossing other people around"
(45% vs. 25%), and as "enjoying fighting" (26% vs. 11%). Women police
officers were more often seen as "weak" (33% vs. 18%).

TABLE 4.5
Shifts in Knowledge about Plainclothes Versus Uniform Police as a Function
of Watching TV Police Drama Episodes, Broken Down by Viewing Habits and
Previous Program Exposure

	Group 1 "The Bill"		Group 2 "Juliet Bravo"		Group 3 Control	
	Pretest	*Posttest*	*Pretest*	*Posttest*	*Pretest*	*Posttest*
Total TV Viewing (per day)						
Under 4 hours	26.0	25.9	25.6	25.6	26.6	26.2
4 hours and over	25.8	26.0	26.2	25.4	25.7	26.2
U.S. Police Drama Viewing						
Heavy	25.4	25.4	25.3	25.4	25.1	24.6
Light	26.1	26.2	26.0	25.5	26.4	24.6
U.K. Police Drama Viewing						
Heavy	26.0	25.7	26.2	26.1	26.2	26.8
Light	25.9	26.1	25.8	25.3	26.1	26.0
Factual Police Program Viewing						
Heavy	25.9	25.4	25.4	25.4	26.3	26.2
Light	25.9	26.3	25.6	25.6	25.9	26.2
Amount of Viewing Test Program						
Heavy	26.0	26.0	25.4	26.1	26.0	26.1
Light	25.8	26.0	26.0	25.3	26.9	27.1
Ever Seen Test Episode Before?						
Yes	25.9	25.7	25.5	25.7	–	–
No	25.9	26.3	26.1	25.5	–	–

There were few marked changes in rate of endorsement of attributes
following viewing of the police drama episodes. Among the children who
watched an episode from "The Bill," increased percentages felt that both
men and women police officers were clever, and an increased percentage
thought that women officers were strong. These results are summarized in
Table 4.7, which shows those attributes on which the most substantial shifts
of opinion were observed to occur.

Among children who watched an episode from "Juliet Bravo," decreased
percentages thought that men officers were very fit, whereas increased
percentages thought that they liked to boss people around, enjoyed

TABLE 4.6
Shifts in Knowledge about Plainclothes Versus Uniform Police as a Function
of Comprehension of TV Police Drama Episodes

	Group 1 "The Bill"		Group 2 "Juliet Bravo"		Group 3 Control	
	Pretest	Posttest	Pretest	Posttest	Pretest	Posttest
Comprehension of Test Episode						
Low	25.1	25.1	24.9	24.5	–	–
High	26.8	26.8	26.8	26.4	–	–

TABLE 4.7
Perceptions of Men and Women Police Officers Before and After Viewing
Police Dramas

	"The Bill"		"Juliet Bravo"		Control	
	Before %	After %	Before %	After %	Before %	After %
Men Police Officers						
Very fit	92	91	89	75	84	92
Clever	77	93	84	91	78	88
Like to boss people around	47	42	42	53	45	46
Enjoy fighting	28	29	29	37	20	24
Weak	19	17	17	25	16	13
Women Police Officers						
Clever	85	94	86	89	87	83
Very fit	80	87	85	87	85	93
Strong	55	73	58	70	76	72
Enjoy fighting	8	17	15	22	10	11

fighting, and were weak. At the same time, more children, after viewing this program, thought that women officers were strong. It was a feature of this episode that the female police officer at the center of the story kept herself fit by jogging in the mornings. The male officers, on the other hand, were out of shape. During one incident in which the female officer and a male colleague had to chase up a flight of stairs, she left him gasping for breath. It would seem, therefore, that we have here an example of a (short-term) shift of opinion about male and female police officers that directly ties in with the content of the program shown to the children.

It needs also to be noted that there were some marked shifts of opinion among children in the control group, who, of course, did not watch anything. This does, therefore, raise the question of how stable such impressions are anyway. Later in this chapter we discuss the view that television may act as an opinion "stabilizer" as much as a force to shift opinions. Perceptions that are susceptible to random or chance fluctuations because they are ill-informed or poorly developed, may become more stable (if not necessarily more accurate) as a function of television viewing experiences. This effect may be especially likely to occur among young viewers for whom television is the only or the principal source of information about a social group, event, or issue.

The Structure of Children's Perceptions of Police

The foregoing assessments examined children's perceptions of different attributes of police*men* and police*women* on an attribute-by-attribute basis. Changes in the endorsement of individual attributes before and after watching police drama episodes provided some indication of short-term influences of such material on young viewers' perceptions of the character of the police. With a few, but certainly not all, of these changed perceptions it was possible to match them up with aspects of program content. To what extent, however, do children's perceptions of the police group together to form a more structured profile? To answer this question, a statistical technique called *factor analysis* was used to find out how these specific perceptions of the police might cluster together to form a more cohesive whole.

The analyses were computed separately on children's previewing and postviewing perceptions of police*men* and police*women*. The findings are summarized in Tables 4.8 and 4.9. As well as having intrinsic interest, the factors reveal certain changes in the way children's perceptions of the police were structured possibly as a result of watching a police drama episode. The results here are derived from both viewing groups combined together into a single sample.

Looking first of all at perceptions of police*men*, these were initially grouped into five factors to which the following labels were given: argumentative, goodness of character, strength, professionalism, and fitness. Analysis of postviewing data produced a reduction down to just three factors: argumentative, goodness of character, and strength. The first factor, argumentative remained largely unchanged, but was joined in the second analysis by the item is weak. The positive loading of this item with others such as gets angry easily, tends to act tough with people, and likes to boss people around may at first seem an odd finding. Rather than reflecting some kind of physical weakness, however, it may imply a perception of weakness of character on the part of an officer who may like to act tough and boss others around, but who is really only doing so because he is insecure and defensive.

TABLE 4.8
Perceptions of Characteristics of Policemen

	Factor 1: Argumentative	Factor 2: Goodness of Character	Factor 3: Strength	Factor 4: Professionalism	Factor 5: Fitness
Previewing					
Gets angry easily	.74621	−.13911	.13008	−.08459	.15046
Likes to boss people around	.66801	−.41161	.02823	−.02153	−.12645
Never listens to other people's point of view	.64822	−.01402	−.30186	−.14246	.08128
Tends to get tough with people	.62459	−.36312	.12316	−.04553	−.13050
Enjoys fighting	.56630	.04254	−.32376	−.23945	−.10383
Is helpful to people	−.18629	.72995	.07237	.09937	−.08716
Is kind	−.24895	.71945	.06309	.07256	−.04393
Is brave	.18074	.51241	.45573	.18100	−.02524
Is clever	−.14864	.49170	.29764	.18644	.30475
Is strong	.10255	.16805	.75250	−.09595	−.06213
Is weak	.30200	−.04727	−.62171	−.19300	.09996
Gets on well with other police officers	−.13913	.18079	−.24829	.77521	−.08571
Is good at taking orders	−.09742	.07145	.23192	.72833	−.07358
Is hardworking	−.17069	.16058	.43319	.54705	.23004
Is very fit	.02093	−.04826	−.11646	−.07613	.89082
Postviewing					
Gets angry easily	.75394	−.16395	.22753		
Likes to boss people around	.71261	−.13577	−.00486		
Tends to get tough with people	.70181	−.28138	−.15290		
Enjoys fighting	.66500	−.08910	−.15547		
Never listens to other people's point of view	.64280	−.03784	−.22179		
Is weak	.50793	−.04076	−.49921		
Is helpful to people	−.24998	.65724	.10047		
Gets on well with other police officers	−.05906	.64610	−.02257		
Is kind	−.25913	.64123	.15852		
Is good at taking orders	.06456	.62512	.11572		
Is clever	−.13547	.61073	.27410		
Is hardworking	−.32843	.59162	.22510		
Is strong	−.09947	.32242	.81540		
Is very fit	−.04174	.32242	.65558		
Is brave	−.06085	.49025	.59542		

74

TABLE 4.9
Perceptions of Characteristics of Policewomen

	Factor 1: Argumentative	Factor 2: Cooperative	Factor 3: Strength of Character	Factor 4: Dedication	Factor 5: Fitness
Previewing					
Gets angry easily	.75516	.05282	−.11085	−.02863	.15016
Likes to boss people around	.73866	−.18637	−.03158	−.09813	.01176
Tends to act tough with people	.70183	−.18637	−.03158	−.09813	−.13469
Is kind	−.04706	.74538	−.01143	.24231	−.01661
Is helpful to people	.03258	.68288	.23852	.17057	.02169
Gets on well with other police officers	−.16530	.63209	.10652	−.07016	.02169
Enjoys fighting	.40319	−.45957	−.11391	.21876	−.08441
Is hardworking	−.09489	.38422	.36520	.24675	−.29368
Is weak	.30100	−.05522	−.68968	.03679	−.20787
Is strong	.15053	.03834	.66209	.38872	.05017
Is brave	.06000	.28904	−.42191	.31697	.33843
Never listens to other people's point of view	.37592	−.26511	−.42191	.31697	.33843
Is clever	.00955	.04128	.18188	.68837	.08234
Is good at taking orders	−.27956	.23150	−.03310	.60547	−.13017
Is very fit	−.02365	.11895	.02186	.00920	.87937
Postviewing					
Tends to act tough with people	.78383	−.09634	.07951		
Gets angry easily	.76726	−.09842	−.07584		
Likes to boss people around	.75449	−.03463	−.07584		
Enjoys fighting	.64582	.13333	−.38864		
Never listens to other people's point of view	.60649	−.17312	−.28685		
Is strong	.07690	.83523	−.08083		
Is very fit	−.08511	.78221	.13815		
Is brave	.08844	.47424	.46645		
Is clever	−.28946	.41722	.22509		
Is hardworking	−.28946	.41722	.22509		
Never listening to other people's point of view	.25007	.41317	.26454		
Is kind	−.21533	.03714	.75373		
Is helpful to people	−.13678	.14444	.69515		
Gets on well with other police officers	−.18869	.21913	.51535		
Is good at taking orders	−.00050	.41244	.48332		

The second factor, *goodness of character*, survived and merged with items from the previewing professionalism factor. What may have emerged here then is a basic dichotomy into good policemen and bad policemen. Finally, the *strength* factor and fit factor merged during the second-wave analysis and was joined also by "is brave" from the first-wave goodness of character factor.

Turning to perceptions of police*women*, before viewing the police drama episodes, the children's impressions divided into five groupings labeled argumentative, cooperative, strength of character, dedication, and fitness. After viewing, three factors only emerged. Once again, argumentative was a major cluster, with the original dedication factor becoming professionalism to reflect a merging with it of certain strength of character items. Finally, a cooperative factor emerged again, but in a cleaner fashion.

The two sets of results exhibit a consolidating of perceptions into fewer, more clear-cut factors, with component items showing a more logical, internal consistency. If such results are to be taken as evidence of an influence of watching television police dramas on children's perceptions of the police, the nature of this influence here takes the shape of a qualitative restructuring of impressions into a cleaner, more concise, logically consistent form.

PERCEPTIONS OF THE POLICE AND CRIME

The children were asked two sets of questions about the police and crime. They were given a list of 16 different types of crime or disturbances and asked, for each one, first, how often they thought the police had to deal with this sort of occurrence, and second, how often the police solved the crime or resolved the problem. Table 4.10 summarizes the results for the first question and Table 4.11 those for the second question.

The children perceived that police had to deal with car thefts and burglaries, speeding and drunken driving, and vandalism against property the most often. The least common forms of crime for the police to deal with, as far as these children were concerned, included murder, bank robberies, and suicide or suicide attempts. These results provide an interesting profile of children's views about police work. The types of crimes that finished at the top of the list tended not to be the ones popularly associated with the crime-busting work of television cops and detectives.

Just a few of these impressions changed after viewing episodes from the two police drama series. Children who watched an episode from "The Bill" decreased in the extent to which they thought police had to solve drug-related crimes and increased in the extent to which they thought that the police had to deal with kidnapping cases and trouble at football matches.

TABLE 4.10
Frequency With Which Police Have to Deal With Different Crimes

	"The Bill"		"Juliet Bravo"		Control	
	Pretest %	Posttest %	Pretest %	Posttest %	Pretest %	Posttest %
Car thefts and burglaries	97	98	99	99	96	95
Speeding and drunken driving	96	91	95	97	92	85
Vandalism (e.g., damaging property)	94	91	91	87	85	87
Shoplifting	86	93	91	95	95	93
Attacks on old people	83	87	79	79	83	73
Racial abuse and attacks	85	81	76	81	82	78
Attacks on young people	75	74	73	81	72	67
Rows and fights in families	76	77	74	80	60	63
Drug dealing	84	71	76	62	66	52
Rape	79	75	69	68	72	65
Trouble at football matches	63	72	73	76	65	74
Crowd trouble at demonstrations	64	68	64	70	49	52
Suicide and suicide attempts	47	47	41	54	50	42
Bank robberies	55	52	34	43	40	33
Kidnapping	41	49	42	37	38	32
Murder	43	40	36	39	43	29

Note. Percentages saying police often have to deal with these crimes.

The children who watched an episode from "Juliet Bravo" increased most markedly on three items: dealing with suicides, attacks on young people, and bank robberies. Some of these shifts of opinion reflect plot events in the programs. The main plot feature of "Juliet Bravo" concerned a suicide case, whereas a kidnapping was a main plot feature of "The Bill."

It was the children in the control group, however, who shifted in their opinions the most. An increased percentage here thought that the police have to deal with trouble at football matches, whereas decreased percentages thought that the police have to deal with suicide cases, attacks on old people, or murder.

There was little difference in perceptions of frequency of crime between pretest and posttest among different demographic subgroups. The one area where differential perceptions did show up was the perceived prevalence of

TABLE 4.11
Frequency With Which Police Solve Different Crimes

	"The Bill"		"Juliet Bravo"		Control	
	Pretest %	Posttest %	Pretest %	Posttest %	Pretest %	Posttest %
Speeding and drunken driving	95	89	95	90	89	99
Shoplifting	87	88	85	86	84	82
Car thefts and burglaries	76	79	80	79	84	83
Trouble at football matches	78	73	76	81	74	73
Attacks on old people	71	70	78	84	70	66
Rape	77	63	71	76	66	62
Racial abuse and attacks	64	63	71	80	63	66
Drug dealing	72	71	70	70	71	70
Kidnapping	70	74	68	68	61	68
Vandalism (e.g., damaging property)	70	65	68	73	61	68
Rows and fights in families	67	71	70	80	66	71
Crowd trouble at demonstrations	69	78	74	79	63	65
Attacks on young people	68	71	67	79	66	67
Bank robberies	67	61	58	62	56	59
Suicide and suicide attempts	59	65	60	65	59	55
Murder	63	57	53	56	52	54

attending to drug-dealing matters. Here, girls consistently rated the prevalence as greater than did boys. From pre- to posttest there was generally a reduction in the numbers of boys and girls who perceived drug dealing as a matter with which the police frequently had to deal in the two program groups. In the control group, however, girls' opinions remained unchanged, whereas for boys there was a marked increase (from 63% to 98%) in perceptions of police often having to handle drug-related crimes.

There were just three further marked shifts of opinion across tests, all of which occurred among girls who had viewed one or other of the two programs. The perception that the police often had to deal with "suicides or suicide attempts" become more widespread among female viewers of "Juliet Bravo" (34% to 61%), and likewise in respect of "attacks on young people" among female viewers of both "The Bill" (67% to 86%) and "Juliet Bravo" (66% to 90%). All of these factors featured in the respective program.

Turning to how often the police solve crimes of different kinds (see Table 4.11), children thought that the police had the greatest success with driving offenses, shoplifting, and trouble at football matches. It is notable, however, that overall, the majority of children believed the police were effective with all the types of offense listed.

Perceived effectiveness increased among children who watched "The Bill" in respect of dealing with suicides, and among children who watched "Juliet Bravo" in respect of attacks on young people and rows and fights in families. This perceptual shift, once again, links in with the narrative of "Juliet Bravo," which depicted police officers becoming involved in dealing with a family row. Controls also shifted on two items of note, speeding and drunken driving, and attacks on young people, on both of which percentages saying police were effective increased.

On breaking down beliefs about police crime-solution rates by age we found some marked differences as a function of this variable. In most cases the older children believe the police solve specific crimes much less than do the younger children. These different beliefs and perceptions are shown in Table 4.12.

Another feature of the table, which we have had occasion to note before, is the much greater variability between pre- and posttest for control subjects who were not exposed to an intervening police drama program, compared to the magnitude of shifts for those children who were exposed.

The youngest children believed that the police solve crimes involving car thefts and burglaries and vandalism much more frequently than did the older children. Racial abuse was felt to be solved not at all frequently by the 15- to 16-year-old children in "The Bill" group, but to be solved frequently by the same age group in "Juliet Bravo." The control group, on this issue, was nondisambiguating because the 15- to 16-year-olds in this group totally agreed with the assertion that police often solve this crime, but eventually (posttest) only 67% of respondents agreed with the assertion.

The differences between the two programming groups, and the two programming groups and the control should not be dismissed. The variability could be indicating malleability of opinion within and between age groups. The greater stability (smaller magnitude of change) within the program groups relative to the control groups then becomes pertinent when trying to establish the role of television in creating and/or sustaining beliefs, opinions, and attitudes.

When we broke down the global responses for solution of crimes by gender we found much less variability than with age. Table 4.13 presents the crimes where males and females tended to differ either in terms of pretest scores, or in pretest/posttest shift direction or magnitude.

Interesting points to note in this table are the responses of boys and girls to the crime of suicide. The boys began by believing that police solve this

TABLE 4.12

Perceived Frequency of Police Solving Specific Crimes, as a Function of Age, Broken Down by Program Viewed (Percentages)

		Age							
		9-10		11-12		13-14		15-16	
Crimes	Program Viewed	Pretest %	Posttest %	Pretest %	Posttest %	Pretest %	Posttest %	Pretest %	Posttest %
Car thefts and burglaries	"The Bill"	83	91	82	89	93	89	41	41
	"Juliet Bravo"	83	90	93	92	78	94	63	79
	Controls	100	82	94	82	96	91	100	67
Kidnapping	"The Bill"	61	78	56	68	89	71	73	82
	"Juliet Bravo"	62	72	80	76	56	61	74	58
	Controls	53	71	52	61	73	70	22	89
Vandalism	"The Bill"	100	87	82	71	64	71	32	27
	"Juliet Bravo"	79	72	64	72	67	83	58	63
	Controls	77	82	79	73	96	48	100	78
Attacks on old people	"The Bill"	83	87	79	82	79	68	41	41
	"Juliet Bravo"	79	83	92	84	61	83	74	84
	Controls	82	82	79	58	83	65	100	67
Rape	"The Bill"	78	74	82	75	86	50	59	55
	"Juliet Bravo"	69	72	80	92	67	61	68	74
	Controls	77	88	67	52	74	61	89	56
Racial abuse and attacks	"The Bill"	83	70	68	71	75	57	27	55
	"Juliet Bravo"	72	79	72	84	61	72	79	84
	Controls	71	82	76	70	91	48	100	67
Crowd trouble/demonstrations	"The Bill"	65	83	57	79	82	71	73	82
	"Juliet Bravo"	72	86	68	68	78	78	79	84
	Control	35	71	49	58	48	57	78	100

TABLE 4.13

Percentage of Males and Females Who Believe the Police Often Have to Deal With the Listed Crimes, Broken Down by Program Watched

	Programs Viewed											
	"The Bill"				"Juliet Bravo"				Controls			
	Male		Female		Male		Female		Male		Female	
	Pretest %	Posttest %	Pretest %	Posttest %	Pretest %	Posttest %	Pretest %	Posttest %	Pretest %	Posttest %	Pretest %	Posttest %
Drug dealing	76	66	67	79	62	64	82	79	56	63	85	81
Suicide	68	58	48	76	60	64	61	66	61	42	56	68
Attacks on old people	61	68	86	74	76	89	82	76	66	63	73	68
Trouble at football matches	83	75	71	71	85	85	63	76	78	78	71	68
Attacks on young people	64	64	74	81	64	76	74	84	51	81	81	73
Rows and fights in the family	76	71	55	71	70	81	71	79	56	66	76	76

crime more often than did the girls, but in posttest, the boys' beliefs dropped, whereas the girls' beliefs increased. Quite the opposite happened in respect of perceptions of attacks on old people. Also, this latter pattern held true for both program groups, but not for the controls.

Likewise, for the crimes of drug dealing and attacks on young people, boys' and girls' pretest beliefs were quite different, with girls believing that police solve this crime much more frequently than did the boys (averaging over program and control groups).

OPINIONS ABOUT THE POLICE

Finally, the children were given a list of 22 opinion statements about the police to which they were asked to respond in terms of 5-point agree–disagree scales. These opinions were checked both before and after viewing the police drama episodes. Shifts of opinion were most commonplace among children who watched the episode of "Juliet Bravo" (see Table 4.14).

Out of the 22 items, substantial shifts in opinion (12% or more) occurred on 9 of them among the "Juliet Bravo" group. Shifts on just 2 items occurred for children who watched "The Bill" and likewise among those children in the control group. "Juliet Bravo" viewers increased in the extent to which they thought that "police women are better in cases where young children are involved than are policemen"; "There are not enough police in

TABLE 4.14
Attitude Toward the Police Before and After Viewing Police Dramas

	"Juliet Bravo"	
	Before %	After %
Policewomen are better in cases where young children are involved than policemen	59	76
The police should try to encourage more women to join	48	74
There are not enough police in big cities	32	55
Most young children today are frightened of the police	32	46
There is just as much crime in small towns and the country as there is in big cities	37	52
There is more chance of a policeman getting promoted than a policewoman	58	43
Policemen are better at telling people what to do than policewomen	68	36
You have to be good at fighting to be in the police force	65	35
Policemen are better at catching criminals than policewomen	35	23

Note. Percentages are of those children who agreed strongly or slightly with each statement.

big cities today"; "Most children today are frightened of the police"; "The police should try to encourage more women to join"; and "There is just as much crime in small towns and the country as there is in big cities." There were marked decreases in percentages who thought that "Policemen are better at catching criminals than policewomen"; "You have to be good at fighting to be in the police force"; and "There is more chance of a policeman getting promoted than a policewoman."

The perceptual shift relating to women police officers being better at handling cases in which children are involved could be linked to the fact that in the "Juliet Bravo" episode used in this study, WPCs were automatically sent to deal with the main case because a child was missing. The decrease in extent to which children in the "Juliet Bravo" group felt that policemen are better at telling people what to do than police*women* can be related to the narrative of this episode in which a woman police inspector pulls "rank" and really takes over the case.

Among children who watched "The Bill," the only two opinions showing any marked shift from pre- to postviewing were that "being in the police force is a good job to have," which increased (48% to 58%), and "plainclothes detectives are cleverer than uniformed police," which decreased (51% to 26%). This result can be seen to relate to the narrative of the episode as the crime is solved by a uniformed woman police inspector after a plainclothes detective proved unable to get cooperation from the main witness.

Age Differences.   There were just a few variations in opinion shifts from pretest to posttest as a function of age (see Table 4.15). Older children, aged 11 and over, who watched an episode from "Juliet Bravo" exhibited an increased perception of the friendliness of the police. Children in the 11- to 14-year age range showed the greatest likelihood of opinion shifts in this way.

There were marked variations also in opinion shifts regarding the perception that being in the police force is a good job. Children ages 11–14 who watched "The Bill" had much more widespread favorable opinion after watching this program than beforehand. The same finding was true of 15- to 16-year-olds who watched "Juliet Bravo." In contrast, 13- to 14-year-olds who watched the latter episode became less likely to look favorably on being in the police force.

DISCUSSION

This chapter reported on an experimental study that explored the impact upon children's knowledge, attitudes, and beliefs of two dramatic television

TABLE 4.15
Percentage of Children Agreeing "Strongly" or "Slightly" With Attitude Statements About the Police, as a Function of Age Broken Down by Program Viewed

	Programs Viewed											
	"The Bill"				*"Juliet Bravo"*				*Controls*			
Statement	*9–10* %	*11–12* %	*13–14* %	*15–16* %	*9–10* %	*11–12* %	*13–14* %	*15–16* %	*9–10* %	*11–12* %	*13–14* %	*15–16* %
Being in the force is a good job to have												
Pretest	61	57	36	36	52	60	61	37	41	58	52	33
Posttest	70	75	63	46	45	68	39	63	24	61	52	56
The police today are more friendly than they used to be												
Pretest	57	61	32	27	76	56	61	26	59	58	65	33
Posttest	74	61	32	36	69	80	33	42	47	70	52	44

84

narratives. Episodes from two well-known police drama series on British television were used as stimulus materials. The study examined what effects viewing such programming would have on pre-teenage and teenage children's perceptions of aspects of the real world dealt with by the programs.

This "effects analysis" formed the second part of a two-stage study. The first part, described in chapter 3, investigated the children's ability to follow the story line of each drama episode. Story line comprehension was found to be fairly good among children generally, but did vary with certain personal and experiential characteristics of young viewers. In particular, comprehension improved significantly with the age of the child. In the current stage of analysis, program comprehension was examined again, but this time as a mediating factor in relation to television's effects upon children's perception of social reality.

The aspect of social reality under examination here related in particular to children's perceptions of the police and police work. We wanted to find out if young viewers' attitudes and beliefs about the police were in any way shaped or altered as a result of what they saw in the program episodes shown to them.

At the outset, we did not expect to find great changes in children's impressions of the police as a consequence of watching a single police drama episode. In the event the results confirmed this view and provided no clear-cut indication of any television influences.

It will be recalled that all the children who participated in this study, both those who were shown the television programs and those who were not, were tested on two occasions, 1 week apart, with a questionnaire that attempted to measure their perceptions of the police and the work that is done by the police force. Comparing the responses given across the two test sessions revealed that some perceptions and attitudes hardly changed at all, whereas others exhibited marked shifts. Adding to this complex array of findings was the fact that attitude shifts occurred among control children as well as among those who watched one of the two police drama episodes. How are these findings to be explained?

One explanation could be that in respect of those aspects of social reality where their firsthand experience is limited or nonexistent, children's beliefs, attitudes, and ideas are both unstable and malleable. Where exposure to mass media information is also minimal (as in the case of the control group children in this study), these beliefs, attitudes, and ideas remain relatively unstable and subject to random fluctuation because they lack any firm anchor points.

Where exposure to mass media information does occur, however, such as by watching a television program — either dramatic or factual — about the topic in question, these relatively loosely held beliefs and ideas may be subject to change, but in a principled way. This is illustrated in this study among children in the two viewing groups whose beliefs about and perceptions of the police shifted in line with attributes and events depicted in the two programs.

This line of reasoning thus posits that television exposure has the ability to stabilize certain beliefs about aspects of the real world that are relatively firmly grounded, while being able to change those not so strongly held. The children in the control group did not have the benefit of television confirmation or denial for their police-related beliefs, which thus remained fluid and open to unsystematic shifts.

Another mode of explanation could be derived from a cognitive information-processing perspective and in particular the notion of construct accessibility. Social groups, objects, or events that are repeatedly depicted in the mass media may be primed so as to become more accessible in the semantic memory store of world knowledge. This represents a cognitive process through which particular memory constructs are activated and reactivated affecting the degree to which an individual will call upon them when placed in a position of perceptual judgment about a social entity. Through this process, diverse sets of information about an entity may become organized into a more coherent body of knowledge or opinion (Higgins & King, 1981). The consolidation of children's perceptions of and attitudes to the police contingent upon exposure to a police narrative drama on television may exemplify such a cognitive process (see Sanbonmatsu & Fazio, 1991).

Knowledge Changes

Children's knowledge about the roles of the police were explored in relation to their ability, before and after viewing test program episodes, to distinguish correctly between the jobs done by uniformed and plainclothes police officers. No overall knowledge changes of any significance were found. The only factors that made any difference to knowledge levels were the age of the children, their ability to comprehend the program, and whether or not they had had experience themselves of being victims of crime or knew of people who had been victimized. One writer has already reported that children who are good at program comprehension tend to have a more integrated and coherent outlook on the world (Pingree, 1983). Older children and those who said they had had victimization experience exhibited higher knowledge levels. Although exposure to the test episodes made no difference to knowledge levels, nor were there any significant relationships between reported viewing of different program categories (including crime drama) and knowledge scores, there were "effects" due to comprehension of the episodes such that those children who were found to demonstrate good comprehension also produced high knowledge of police matters. The direction of causality here, if there is one, is, of course, obscure.

Perceptions of Police

The children were asked for their perceptions of the roles played by male and female police officers. This was an especially pertinent range of questions to ask because the two drama series episodes used in this study featured female police officers in positions of authority. An initial tendency to perceive characters in gender-stereotyped ways was consistent with earlier findings (Reeves & Greenberg, 1977; Reeves & Miller, 1978). Such gender stereotyping is known to become established very early in life (Davidson, Yasuna, & Tower, 1979; Mayes & Valentine, 1976) and may therefore be difficult to shift.

In the present study, there were few significant changes in the rate of endorsement of different characteristics of either men or women police officers as a function of watching either of the police drama episodes. The main changes that did occur among the two viewing groups were in respect of attributes of police officers that related to specific aspects of the programs. In some cases, however, the absence of change in opinion was perhaps more significant as a result than substantial opinion change. The best example of this was the perception of women police officers as "very fit." This view shifted least by a well-marked margin in the case of those children who watched "Juliet Bravo." Both the controls and children who saw "The Bill" exhibited more substantial opinion shifts on this item. This result reinforces the opinion stabilizing hypothesis of television program effects suggested earlier, an effect that may be underpinned by a cognitive "priming" process (Sanbonmatsu & Fazio, 1991).

This hypothesis was given further support by later factor analyses of perceptions of the police carried out before and after viewing the two police drama episodes. For perceptions of police*men* and police*women* factor analyses yielded fewer factors for postviewing perceptions compared with previewing perceptions, suggesting a consolidating of children's impressions of the police by television drama portrayals, at least during the period immediately after viewing.

Perceptions of the police and crime provided further evidence of consolidation of impressions of the police, on this occasion in connection with beliefs about the kinds of crimes the police have to deal with. Children in the control group exhibited the greatest shifts in belief of the three groups. The main perceptual shift for the two viewing groups occurred in respect of two items: "kidnapping" and "suicides"—which were prominent features of the plots.

Opinions About the Police

The children's opinions about the police exhibited a number of shifts more often among those who watched "Juliet Bravo" than those who watched

"The Bill." Quite a few of these shifts were linked logically to the events depicted in the programs. Children's impressions of policewomen improved substantially on a number of characteristics in the light of watching the episode of "Juliet Bravo," which featured a woman police inspector in a position of authority over a station occupied largely by policemen. Police-women were more often seen to be competent in catching criminals and as having good chances of promotion after viewing the episode. At the same time, there was a reduction in numbers of children who believed that men were better at telling people what to do than women in the police. These findings illustrate the potential of television dramas to effect short-term shifts in children's opinions where the latter have a specific and direct link with portrayals in the dramatic narrative.

In the introduction to this chapter we listed a number of factors that earlier research had identified as important mediators of television's possible effects on beliefs about crime and the police in reality. These were: television viewing patterns, perceptions and comprehension of television content, judgments about different types of crime, and personal experienc-e(s) with crime and the police.

The variables listed here did not uniformly emerge as significant media-tors of children's responses to crime drama programs in the current research. Television viewing patterns have been linked with real-world perceptions in relatively simplistic and more complicated ways. Survey results reported by Gerbner and his colleagues, for example, examined relationships between crude measures of reported television viewing and perceptions of crime in the real world. Their findings indicated that heavier amounts of television viewing were associated with certain inaccurate and systematically distorted views of the world (Gerbner et al., 1977, 1978, 1979). More sophisticated analyses of the same secondary data sources by other writers failed to replicate Gerbner's results (Hirsch, 1980; Hughes, 1980). In the United Kingdom, researchers argued that measures of total amount of viewing disguise many of the subtleties of the viewing experi-ence. It is important also to investigate the types of programs individuals watch, because different program content may convey different messages about the world (see Wober & Gunter, 1988).

The current research obtained information from children both about their overall claimed viewing and about reported viewing of specified program types. Viewing patterns as reported by these young respondents were found to have only marginal links with their perceptions of crime and the police.

Children's abilities to understand program content improves with age (W. Collins, 1973, 1979) and has been found to mediate young viewers' responses to television programs (Pingree, 1983). Age was found in our research to be significantly related to levels of program comprehension, and comprehension of program content in turn mediated level of knowledge gain about certain aspects of police work as a function of exposure to a police drama episode.

Judgments are made by viewers about different types of crime. These judgments have been found to occur at different levels that are differentially sensitive to influences by television content (Tamborini et al., 1984). We found that base-level perceptions of police involvement in dealing with and success in solving different kinds of crime varied with the type of crime. There was little evidence of any systematic shifts in these perceptions contingent upon watching police drama episodes.

Finally, direct experience of crime or the police, which has been found elsewhere to be an important mediator of television's supposed cultivation effects (Weaver & Wakshlag, 1986), was found in this research to be significantly related to program comprehension, but had a less visible effect on changes in belief contingent upon viewing the police drama episodes.

Elsewhere, exposure to television depictions of crime has been found most powerfully to affect perceptions of real-life crime and feelings about personal safety in respect of hypothetical situations similar to ones depicted in television drama. Television has its most profound effects when direct sources of information about the police or crime are limited or missing altogether (Tyler, 1980; Weaver & Wakshlag, 1986). Thus, British viewers' perceptions of crime rates in U.S. cities were related to their reported viewing of U.S.-produced crime drama series, whereas their perceptions of crime in locations nearer to home were not related in any significant degree to their television viewing (Gunter, 1987b).

This research reveals that children hold varied beliefs about the police and their work in dealing with crime. Watching police drama episodes appears to have some short-term effects on particular perceptions that concern police characteristics that featured strongly in the programs. These effects were mediated by certain other factors, but it is clear that single episodes provide insufficient viewing experience to generate widespread and significant shifts in children's real-world perceptions. Many of these perceptions appear to be unstable anyway, and if anything, television programs that contain relevant content can act to stabilize otherwise highly changeable beliefs.

5

Science Programs With Single Themes: Evaluation, Comprehension, and Cognitive Impact

Although it is true that television is predominantly seen and conceived of by its audience as an entertainment medium, nonetheless, for many viewers, it is also recognized as a major source of information, embodying functions to inform, explain, and educate (Johnsson-Smaragdi, 1983; Rubin, 1977, 1979). Most broadcasters take this additional role seriously as can be seen from the scope and diversity of television's programming. Information about events in the known world is communicated by regular news and current affairs programs; the world of the unknown is explored by various nature and science programs that often depict the unseen and the unimagined. Both types of programs can command large viewing audiences. Before television, both these worlds were less directly and vividly available to the majority of the population. With the advent of television, however, both are now easily apprehended through the "window on the world" offered by the television set in nearly everyone's living room.

There can be little doubt that television has the potential to enlarge people's awareness and stock of knowledge of world events. This enlightenment can occur in response to a variety of different program formats. Thus, within the gamut of programming we can identify programs that impart information incidently on the back of entertainment (e.g., drama series/serials and quiz or talk shows); programs that are clearly highly constructed, didactic, and manipulated along educational lines (e.g., programs made especially for schools or instructional purposes); and, somewhere in the middle of these two extremes, programs that try to convey important scientific and technological information in popular ways. The latter comprise many widely viewed general interest magazine and documentary films. In short, then, television makes available many different types of "knowledge." These may comprise essentially unrelated facts, as in the general knowledge questions posed in game and quiz shows; knowledge about the people and social structures that constitute the social world we inhabit, through drama portrayals or factual reports in the news; and information that is essential to a fuller appraisal of our physical and sociotechnological world, as in factual programs about science and technology.

To what extent, however do children take advantage of these learning opportunities on television? Chapter 4 looked at what children understand and learn from TV drama. This chapter turns the spotlight on the extent to which children "pick up" any of the content of "informational" television. Factual programs can attract large audiences, given advantageous scheduling, but often attempt to treat serious subject matter in an entertaining fashion. Does the "entertainment" versus "information" orientation to television intercede to prevent the uptake and comprehension of such content (see e.g., Salomon, 1979, 1983a)? Does the medium precipitate "watching," but not "learning" (as suggested by Singer, 1980), or can it be shown that informational television does have demonstrable impact?

Evidence for children's learning from factual television programs derives largely from research on children's learning from news and current affairs broadcasts, and their acquisition of knowledge and skills from consciously contrived educational programs. This chapter is specifically concerned with the way in which children process information offered by educationally oriented programs that are available on mainstream television, particularly those that are science-based.

EDUCATIONAL TELEVISION

This is one area of programming that shows clearly that children undoubtedly can learn from television. The greatest volume of such programming in this field has occurred in the United States, although Britain has produced its own well-regarded programs, such as "Play School" and "Play Bus" for younger children ages 4 to 6, and "Blue Peter" for older children, which attempt to provide information in an entertaining way to a home-based audience.

In the United States during the late 1960s and early 1970s a number of highly innovative and popular educational television programs were researched, developed, and broadcast. The chief feature that served to differentiate this new crop of programs from previous ones was an awareness and deliberate exploitation of the unique powers of television. The dominant force behind these innovative programs was the Children's Television Workshop (CTW)—a marriage of educational advisors, professional researchers, and television producers that, according to Lesser (1974), was a "howling success." By a process of formative and summative research, producers of these programs knew who was watching, what the audience found appealing, and what was being understood or misunderstood.

There were three major flag ships of this potent combination of, on the one hand, a methodological and analytic-scientific approach to programming, and on the other, the deliberate employment of the intuitive–creative methods of television production: "Sesame Street," "The Electric Company," and "Feeling Good."

"Sesame Street" was designed to prepare children for school by developing both factual knowledge and thinking skills, specifically as they related to symbolic functions, cognitive processes, and physical and social environments. More specifically, "Sesame Street" was designed to develop skills with letters, numbers, and geometric forms; order, classification, and relationships; and exploitation of the natural world. Basic to all program production was that, before broadcast, prior research had to have shown that the programs had demonstrable ability to attract attention, to appeal to the audience, and to be comprehensible.

Following broadcasting of these programs numerous studies were conducted to assess and evaluate their success. A study by Ball and Bogatz (1970) of "Sesame Street" is representative. Ability on content issues of the program showed improvement over a 1-year period, and such improvement was a direct function of the amount of "Sesame Street" watching engaged in. In a later study, Bogatz and Ball (1972) basically found the same positive results on an increased number of objectives, but also uncovered the fact that although viewers could learn basic skills and knowledge, they had more difficulty with complex skills. Overall, however, Ball and Bogatz concluded that television, although being explicitly entertaining, can still educate young children in both the cognitive and the attitudinal domains.

Certain researchers it must be said (e.g., Cook & Conner, 1976; Liebert, 1976) have been less sanguine about the specific effects of "Sesame Street," arguing that in addition to viewing factors, parental encouragement was vital. On balance, however, the weight of evidence clearly supports the contention that programs devised for home consumption and that maximize the power of television's unique characteristics can eventuate in learning. As Bryant, Alexander, and Brown (1983) pointed out, "Sesame Street" was the first mass-audience educational television that attempted, and succeeded, in "education by entertainment" and demonstrated that "learning can be fun," by utilizing a magazine format with a variety of special production techniques. In other words, children could both laugh and learn at the same time.

"The Electric Company" was a program designed to increase reading skills among primary school children. It again used a magazine format and a variety of attention-grabbing production techniques. Once again, Ball and Bogatz (1973) were one of the chief research teams concerned with evaluating this informational program. They found that on 17 of 19 reading skills tested, viewers of "The Electric Company" outperformed nonviewers. Although less supportive in certain respects, an independent evaluation by Sproull, Ward, and Ward (1976) again found that children were responsive to the program series, and demonstrated learning from it.

"Feeling Good" was designed to motivate viewers to take steps to enhance their health in 11 basic areas, such as cancer, alcohol abuse, cardiac disease, nutrition, mental health, and prenatal care. The overall aim of the program was information accumulation and positive attitude change. Achievement of desired goals was somewhat fragmentary (Bryant et al., 1983) but this may have been for other than purely educational or television production reasons.

THE IMPACT OF TELEVISED SCIENCE

The current research focused on a particular type of educational broadcast, namely programs concerned with science and technology topics. Previous research had provided important insights into styles of production conducive to children's learning about science from television. Particularly relevant was work done on "3-2-1 Contact," an educational program targeted at children in the United States. It was a series about science and technology for children ages 8–12, aimed at getting them to enjoy science and to engage in scientific activity, and to help them learn different styles of scientific thinking. The programs were presented in a magazine format, presenting themes based on opposites, with continuing features such as mystery adventure, animation, live action film, music, comedy, and special effects. Mielke and Chen's (1980) early assessment of this program series is essentially positive, indicating that large audiences were attracted to the program and that its aims and objectives were, generally, realized.

Mielke and Chen (1983), in discussing the impact of "3-2-1 Contact," pointed out that animal behavior and the human body have high interest and curiosity value for children in informational television. Other findings in the formative phase of research into "3-2-1 Contact" are also interesting. Plotted drama was preferred over segmented magazine format as a general program type. Thus, the challenge to producers may be to investigate new ways of incorporating instructional content into a plotted drama format where a problem is posed and resolved through relations between various recurring characters. Additionally, the dramatic development of a problem and its resolution can help motivate the perceived need for a scientific approach or piece of information on the part of the viewer.

One interesting finding by Mielke and Chen (1983) was that children held both positive and negative perceptions of scientists and the work of science. This ambivalence in young children mirrors that found in adolescents (e.g., Mead & Metraux, 1957) and in adults (Royal Society, 1985), and is discussed later in this chapter.

But what about prime-time science programs made for the popular audience? Do programs that convey information of a scientific nature but that are intended to be broadcast to mass audiences have equal impact and learning outcomes?

THE ROLE OF SCIENCE ON MAINSTREAM TELEVISION

There is currently a feeling that for an intelligent democracy the mysteries of science must be laid bare and the knowledge produced by scientists increasingly passed into the public domain. A chief vehicle of this transfer is held to be television. To date, however, there is little research on how well children learn from science programs that are broadcast as general television programs, as distinct from science programs designed for schools.

Although very little experimental investigation of television science has been undertaken, there is a literature available from more sociological and "head-counting" quarters. For example, Jones, Connell, and Meadows (1971) surveyed the presentation of science in the public media. Responses to particular programs have been investigated (e.g., Ryder, 1982) and the ways in which science programs are made has also been a focus of attention (e.g., La Follette, 1982; Silverstone, 1985). In general, the research that is available concerns society's attitudes to or perception of science and science on television. Little, if any, work of an experimental nature has been concerned with children's learning from science programs, broadcast on television in or around peak viewing slots.

There are, however, pockets of research that suggest an association between scientific knowledge and watching science-based television programs in adults. One such study is that conducted by Lucas (1987), that investigated public understanding of radioactivity and nuclear waste. Although he found that, overall, such understanding was low in a sample of 1,033 adults over the age of 15, he did find that "correct" answers were positively associated with frequency of viewing any of the science programs "Horizon," "Tomorrow's World," "The Natural World," and "The Sky at Night." On the other hand, there was no such positive relationship with watching television news or current affairs programs, although there was with reading newspapers.

The study discussed here serves to indicate the potential of television in knowledge growth in the domain of science. Other research, concerned mainly with attitudes and perception, rather than knowledge, paints a less appealing picture of the outcome of watching science on prime-time television. Gerbner (1987), within his on-going cultural indicators studies, assessed the portrayal of science and scientists on prime-time television in the United States. His studies also analyzed survey data to discover what contributions television makes to conceptions of science held by different groups of viewers. Gerbner found that after leaving school most of his respondents encountered science and technology most often on television, not in informative science and documentary type programs, but rather through prime-time entertainment. Such is likely to be the case in the United Kingdom also. Gerbner's study was based on detailed analysis of a 10-year sample of network prime-time dramatic programs telecast between 1973 and 1983. A sample week from each season showed 174 programs in which science, technology, or medicine were major themes; 410 programs in which they were minor themes; and 252 programs with no such themes. The study found that certain images of science, technology, or medicine appeared in 7 out of every 10 prime-time dramatic programs. On average, in addition to news and documentary footage, it would appear that the average prime-time viewer will see a dozen doctors and two other scientists each week. Although doctors are highly regarded, scientists are more negatively evaluated—seen as less sociable, older, "stranger," and more likely to be foreigners. As Gerbner (1987) said, the image of the scientist was "somewhat foreboding, touched with a sense of evil, trouble, and peril" (p. 112).

Having established the image of science portrayed on prime-time television, Gerbner assessed whether a heavy diet of such programming as opposed to a light diet had observable effects on the ideas and behaviors of viewers. On the basis of a telephone survey of 1,631 respondents, Gerbner was able to show that the more people watch television the less favorable they are about science. Heavy viewing as opposed to light viewing tended to enhance anxiety and erode or inhibit appreciation of the benefits of science.

An altogether more positively toned research finding has been presented by Elliott and Rosenberg (1987), again with a U.S. sample. Using what they called a *media dependency theory approach*, these researchers found that feeling competent about handling scientific information and being enthusiastic about scientific and technological advances are strongly related to exposure to media science information.

Television reportedly represents an important source of information about science for many people. The public's knowledge about science can be shaped by factual programs (magazine shows, documentaries) that focus on science topics and themes. Impressions of scientists and the work that they do may even be influenced by dramatic portrayals. Whatever television's effects in this realm, recent U.K. evidence has indicated that the public has an appetite for science and is interested to see it covered by television.

In the United Kingdom, television is regarded by many people as their main source of scientific information. In addition, 7 out of 10 people in Britain claim to be "very" or "fairly interested" in science and technology topics. Asked their views on the amount of coverage of science on television, 55% said the level was about right, with 26% saying there was too little coverage. Three percent wanted less science, whereas 16% had no opinion either way (IBA, 1986). In another, comparable study, IBA research found that the great majority of viewers felt they should be informed about science; 78% agreed that "people should be informed about the things scientists are doing" (Gunter, 1988).

In terms of program topic interest, the most popular science topics concern biological, medical, and health matters. There is a healthy interest also in geology, car technology, weather forecasting, and space exploration (e.g., Gunter, 1988). Most respondents (78%) felt that a lot could be learned about these topics from such programs. A perplexing finding, however, cited by both Svennevig (1988) and Gunter (1988), is the unusual perception held by viewers of "science," and where it can be found in the schedules. Often they did not see it in explicitly scientific programs but did find it in programs where, on conventional definitions of science, none existed (e.g., a quiz show that featured general knowledge questions about science; drama series with science themes or portrayals of scientists).

Although viewers widely acclaim television as their chief source of science information in this field, and seem to be satisfied with its delivery, there remains widespread scientific ignorance and illiteracy among adult populations (e.g., Miller & Barrington, 1981). One of the latest reports indicating this gap between interest in, appreciation of, and attention to televised science on the one hand and learning from such programming on the other is the cross-cultural study conducted by Durant, Evans, and Thomas (1989) and Evans and Durant (1989). Having sampled 2,009 British and 2,041 U.S. adults over 18 years of age in 1988 these researchers concluded that although both populations were interested in science, technology, and medicine, their understanding of such subject matter was low. Working on the assumption that people who were interested in a particular issue would tend to be relatively well informed about it, they asked respondents to say how well informed they were about a number of issues and then tested knowledge of that issue. As might be expected, self-reported interest and "informedness" matched for sport, politics, and films, but interest and knowledge did not match for science, technology, and medicine.

The major finding to emerge from this research that has looked at adults' perception and opinion of, attitudes to, and learning from television-based science, is that although the public is largely uninformed it is also largely interested in science on television. This major finding stimulated our work with children. We were addressing the same issues but from a slightly different perspective. We were concerned to find out (a) whether children liked, watched, and appreciated science-based television programs, and (b) whether they could learn from them. Answers to these questions would be interesting in themselves and would also be of potential help in understanding the adult data outlined here because the mismatch between espoused interest in science programs and objective understanding of such content, makes it unclear whether popular informational (science) programs can generate knowledge growth.

The orientation adopted was that the impact of science programs depends on many features of the process of production and the constraints of the particular medium, the content of the program itself, and its reception by the viewer. This reception depends on a multiplicity of contexts such as other programs that the children watch, the viewer's preconceptions formed by all other sources of influence, and his or her motivations for viewing.

Within this framework, we were concerned to elicit the attributes of programs that affect the appeal and comprehension of science presentations: What formats are most appropriate for science presentation in popular television? What type of information is best recalled and comprehended? and What is the competitive appeal of science programs in a home-viewing environment?

METHOD

The details of the methodology used in this experiment were described in chapter 2, however, a summary of the main components of the study is provided here to remind readers of how it was carried out.

The experiment employed a pretest, program exposure, posttest format in which groups of children were tested for their recall and comprehension of program content and for any impact the program had upon their science general knowledge. There were 129 children tested, but only 111 appeared for both the pre- and posttests. Two age groups were represented: There were 55 8- to 9-year-olds and 56 14- to 15-year-olds. They were evenly divided between males and females, and 27 did not have English as their first language.

Two programs were used as test materials, "Body Matters" and "Erasmus Microman." The former program was produced for the general family audience, whereas the latter was especially made for a youth audience. Both programs had one important feature in common in that they focused on one topic only per edition. The "Body Matters" program used in this experiment explored the structure of the human skeleton, and the "Erasmus Microman" program investigated Michael Faraday's attempts to produce electricity. The children's program was presented at a slower pace than the family audience program, and used a more dramatized style with actors playing roles. The family program was presented before a live studio audience by professional people (qualified medical doctors) in a more factual fashion.

Both programs were analyzed in depth so that detailed questionnaires could be designed to probe children's understanding of their respective contents and general knowledge growth contingent upon watching.

During a prescreening phase, all children were given a general knowledge questionnaire that contained questions on a range of subjects (history, geography, science, current affairs). Pilot work had established difficulty levels for the questions. From this benchmarking exercise it was estimated that the youngest children would be able to answer correctly only about 20% of the questions, whereas the oldest should have been able to get about 80% correct. About 25% of the items on the questionnaire dealt with matters covered in the programs.

Viewing of the programs took place 7 days after the prescreening tests, and the children were then tested again for a second time immediately after they had watched one of the two programs. The posttest measured the children's comprehension of the program they had watched, their recall of its informational content and knowledge growth on those questions used in the pretest that dealt with program-related topics, their subjective impressions about learning from such programs, and their general opinions about science programs on television.

ATTITUDES, COMPREHENSION, AND KNOWLEDGE GROWTH

The result are presented in four parts. The first part examines the children's general attitudes toward science programs on television, whereas the second part explores attitudes toward the two test programs that were shown to different groups of children. The third part examines the children's general comprehension and recall of test program content and the fourth part looks at specific science knowledge growth contingent upon viewing either of the two programs.

Attitudes Toward Science Programs in General

Before examining the children's responses to the specific programs they had just been shown, we were interested to find out if science programs in general were well received or not. These responses should reflect more enduring attitudes to this type of television programming. We also wished to know whether attitudes toward science on television varied among boys and girls, different age groups, and as a function of other attributes of young viewers. Table 5.1 presents the relevant findings and the questions in their entirety.

Most of the children felt that science programs could help viewers learn new things and that they might inform about things viewers might need to know. A majority of the children also perceived science programs as generating cognitive activity, by "making you think." This last viewpoint

TABLE 5.1
General Opinions About Science Programs on Television

Attitude Statement	All %	Age		Sex		Language Ability	
		8–9 %	14–15 %	M %	F %	English as First Language %	English as Second Language %
Programs like this help you to learn new things	91	95	88	84	98	93	82
Programs like this tell you about things you might need to know	80	86	75	80	80	77	100
It is easier to learn from television than from books	70	59	77	69	71	66	67
Programs like this make you think	68	81	57	69	67	64	82
Programs like this should be put on BBC 2 or Channel 4	46	41	48	45	46	44	50
Programs like this should only be shown as school programs in school	43	30	52	42	43	39	46
I try to watch a lot of these kinds of programs	42	69	15	46	39	35	46
There should be more programs like this on television	38	60	18	37	38	52	10
I usually switch over or go out of the room when these kind of programs are on	38	21	56	39	37	43	36
These kind of programs go on for too long	31	22	39	31	30	31	32
There are too many information programs on television nowadays	30	30	30	30	30	29	32
I often talk about these kinds of programs with my family and friends	23	34	11	26	20	19	29

Note. Percentages are summed over those children who "strongly agreed" or "agreed" with each attitude statement.

was especially widespread among the youngest age group (8–9). Most children, especially teenagers, thought that television was a relatively easy medium to learn from, certainly when compared with books. This finding corroborates earlier research (Salomon, 1983b) that revealed that this mental set toward television is commonplace among children and can contribute toward poor memory for program content.

On most of the remaining attitudes, which were held by varying sized minorities of the sample, there were marked differences between the younger and older children in the views held. The younger age group, for example, was much more likely than the oldest group to say that they try to watch a lot of science programs and that there should be more of these programs on television. The youngest children were also markedly more likely to report talking to members of their family or to friends about science programs, although, only a minority even of the younger ones said this.

Older children tended to exhibit more cynical attitudes about science on television. They were more in favor of restricting science to minority television channels or to programs made especially for schools. They were also more likely to switch channels to avoid science programs. There was, however, no widespread rejection of information programs per se, nor did any more than a minority of either age group feel that science programs went on for too long. The impression with which we were left was that it was either the content or perhaps the presentation style of science programs in particular, to which older children were objecting.

Program Appreciation Patterns

To shed more light of the structure of children's general opinions about science programs, we subjected their attitudinal responses to further statistical analysis. Principal Components Factor Analyses with Varimax Rotation yielded three factors which were labeled as Factor 1: program attraction, Factor 2: program utility, and Factor 3: home–school comparison (see Table 5.2).

Program attraction was defined by the following statements: "These kind of programs go on for too long," "There are too many information programs on television nowadays," "I usually switch over or go out of the room when these kind of programs are on," "There should be more programs like this on television," "I try to watch a lot of these kind of programs," and "programs like these should be put on BBC 2 or Channel 4."

The *utility* factor displayed high association between responses to statements such as "I often talk about these kind of programs with my family or friends," "programs like this tell you about things you might need to know," "programs like this make you think," and "programs like this help you learn new things."

TABLE 5.2
Structure of Children's Perception of Television Programs

Statements	Attraction Factor 1	Utility Factor 2	Home–School Factor 3
These programs go on too long.	.75803	−.11117	.12541
There are too many information programs on TV nowadays.	.75029	.00996	.24482
I usually switch over or go out of the room.	.70728	−.24545	−.01361
There should be more programs like this on TV.	−.53804	.52020	−.10955
I try to watch a lot of these kind of programs.	−.52484	.50929	−.18766
Programs like these should only be on BBC2/Ch. 4.	.48087	.04720	.43542
I often talk about these kinds of programs.	.23898	.69673	−.06929
Programs like these tell you about things you should know.	−.11697	.62984	−.26611
Programs like these make you think.	−.42410	.58713	.20927
Programs like these help you learn new things.	−.21319	.52607	.18298
Easier to learn from TV than from books.	−.00800	−.15388	.77149
Programs like these should only be shown in school.	.27106	.03369	.68141

Finally, the *home-school* comparison factor was defined by two statements: "It is easier to learn from television than it is from a book" and "programs like these should only be shown as school programs in school."

These factors seem to have coherence in that they recognize that children (and adults for that matter) can have views about specific television programs (Factor 1), which they know exist and value at a cognitive level but toward which they have no behavioral commitment (except perhaps avoidance) (Factor 2) and that therefore may or may not enter into a comparison level of alternatives in attitudinal attraction (Factor 3). These factors were treated later as independent variables to see if such attitudinal clusters predicted recall, comprehension, and knowledge growth following program exposure.

Attitudes to "Body Matters" and "Erasmus Microman"

A second battery of statements was provided in order to measure the children's attitudes toward each of the two test programs used in this experiment. These views were obtained from the children shortly after they had watched either "Body Matters" or "Erasmus Microman."

The attitude statements that exhibited noticeable differences as a function of either program, age, gender, or fluency in English are presented in Tables

5.3, 5.4, and 5.5. Those attitude statements showing no differences in response among sample subgroups are not shown but they are commented on later where appropriate.

Both programs were rated highly by most children for what they felt they could learn from it. A majority also felt there should be more programs of this sort on television. At the same time, however, many children found the entertainment orientation too much to handle. There was further concern, more especially in the case of "Body Matters," about the kind of detail covered on one topic. Reinforcing the latter view, many children indicated a preference for coverage of more than one topic in a program, particularly those who watched "Erasmus Microman." As Table 5.3 shows, however, opinions about each program varied considerably with the age of the child.

Age. Broadly, younger children were more favorably disposed to more science programs being shown on television and to such programs having more than one in-depth topic per week, that is, being more magazinelike, and were considerably more likely than older children to say that the

TABLE 5.3
Age Differences in Attitudes Toward Body Matters ("BM") and "Erasmus Microman" ("EM")

	Program Viewed					
	"Body Matters"			"Erasmus Microman"		
		8–9 Years	14–15 Years		8–9 Years	14–15 Years
Attitude Statement	"BM" All %	%	%	"EM" All %	%	%
I feel I could learn a lot about my body ("BM") electricity ("EM")	75	81	69	70	83	57
There should be more programs like this	54	69	39	66	91	40
Sometimes "BM"/"EM" tries to be too amusing/like school	51	25	77	59	57	60
It is better if more than one topic is covered each week	39	50	27	62	74	50
The presenters in "BM"/"EM" try to tell you too much	46	56	35	44	57	30
Telling you about something in a lot of detail is boring	55	44	65	32	17	47
"BM"/"EM" is the best science program on television	35	50	19	48	83	13
You have to be clever to understand "BM"/"EM"	33	50	15	25	30	20

Note. Percentages are summed over those children who "agreed strongly" or "agreed" with each attitude statement.

particular test program they had watched was the best such program on television. This latter result may reflect the generally less critical attitude of younger viewers as opposed to older viewers. Younger children also felt that they could learn more from the program's content than did the older children. The responses relating to the amount of information imparted by presenters, number of topics covered, and being able to learn a lot indicate that, with increased age, children feel able to tackle a greater volume of more complicated information, possibly because their ability to process in-depth, and thus more complex material, improves. Responses to the statement that the test program watched was the best science program on television showed a marked downward trend from positive to negative with age, suggesting that by age 14–15 a more selective attitude to science-based television may be beginning to develop. There is some further indication that older children want to be challenged by science program. A noticeable contrast between ages is seen in respect of the perception of how clever you need to be to understand the test program. The older children did not feel that you had to be clever to understand such programs to the same extent as did younger children. Alternatively, this finding could reflect the view, expressed by Salomon (1983b), that older children do not see television as a difficult medium, compared to, for example, books and reading.

Gender Differences.   A number of differences in opinions about science programs were recorded between boys and girls, some of which were quite substantial. These are presented in Table 5.4.

Contrary to conventional stereotypes, females agreed with positive statements concerning science programs more than did males and less frequently with negative statements, and markedly so for "Erasmus Microman." Girls were much less likely than boys to say that the presenters in this program try to tell you too much or use difficult language. Although the boys' perceptions of science-type programs were fairly uniform, the girls seemed to vary hugely as a function of the type of program that was being referred to. In "Body Matters," the information is provided by "studio experts" (two males and one female) with the males taking a dominant role within the program. In "Erasmus Microman," a boy and girl participate equally in the experiments, thereby presenting more of an appropriate role model for girls to identify with. This suggests that girls may be more selective in what appeals to them or that both programs provide appropriate role models for boys but only "Erasmus Microman" performed this function for girls. However, once again, against the stereotype, the girls were more likely than boys to say that they felt they could learn equally from programs that cover medical/ bodily matters ("BM") and more 'hard-nosed' subject matter such as electricity ("EM").

TABLE 5.4

Gender Differences in Attitudes Toward "Body Matters" ("BM") and "Erasmus Microman" ("EM")

	Program Viewed			
	"Body Matters"		"Erasmus Microman"	
	Male	Female	Male	Female
Attitude Statement	%	%	%	%
I feel I could learn a lot about my body ("BM") electricity ("EM") from such programs	64	85	65	73
Sometimes the presenters use words that are difficult to understand	60	58	42	18
"BM"/"EM" rarely covers topics that interest me	56	55	52	18
Telling you about one thing in a lot of detail is boring	52	55	42	23
Presenters in "BM"/"EM" try to tell you too much	48	46	58	18

Fluency in English.   As explained earlier, the two programs featured in this experiment differed in a number of ways—especially in format and presentational styles. Because the delivery rate of information and mode of presentation differed between the two programs (and as it does across science programs generally) it was relevant to ask if children without English as a first language experienced any difficulties relative to those children who did have English as a first language. Table 5.5 presents the findings.

The results show that perceptions of the two programs did vary with the language ability of the children on several factors relating to level of interest and difficulty of language used in each program. Those children for whom English was a second language showed a much stronger preference for the family-oriented show, "Body Matters" than for the children's program, "Erasmus Microman," as evidenced by their responses to the items: "There should be more programs like this," and "(this) is the best science program on television." It was also clear that these same children perceived greater detail in "Body Matters" than in "Erasmus Microman" and were more likely to say of the former that "you have to be clever to understand (it)." Despite these responses, however, children with ESL widely felt that neither of these programs regularly covered topics of interest to them. Thus, they appeared to have a lower level of general interest in science topics than did children with English as a first language, despite their stronger preference for "Body Matters."

TABLE 5.5
Language Ability and Attitudes Toward "Body Matters" ("BM") and "Erasmus Microman" ("EM")

| | Program Viewed | | | |
| | "Body Matters" | | "Erasmus Microman" | |
Attitude Statement	English as a First Language %	English as a Second Language %	English as a First Language %	English as a Second Language %
"BM"/"EM" rarely covers topics of interest to me	48	72	33	100
There should be more programs like this	43	83	65	25
Programs giving a lot of detail are boring	63	33	37	0
"BM"/"EM" is the best science program on television	28	56	47	0
You have to be clever to understand "BM"/"EM"	25	56	25	25

PROGRAM COMPREHENSION

From the information just presented it can be seen that the children exhibited varying subjective impressions about science on television and about the two specific science programs that they watched for the purposes of the current experiment. Included among these impressions were opinions about what could be learned and how easy or difficult it was to learn from such programs. The real test, however, of how well children learn from science programs would be an objective measure of what informational content they can remember and understand after viewing, and whether their knowledge of science grows as a result of watching such programs. The next part of this chapter reports the results of this type of assessment.

To what extent could children understand the content of such programs and recall details that had been explicitly presented during its transmission? We distinguished between understanding or comprehension, on the one hand, and recall or memory, on the other. Comprehending material was taken to mean having the ability to go beyond the information actually presented and to reason with the general principles implied by the presentation of specific details. Memory was conceptualized as the ability to recall to mind those specific details given out in the program the children had just seen. Although conceptually distinct, it is clear that recall and comprehension are nonetheless closely associated. We tested both abilities by means of open-ended (OE) and multiple-choice (MC) questions.

Overall Comprehension and Recall Levels

Overall, the children demonstrated a high standard of both comprehension and recall of program content. In terms of comprehension of program content, collapsing across both types of question (OE or MC) and all demographic and background factors, the children scored 63% correct on questions that asked them to reason about or problem solve in terms of details given out in the program. Clearly then, the children were able to understand the program's content.

In terms of recall, overall the children scored a creditable 64.5% correct answers. Not only were they able to reason about the program, but, at least in the short term, they were also able to remember details of what was shown and spoken about.

Performance Differences Among Children

A number of differences emerged among the children in terms of their program comprehension and recall. In particular, age emerged as an important variable. Older children did better than younger children on every measure taken. However, it should be noted that older children also had much higher background knowledge at the outset (as shown by their general knowledge pretest scores) than did younger children, and it is known that relevant general knowledge is a good predictor of information pick-up from television (Findahl & Hoijer, 1985; Gunter, 1985b; Robinson & Sahin, 1984). In fact, younger and older children were closest on questions that may be indicating that the problem of learning from television for the younger child is not one of encoding the material, but rather of storing, organizing, and retrieving it. Where younger children did not have to retrieve information, but merely to recognize it (MC questions), their performance was closer to that of older children. With OE questions, where children may not have had knowledge into which new information could readily be slotted, they exhibited retrieval deficits because multiple access routes to the material may not have been available. Younger children also found the physical act of writing and spelling as opposed to ticking a box more daunting than older children, which could have inhibited their performance on the OE questions. Whatever the cause, however, age clearly remains a very powerful effect on children's ability to pick up and then to articulate information from informational television (see Table 5.6).

In terms of program content and presentation factors, both age groups were better able to "recall" information from "Erasmus Microman" than they were from "Body Matters," although there was little variation in terms of their ability to "comprehend" information from either program (see Table 5.6). The "Erasmus Microman" sample also achieved lower scores in

TABLE 5.6
Percentage Correct Recall and Comprehension Scores From the Two Science
Programs

Program Viewed	Age	Pretest General Knowledge %	Posttest Recall Total %	Posttest Recall OE %	Posttest Recall MC %	Posttest Comprehension Total %	Posttest Comprehension OE %	Posttest Comprehension MC %
"Body Matters"								
	8–9	27	43	43	44	55	31	68
	14–15	70	64	58	70	74	65	76
"Erasmus Microman"								
	8–9	18	66	59	75	51	30	65
	14–15	55	85	87	81	71	60	79

the general knowledge pretest, thus indicating, perhaps, that they had to work harder at retrieving relevant information from their test program than the "Body Matters" sample. This suggests that the format and content of "Erasmus Microman," in terms of presenting information, might have been more appropriate for the child audience it was intended for, than "Body Matters," whose target audience is adults and/or families.

Gender had no significant effect whatever on recall or comprehension for either of our program groups, with boys scoring 67% correct recall and 63% correct comprehension, whereas the girls scored 64% and 64% respectively. This noneffect of respondent gender is mildly surprising given that science programs were being investigated and it is generally assumed that girls are socialized away from the hard sciences at a very early age. There is little or no evidence for girls being "switched off" by science here, where the issue is recall and understanding of prime-time television science programs. Boys and girls did not differ in general knowledge either: During the pretest, the boys scored 45%, whereas the girls turned in a score of 42%.

Fluency in English also proved to be nondiscriminating in terms of either total recall or comprehension, or in terms of general knowledge. ESL children scored 44% on general knowledge, 70% on recall, and 63% on comprehension, whereas those children with English as a first language scored 48%, 69%, and 67%, respectively.

Children's performance was analysed further by carrying out analysis of variance tests (ANOVA) on OE and MC recall and comprehension scores as a function of each demographic variable (age, gender, and fluency in English) and by program. For simplicity, the F statistics only for each ANOVA are summarized in Table 5.7.

As can be seen, age was a statistically significant effect, with older children doing better than younger children in all cases. Meanwhile, confirming our earlier observations, gender did not emerge as a reliable

TABLE 5.7
Summary Table of *F* statistics for Recall and Comprehension as a Function
of Age, Gender, and Language Ability

	Posttest			
	Recall		Comprehension	
Program viewed	OE	MC	OE	MC
"Body Matters"				
Age	11.265*	13.386*	32.317*	5.946***
Gender	<1	<1	<1	<1
Language ability	4.800***	14.263***	27.813*	15.441*
"Erasmus Microman"				
Age	23.692*	1.266	6.364**	12.133**
Gender	<1	<1	3.031	<1
Language ability	1.712	<1	<1	2.067

Note. $F(1,56)$ for "Body Matters." $F(1,51)$ for "Erasmus Microman." $*p<.001.$ $**p<.01.$
$***p<.05.$

effect in any of the analyses. Fluency in English, however, did show up in
this more detailed analysis to be a factor of some importance. Thus, with
"Body Matters," having English as a first or second language seemed to
make a difference, with those children who had English as a first language
doing better on recall and comprehension of program content. With
"Erasmus Microman," fluency in English appeared statistically to make no
difference to recall or comprehension under either of the two questioning
modes (OE or MC). It is possible that the simpler language level of this
children's program rendered it easier to follow for those children whose
fluency in English may have been less competent.

The Effect of Background Viewing Habits
on Recall and Comprehension

In addition to the demographic factors of age, gender, and fluency in
English, it is possible that the nature and amount of television viewing that
the children undertook could affect their ability to learn from informational
television. This was investigated in a number of ways.

Previous Viewing of Specific Test Program.   The first approach we took
was to argue that if there were long-term effects of single exposure to a
specific program then children who had previously seen the programs with
which we presented them during the experiment should perform better than
those children who had not previously seen the program. In the event, the
results were mixed. As Table 5.8 shows, when we divided our samples into

TABLE 5.8
Percentage Correct Recall and Comprehension Score as a Function of
Having Previously Viewed the Presented Program

| | Pretest | Posttest | | | | | |
| | General Knowledge | Recall | | | Comprehension | | |
Program Viewed		Total	OE	MC	Total	OE	MC
	%	%	%	%	%	%	
"Body Matters"							
Previously Viewed	56	67	64	69	73	61	76
Not Previously Viewed	45	53	48	53	62	44	71
"Erasmus Microman"							
Previously Viewed	24	72	70	76	55	35	68
Not Previously Viewed	43	77	76	79	64	50	74

those who had viewed each specific program previously and those who had not, this seemed to have an effect on those children who watched "Body Matters" but not for "Erasmus Microman" viewers.

Although it is possible that the "Body Matters" data could be taken to support the view that learning from television programs persists over time, the "Erasmus Microman" data cast doubt on this assumption. It would be difficult to sustain the hypothesis of long-term effects unless we posited an interaction with type of program, such that seeing a program like "Body Matters" precipitates long-term learning, whereas a program like "Erasmus Microman" has no such effects. Although this is a possibility because the content, format, language complexity level, and target audience all differ with respect to the two programs chosen for presentation, a simpler explanation would be one based on sampling artifacts.

As can be seen from Table 5.8, background knowledge differed between those children who had seen the program episode before and those who had not for our two program groups and in different ways. Thus, it would seem that any effect due to having seen the specific episode shown before was swamped by the more powerful factor of the general knowledge individual children brought to their viewing.

Previous Viewing of This Type of Program.   The swamping effect of preexisting knowledge was also seen when we investigated whether watching "Body Matters" or "Erasmus Microman" generally, rather than just the specific episode we had chosen to present to the children had an effect on recall and comprehension of the content of the specific program seen. The theoretical basis of this investigation was the possibility that children would demonstrate "learning how to learn." That is, by being exposed to "Body Matters" or "Erasmus Microman" on a regular basis, a growing familiarity concerning the program's format, style and "way of doing things" could develop that would lead to ease of learning of new material presented in that program. However, just the opposite seemed to be the case because there was a suggestion of an inverse relationship between frequency of viewing the programme ("nearly always," "most of the time," "occasionally," "never") and both recall and comprehension performance, such that the more children had reportedly watched each television series, the poorer their recall and comprehension was of the specific program presented. And this was most marked with the children's program—"Erasmus Microman."

When we looked at general knowledge, however, the relationship was much more linear. Those children with high initial knowledge performed better on both recall and comprehension, in both programming groups, irrespective of amount of prior viewing of this program.

Heavy and Light Viewing of Science Programs in General. Still pursuing the same line of reasoning mentioned earlier and in opposition to the argument that heavy viewing of television is antithetical to both social and academic learning, we went on to investigate if heavy viewing of science-type programs in general could eventuate in the development of schema and strategies that would facilitate the uptake of the type of information contained in such programs. However, a glance at Table 5.9 reveals that there was little support for this view: If anything, the lighter viewers of science-type programs produced the better performance.

An interpretation of Table 5.9 could be that heavy science program viewers are in fact heavy television viewers per se, and as a result their information pick-up skills have been blunted. This reasoning would be in line with the notion that heavy viewing undermines the cognitive ability to learn new information. However, the actual level of both recall and comprehen-

TABLE 5.9
Mean Percentage Correct Recall and Comprehension Score as a Function of Heavy and Light Viewing of Science-Type Programs

Program Viewed	Intensity of Viewing	Pretest General Knowledge	Posttest Recall Total	OE	MC	Comprehension Total	OE	MC
		%	%	%	%	%	%	%
"Body Matters"								
	Heavy	38	51	49	53	55	38	71
	Light	50	54	51	57	61	50	72
"Erasmus Microman"								
	Heavy	22	70	62	77	50	31	68
	Light	44	79	79	79	64	52	75

sion even for heavy viewers constituted a respectable standard of performance.

And indeed when we went on to perform finer grained analyses, looking at viewing factors as the independent variables, it was seen that viewing habits did have certain specific relationships with recall and comprehension scoring. Viewing proclivity was a significant differentiator in certain specific conditions. The F statistics associated with these analyses of variance are presented in Table 5.10.

With these more detailed analyses it is still clear that, having seen the actual program presented in the experiment had little effect, making a difference only for "Body Matters" and only on open-ended recall with "seen before" viewers performing better.

Likewise, a history of viewing the television series from which these particular programs were taken had little effect, but did significantly differentiate between children on their MC "Body Matters," with "occasional" viewers doing best, and on their OE comprehension of "Erasmus Microman," with respondents claiming "never" to have seen it before doing best.

In terms of reported general science program viewing (heavy vs. light) it emerged that heavy and light viewers did not differ in their performance on recall or comprehension of "Body Matters," but for "Erasmus Microman," OE recall and comprehension were related to this viewing factor such that light viewers of science programs did better.

TABLE 5.10

Summary Table of F statistics for Previous Viewing Experience and Science Program Content Recall and Comprehension

Program Viewed	Viewing Factors	Posttest			
		Recall		Comprehension	
		OE	MC	OE	MC
"Body Matters"					
	Science viewing	<1	<1	2.164	<1
	Seen test program	3.942***	2.162	2.954	1.048
	Ever watched test program	2.596	5.087***	<1	<1
"Erasmus Microman"					
	Science viewing	5.424**	<1	4.887***	1.965
	Seen test program	<1	<1	3.095	1.226
	Ever watched test program	3.811	<1	7.140**	1.026

Note. $F(1,56)$ for "Body Matters." $F(1,51)$ for "Erasmus Microman." *$p<.001$. **$p<.01$. ***$p<.05$.

KNOWLEDGE GROWTH

In this phase of the study we were interested to find out if the program the children had watched had produced certain predefined, specific learning effects. These learning effects we termed *knowledge growth* because, by using as pretest questions, items from the program that we knew the children were going to see, and then presenting these questions again after viewing, we had two scores on identical items that we could compare directly. This would serve to give an unambiguous estimate of learning from specific television programs. In addition, we were interested to see if any of the demographic or previous viewing habits that we have discussed before would serve to influence any knowledge growth that may be exhibited, either working independently or in conjunction. To answer these questions we performed a number of three-way ANOVAs on the scores the children obtained on the key repeated items in the pre- and the posttests, the results of which are presented in Table 5.11.

The key points to note from Table 5.11 are that: (a) test (pretest–posttest score differences) was significant in every case; (b) no interactions involving test appeared, thus indicating that the effect of seeing the program was

TABLE 5.11
Summary *F* statistics for Three-Way ANOVA

ANOVAS	*Significant Factors*	*Program Viewed* "Body Matter"	"Erasmas Microman"
Test X Age X Sex			
	Age	27.78*	14.822*
	Test	72.659*	212.137*
Test X Age X Seen program before			
	Age	13.065*	6.951**
	Seen Before	5.908***	<1
	Test	27.753*	86.527*
Test X Age X Weight of viewing science program			
	Age	12.633*	4.929***
	Test	35.220*	75.390*
Test X Age X Seen test Program before			
	Age	9.442**	8.513**
	Test	30.973*	114.234*
Test X Age X ever/ never watched program			
	Age	31.095*	11.459*
	Test	60.750*	135.510*

*$p<001$. **$p<.01$. ***$p<.05$.

sufficient to produce learning and (c) none of the demographic or viewing factors we chose to look at altered this knowledge growth in any significant way. (In this analysis, "seen program before" refers to whether or not the children had viewed the series from which the test program had been drawn. "Weight of viewing science programs" indexed whether viewers watch a lot of science programs in general not just the series we were specifically addressing. "Seen test program before" related to whether our subjects had actually seen, on some previous occasion, the specific episode we presented them with, or not.)

Table 5.11 also serves to make clear a common and major finding present throughout this volume: Age is an important factor in considering the effects of television. Under this more powerful analysis, age is the only variable (other than test) to show up as a consistent effect. What is interesting, however, is that age and test do not interact. This means, in contrast to the developmental trends in comprehending and understanding television we discussed in chapter 1, that in this experiment, children of different ages were not behaving differentially in their knowledge growth as a result of exposure to a relevant television program. That is, all age groups benefited about equally from exposure to the program, they merely began at different levels or starting points initially.

COMPREHENSION AND KNOWLEDGE— FURTHER ANALYSES

So far in this chapter we have looked at difference scores in comprehension and recall as a possible function of a number of variables such as age, gender, language ability, and a host of previous viewing factors. However, the data are sufficiently rich and suggestive as to allow more probing questions to be asked, such as what is the relative contribution to the overall scores on comprehension and recall of the several factors we have already looked at, and some we have not as yet discussed. These types of question require a different sort of analysis—regression analysis—and this section recounts what we discovered by employing this tool.

Open-Ended and Multiple-Choice Question Performance

From previous analysis of the data it seemed as if the level of general knowledge that children displayed before they were exposed to their television program was related to their eventual performance on OE and MC comprehension and recall questions. Age also seemed to be important. Although the gender and language ability of the children did not seem to make an overall difference, from the tables presented previously it can be seen that they were an important consideration in certain cases. Likewise, previous viewing behavior had certain local effects while failing to obtain the status of a general factor of importance.

In addition to these factors that have already been discussed, on the assumption that liking for a program should produce attention to it, and that attention allocation to a program should produce learning from it, at least when the program is of an informational type, we asked our subjects to rate the program they had just seen for liking. This score for liking (out of 10) could be a useful predictor of recall and comprehension. Finally, although we have not reported it so far, we did find some suggestive evidence that whether a child read a daily or Sunday newspaper made some difference to their OE and MC question performance on recall and comprehension. This finding should not be too surprising because if general knowledge is related to the ability to pick up information then we have to ask where that general knowledge came from in the first place. The answer would seem to lie in exposure to the written word, school, and the audio or audiovisual media. In this sense, then, reading of newspapers should be related to children's knowledge both by affording them the opportunity to exercise their information extraction skills and by actually providing them with information directly. Additionally, reading is related to intelligence level that could underlie the children's level of general knowledge.

The technique of multiple regression allows us to look at all these factors together and to tease out their independent and combined contribution to the overall performance of interest: in this case, OE and MC question recall and comprehension.

However, when we performed regression analysis on data from our "Body Matters" and "Erasmus Microman" samples, as Table 5.12 indicates, the only variable found to be contributing to open-ended recall was general knowledge. This variable swamped all the other variables of interest.

When general knowledge was excluded from the analysis two other variables emerged as significant predictors of open-ended memory performance (see Table 5.13). In the case of "Body Matters," age was the only significant predictor of recall performance, whereas with "Erasmus Microman" reported frequency of reading a daily paper was the sole significant predictor.

From the results just presented it can be seen that although it is possible to argue that children's ability to learn from television is a product of many factors, in this experiment it is fairly clear that the most important consideration is what children bring to the learning experience in terms of background knowledge. When this is partialed out, the age they have reached and their reading experience appears to carry some importance. What this analysis cannot do is separate out whether age is merely a synonym for acquired knowledge or whether age is something over and above accumulation of information. We have argued before that age may in

TABLE 5.12
Multiple Regression (Enter) for "Body Matters" and "Erasmus Microman": Open-Ended Question Performance

Variables	B	SE B	Beta	Correl.	Partial	Partial Correl.	F	Sig.
"Body Matters"								
Seen program before	-1.481	1.012	-.131	-.274	-.124	-.202	2.139	.149
Read a Sunday paper	.795	.437	.266	-.411	.154	.248	3.296	.075
Gender	-.375	.729	-.045	-.115	-.043	-.072	.265	.608
Score for program out of 10	-.047	.181	-.026	-.223	-.022	-.037	.070	.792
Age	-.440	.273	-.329	.611	-.136	-.221	2.590	.113
Read a daily paper	-.428	.463	-.136	-.442	-.078	-.129	.854	.359
General knowledge	.237	.045	1.107	.760	.446	.596	27.569	.000
(Constant)	8.393	4.097					4.196	.045
Multiple R = .79947; R^2 = .63915; Adj R^2 = .58863; SE = 2.62896; F change = 12.652; Sig = .000								
"Erasmus Microman"								
Seen program before	.016	1.420	.001	.170	.001	.001	.000	.991
Read a Sunday paper	-.305	.465	.089	-.304	.067	.097	.432	.514
Gender	-.209	1.005	-.022	-.051	-.021	-.031	.044	.835
Score for program out of 10	.507	.281	.269	-.283	.185	.259	3.244	.078
Age	.452	.333	.302	.617	.139	.197	1.835	.182
Read a daily paper	-.576	-.499	-.157	-.504	-.118	-.169	1.331	.254
General knowledge	.141	.051	.534	.669	.281	.376	7.446	.009
(Constant)	-.494	6.310					.006	.938
Multiple R = .72279; R^2 = .52243; Adj R^2 = .44814; SE = 3.49472; F change = 7.032; Sig = .000								

TABLE 5.13

Multiple Regression (Enter) for "Body Matters" and "Erasmus Microman" : Open-Ended Question Performance (General Knowledge Excluded)

Variables	B	SE B	Beta	Correl.	Partial	Partial Correl.	F	Sig. F
"Body Matters"								
Seen program before	-2.273102	1.235192	-.202544	-.274386	-.192807	-.249539	3.387	.0715
Read a Sunday paper	-.037900	.503466	-.012692	-.411491	-.007887	-.010541	.006	.9403
Gender	-.933754	.890426	-.113800	-.115521	-.109869	-.145284	1.100	.2993
Score for program out of 10	.150929	.218358	.084196	-.223785	.072417	.096337	.478	.4926
Age	.698336	.206184	.521480	.611708	.354854	.428518	11.471	.0014
Read a daily paper	-.470102	.571685	-.149215	-.442876	-.086154	-.114391	.676	.4147
(Constant)	7.575412	5.049995					2.250	.1398
	Multiple R = .66346; R^2 = .44018; Adjusted R^2 = .37432; SE = 3.24223							
"Erasmus Microman"								
Seen program before	.378807	1.510025	.031807	.170859	.027595	.036962	.063	.8030
Read a Sunday paper	.042885	1.069007	.004535	-.051942	.004413	.005915	.002	.9682
Gender	-.738147	.529455	-.202318	-.504151	-.153357	-.201348	1.944	.1700
Score for program out of 10	.445552	.300031	.236579	-.283152	.163352	.213888	2.205	.1444
Age	.295418	.496790	.086738	-.304166	.065412	.087342	.354	.5550
Read a daily paper	1.038440	.272852	.695408	.617737	.418643	.489363	14.485	.004
(Constant)	-3.182362	6.655649					.229	.6348
	Multiple R = .66589; R^2 = .44341; Adjusted R^2 = .37081; SE = 3.73155							

fact be a short-hand way of talking about evolved information-processing strategies or metacognition (e.g., Desmond, 1985) and this goes beyond mere acquired knowledge to date, and refers to the ability (competence) to approach a learning task in an optimal way with the outcome of maximizing the learning that takes place.

It is also clear from these results that the child's gender makes little difference to learning from informational television. Gender did not contribute to the variability in OE question responding either by itself or in combination with any other variables. This result mirrors the absence of main and interaction effects involving the variable of gender in the ANOVA results presented earlier.

Tables 5.12 and 5.13 indicate that liking of a program did not contribute to performance. Although we made the argument for a link between liking and attentional allocation, and for a link between attention and learning, such a link may be tenuous. For example, we know that incidental memory can be clearly demonstrated (i.e., memory for presented material can be shown to be good despite the fact that subjects are not "set" to memorize that material). In terms of television research, D. R. Anderson and Lorch (1983) always challenged the dominant assumption that attention and comprehension are isomorphic. In memory research in general, the relationship has also been challenged (e.g., J. Anderson, 1990).

When we turned our attention to MC question answering much the same picture emerged as that for OE questioning. The results for both "Body Matters" and "Erasmus Microman" can be seen in Table 5.14. In the case of learning from "Erasmus Microman," performance was significantly predicted only by general knowledge. With "Body Matters," however, a slightly different pattern emerged. Although general knowledge was easily the most powerful predictor of recognition memory, age and reported frequency of reading a Sunday newspaper also emerged as significant predictors.

The point of interest here, however, is that in the analysis of "Body Matters," general knowledge, although still the main contributor of variance did not swamp age and, this time, reading of Sunday papers. In fact, children's reading habits can be seen to contribute more to MC question answering than does age.

However, with "Erasmus Microman" the familiar pattern, established for OE question answering, reasserts itself, with general knowledge serving to repress all other possible contributory factors. Only when we performed supplementary analysis with "Erasmus Microman" in which general knowledge was removed from the equation did age appear as a variable of importance [$F(1, 51) = 31.471$, $p < .001$].

The similarity of findings for both OE and MC questioning is the chief characteristic of this regression analysis. It is clear that the learning (comprehension and recall) that children exhibit from watching informa-

TABLE 5.14

Multiple Regression on "Body Matters" and "Erasmus Microman" (Enter): Multiple-Choice Performance

Variables	B	SE B	Beta	Correl.	Partial Correl.	Partial	F	Sig. F
"Body Matters"								
Seen program before	-.485354	.799558	-.061570	-.189278	-.057957	-.085532	.368	.5466
Read a Sunday paper	1.046596	.345750	.498978	-.231455	.289012	.393543	9.163	.0039
Gender	.399221	.576099	.069268	.011357	.066163	.097534	.480	.4915
Score for program out of 10	-.020646	.142935	-.016397	-.098051	-.013791	-.020423	.021	.8857
Age	-.614009	.216221	-.652769	.434408	-.271129	-.372669	8.064	.0065
Read a daily paper	-.513303	.365989	-.231956	.334960	-.133907	-.194554	1.967	.1669
General knowledge	.207041	.035748	1.373544	.619945	.552974	.633649	33.544	.0000
(Constant)	11.688139	3.234845					13.055	.0007
		Multiple R = .73770; R^2 = .54421; Adjusted R^2 = .48040; SE = 2.07535						
"Erasmus Microman"								
Seen program before	-.296404	.904350	-.042241	.145827	-.036487	-.048800	.107	.7446
Read a Sunday paper	-.016939	.317952	-.007880	-.288445	-.005931	-.007941	.003	.9577
Gender	.785770	.640140	.141028	.135793	.136650	.179996	1.507	.2260
Score for program out of 10	.074010	.179486	.066700	-.260001	.045904	.061353	.170	.6820
Age	-.234895	.212550	-.266985	.415842	-.123027	-.162551	1.221	.2750
Read a daily paper	.065673	.296231	.032728	-.209744	.24680	.033030	.049	.8256
General knowledge	.142853	.033060	.914549	.614819	.481037	.541524	18.672	.0001
(Constant)	11.924789	4.017822					8.809	.0048
		Multiple R = .66507; R^2 = .44232; Adjusted R^2 = .35557; SE = 2.22500						

tional television programs, in this case, science-based, is a function of the knowledge they already have and the cognitive skills and strategies they can deploy when exposed to such programs. These factors far outweigh other demographic factors such as gender, and television viewing histories, although there is just a suggestion that reading of verbal material may be a factor in the uptake of information from the visual medium but this awaits further clarification.

Finally, within the analyses, we turned our attention to the mode of presentation (i.e., the way in which the information was presented within the two different programs). On examining the responses to individual questions (both OE and MC), we identified those that produced relatively high and low percentages of correct answers and then examined the way in which the information relating to the question was presented. These findings are presented in Tables 5.15 through 5.18.

For "Erasmus Microman," children were more likely to answer a question correctly if there was a visual demonstration combined with a related oral explanation plus an element of viewer identification in the way in which the information was presented. Repetition of a concept by means of an alternative experiment, thereby allowing the same information to be presented in more than one way also appeared to enhance learning. "Oral" messages unrelated to visuals only seemed to have an effect if the viewer was able to identify with the message in some way. For example, within the program, Michael Faraday was described as being "bad at Maths" and "having left school at 14"; both of these factors are elements that children of today can still identify with.

The "Body Matters" group was also more likely to obtain correct answers to questions where the information was presented both orally and visually and where concepts were repeated by means of an alternative demonstration.

An element of incongruity also helped to facilitate learning; for example, a pint of beer balanced on a rolled up £5.00 note, a presenter standing on a sheet of glass balanced on a set of rolled up £5.00 notes, dancers trying to carry out a routine encased in heavy suits of armor all helped to reinforce the message that bones are relatively light compared to body weight and that they still support heavy weights because of their hollow construction.

Conversely, children rarely provided correct answers to questions related to information that was presented orally with no visual backup and where there was no allowance for viewer identification. While this kind of program analysis tends to be subjective, it is supported by previous research on "Sesame Street," where it has been demonstrated that repetition, viewer identification, appropriate matches between the visual and oral message, and elements of incongruing can all help to enhance learning.

The positioning of the information within the program also appeared to

TABLE 5.15
"Erasmus Microman" (High Percentage of Correct Answers)

Question	Percent Giving Correct Answer	Position in Program	Mode of Presentation
4(OE) Which direction does a compass needle point to? (Ans: North)	87%	2nd ¼	Oral explanation matched to visual, repeated via more than one experiment.
5(OE) What kind of metal was the wire made of that MF used in his experiments (Ans: Copper)	70%	2nd ¼	Oral explanation matched to visual via more than one experiment.
8(OE) How old was Faraday when he left school? (Ans: 14)	98%	1st ¼	Oral only (but this age would be unusual for today's youngsters).
4(MC) What did Faraday say "Nature" used to create electricity (Ans: Thunder + Lightning)	94%	1st ¼	Graphic visual with oral link made shortly after; further reference at end of program with oral/visual match.
8(MC) Why did the filings on the tray move? (Ans: Because there were magnets underneath it)	98%	2nd ¼	Oral matched to visual via one clear step-by-step experiment; child actors participated via questions and answers.
15(MC) Why didn't Faraday use Maths in his experiments? (Ans: Because he wasn't very good at it)	89%	2nd ¼	Oral only (could encourage children to identify with this).
16(MC) Why did the magnet have to go inside the bandaged tube instead of outside it? (Ans: So that is would connect with the metal tube)	91%	3rd ¼	Oral matched to visual via clear step-by-step experiment; child actors encouraged to participate.

Note. n = 53

produce some kind of effect. Children were more likely to give correct answers to questions relating to information presented in the first half of the program than they were in the second half. This was despite the fact that they were presented with a questionnaire shortly after viewing the program, when it could be assumed that they would be more likely to recall items they had just seen at the end of the program. This finding suggests that learning from television is related to concentration spans in that learning is more likely to occur when children are paying most attention

TABLE 5.16
"Erasmus Microman" (Low Percentage of Correct Answers)

Question	Percentage Giving Correct Answer	Position in Program	Mode of Presentation
2(OE) What do opposite poles of a magnet do? (ANS: Attract/ stick together)	30%	2nd ¼	Oral explanation precedes visual demonstration (not simultaneous) viewer makes link.
6(OE) What do similar poles of a magnet do? (ANS: Repel/ push apart)	40%	2nd ¼	Oral explanation precedes visual demonstration (not simultaneous) viewer makes link.
7(OE) What does a dynamo do? (ANS: Generates electricity)	30%	4th ¼	Word mention followed by visual demonstration of effect but no oral explanation to allow link.
10(OE) When Faraday + Baslow designed electric motors, what kind of liquid did they put into the bowl? (ANS: Mercury)	40%	4th ¼	Word mentioned in voiceover, but no explanation of mercury's properties; visually it looked like water.
2(MC) If the boy had stopped pedaling the bike, what would have happened to Erasmus Microman and the girl if they had stayed in the laboratory? (ANS: They would have died from lack of oxygen)	40%	4th ¼	Practical, visual demonstration of effect of pedaling to create electricity but no oral explanation to allow viewer to make link.
18(MC) Why do you think Faraday used *copper* wire in his experiment (ANS: Because copper is a good conductor of electricity)	40%	2nd ¼	Oral explanation with visual showing *effect* of experiment only; visuals do not act as reinforcement of concept.
19(MC) How far back in time did the children go? (ANS: 100–150 years ago)	45%	4th ¼	Oral message only with no reinforcement; requires viewer "recall."

TABLE 5.17
"Body Matters" (High Percentage Correct Answers)

Question	Percentage Giving Correct Answer	Position in Program	Mode of Presentation
7(OE) What kind of creatures have their bones on the outside of their bodies? (ANS: Lobsters/ Shellfish)	76%	1st ¼	Visual practical demonstration with oral explanation related to visual; incongruous element present.
8(OE) What two colors are your blood cells? (ANS: Red and White)	78%	4th ¼	Practical demonstration using large-scale model; oral explanation matches visual.
1(MC) Why was one of the dancers wearing a suit of armor? (ANS: To show how difficult it is to move if our bones were on the outside of our body)	86%	1st ¼	Incongruous visual demonstration matched to oral explanation; reinforced by further demonstrations using other examples.
7(MC) Why was one of the presenters rolling up a £5.00 note? (ANS: To show how a hollow tube can support a heavy weight)	86%	2nd ¼	Visual practical demonstration linked to a previous demonstration; incongruous element; clear explanation presenting difficult concept simply.
14(MC) Why did one of the presenters have a pint of beer in his hand? (ANS: To show how a narrow tube can support a heavy weight)	90%	2nd ¼	Practical demonstration involving audience participation; oral match with incongruous element.
18(OE) What part of your body are you likely to damage if you carry a heavy shoulder bag? (ANS: Your spine)	86%	3rd ¼	Practical visual with clear oral explanation combined with incongruous element.

TABLE 5.18
"Body Matters" (Low Percentage Correct Answers)

Question	Percentage Giving Correct Answer	Position in Program	Mode of Presentation
1(OE) How many bones are there in the human skeleton? (ANS: Over 200)	9%	1st ¼	Oral only: viewer has to rely on recall.
6(OE) What mineral makes your bones grow hard? (ANS: Calcium)	26%	2nd ¼	Mismatch between oral and visual information; need to recall oral for correct answer.
10(OE) What are the cells in your bone marrow called that divide into blood cells? (ANS: Stem cells)	3%	4th	Lots of oral and visual information together but only presents correct answer.
4(MC) If you have an infection, what does your blood do to fight it? (ANS: It produces more white cells).	41%	4th ¼	Viewer needs to make appropriate link between oral and visual explanation to understand cause-and-effect concept.
6(MC) What causes anemia? (ANS: Too few red blood cells in your body)	41%	4th ¼	Viewer needs to make appropriate link between oral and visual explanation to understand cause-and-effect concept.
10(MC) What happens to your bones if the collagen is removed from your body? (ANS: They become brittle and break easily)	40%	2nd ¼	Complex information; oral explanation poorly linked to visual.
13(OE) What would have happened to the little boy called William if he hadn't had a bone marrow transplant? (ANS: He would have died)	33%	4th ¼	Oral explanation only; viewer required to make appropriate links and hypothesize re-cause and effect.

and their minds are still fresh. However, it must be noted that in both programs, concepts presented toward the end of the program were more likely to be rushed through, with more limited visual demonstrations and oral explanations.

DISCUSSION

This chapter looked at children's perceptions and evaluations of, and learning from, informational television. The stimulus for this investigation was the general finding that although adults professed an interest in science on television, their objective knowledge levels of such material was less than acceptable (e.g., Durant et al., 1989). We were interested to find out whether children appreciated science on television, availed themselves of the opportunity to view such material and whether they could learn from it.

Our results are fairly clear. Children across both the age groups studied appreciated that science on television is desirable and beneficial. They appreciated that such programs could communicate important information that they themselves should be aware of. They also believed that science should be part of prime-time television and that it should not be ghettoized on minority channels or only presented in schools programs. They were, in addition, appreciative of the unique techniques that television can utilize in getting its messages across. However, the data reveal that as children get older they become less likely to watch such programs. This was true of both boys and girls studied here.

When we move from appreciation of science programs to their ability to communicate information and children's ability to learn from them, again our findings are quite clear: Children can learn from such programs, at least in the short term. Our research went beyond mere recall of facts given out to testing the children's comprehension of program material by getting them to problem solve in domains related to but not directly addressed by the programs. In terms of both superficial learning, indexed by recall, and deeper conceptual development, measured by comprehension, the children who took part in the experiment reported in this chapter demonstrated knowledge growth contingent upon watching a science program. An interesting finding, not anticipated from previous literature, was that both age groups learned at approximately the same rate. That is, older children (14–15 years) did not demonstrate an ability to acquire or utilize information in a way qualitatively different from younger children (8–9 years). This was shown by the absence of first- or second-order interactions in our three-way ANOVA results.

This lack of clear age differences in qualitative aspects of learning has also been found by Murray (1988) who looked at learning in 7- and

11-year-olds who were required to memorize an illustrated story (pictures and words). Although previous research (e.g., Pezdek, 1980) indicated a clear age-related difference in the ability to integrate both pictures and words into a central amodal memory representation, Murray did not find this. Rather, his 7- and 11-year-olds showed no qualitative differences in accessibility to an amodal representation, although they did exhibit a difference in quantity of recall. Murray argued that the fact that he presented an integrated context (story) rather than discrete pictures and words, as Pezdek had done, could explain the lack of qualitative differences in memory as a function of age. The fact that television is more similar to illustrated stories than to discrete picture/words may offer a similar explanation for our lack of interaction between age and recall test.

It could also be that both age groups in the study presented in this chapter (all over 7 years of age) were beyond the critical stages of cognitive development that would have predicted qualitative differences between the age groups employed here. However, this seems unlikely because if one accepts a stage approach to development (e.g., Piaget, 1970) then the age groups investigated in this research certainly straddle key critical stages. A third alternative explanation is that, unlike a stage account, an information-processing approach to development (e.g., Siegler, 1983, 1991) would predict a quantitative but not necessarily a qualitative difference in recall, which is precisely what was found here.

An alternative account would argue that television programs of this nature are encoded similarly by all children after the age of 7, and what serves to differentiate children of different ages is how they store and retrieve the material, once encoded (e.g., Brainerd, Reyna, Howe, & Kingma, 1990; Flin, Boon, Knox, & Bull, 1992; Siegler, 1983, 1991). On this account, any age differences are due to the later storage and retrieval phases of memory, not the initial encoding stage. If this is the case, then younger viewers should approximate older viewers when aids are given at the retrieval stage, and be most disparate when such retrieval aids are not provided. The OE and MC manipulations used in this study can be conceptualized as addressing this issue. The data indicate that both age groups were least discrepant when being tested by MC questions, and most differentiated when being tested by OE questions. These findings mirror many studies that show recognition memory to be much less age-sensitive than recall memory (e.g., J. Anderson, 1990).

Whatever the final resolution of this debate proves to be, the key point to grasp is that children of a wide age range can be shown to learn from television information programs at least over the short term.

Another finding that was not entirely anticipated was the near-universal absence of a gender effect—either in appreciation of, or ability to learn from, science programs transmitted at prime viewing times. Although the current debate about biological differences in male and female cognitive abilities rages—creating more heat than light (cf. Benbow, 1988; Kimura, 1992; Moir & Jessell, 1991), there can be little doubt that societal influences do serve to push girls away from science and mathematics (e.g., Archer, 1992) which is only now beginning to be corrected. On this basis, we entertained the possibility that these social stereotypical influences would impact differentially upon our male and female subjects in this aspect of the research program.

However, despite the gender stereotyping of school subjects (Archer, 1992) and the observation that boys and girls vary in the type of information program they choose to watch (see Gunter et al., 1991) there can be little doubt, in the light of findings discussed in this chapter, that girls can learn science as well as boys, across the board.

Somewhat surprisingly, we found that many viewing factors that, a priori, one would have thought would be related to learning from science-type programs proved noncontributory. We explored the extent to which having previously seen the actual program we presented them with, having watched the program series before, and having a history of watching a lot of science programs would influence our children's learning from the currently presented program. Although there were isolated relationships between such previous viewing factors and current learning, the overall conclusion that has to be drawn is that these factors are not good predictors of current learning. This overall conclusion, however, may be program specific as there is some evidence that the more complex the program the more important it was to have had exposure to it before. However, the corollary to this does not hold because we found that, overall, those who watched science-type programs most had the poorest learning performance. We have previously acknowledged the possible argument that this may be accounted for by the fact that those children who watch science-type programs most may also be generally heavier television viewers, and this heavy viewing of television overall may serve to blunt information-processing skills (e.g., Winn, 1977/1985, 1987). This argument, however, lacks theoretical and empirical underpinning. It presupposes that television viewing is a cause rather than an effect of information-processing skills acquisition and deployment. Furthermore, information-processing skills, in this argument, are unjustifiably treated as a unitary whole rather than an assemblage of subsystems such as attentional deployment, strategic processing, knowledge activation, and memory monitoring, all of which could be differentially affected by an extensive diet of television. In addition, the "blunting" notion suggests that in some way, watching a lot of television precipitates poorer processing of its content. Just the opposite may be the case—especially with children. By exposure to television and its conventions, children become better at interpreting its symbol systems and presentational formats and thus become more—not less—adapt at extracting its meaning.

Clearly, the general lack of effect of previous viewing found in the current experiment cannot be answered by one study, but it is an issue that we come back to in the final chapter.

Related to this issue is the role that reading plays in learning from television. Although the amount and quality of reading that the children did—in terms of daily and Sunday newspapers, comics, and special interest magazines—proved nonsignificant overall, there was a suggestion that this was an important consideration in the analyses. For example, in the regression analysis we found that reportedly reading a Sunday paper regularly contributed to MC answering on "Body Matters" and that this was even more important than the age of the viewer. However, this reading factor was not significant for "Erasmus Microman." Once again, this issue is addressed for its robustness in the following chapter.

Although we have made much of the fact that scores on the same item increased from pretest to posttest, it could be that this is an artifact of repeated testing and not a function of viewing a related television show. In the absence of a control group (who would receive two testings on the same item but not view the item-relevant program) this issue cannot be decided definitively. However, several reasons exist for the rejection of this possibility. First, children were not told the correct answers until the whole experiment was finished; second, the children received 30 questions within which were embedded the target questions. They had no way of knowing which were the to-be-repeated questions. Third, the item-relevant program occurred 1 week after the initial testing, thus memory for any correct answers incidentally learned, would have had a good chance of fading before priming by the program could occur. The last reason for doubting that our knowledge-gain scores are artifactual is that the appropriately controlled experiment has been conducted (Clifford, Franks, & Reed, in press). In this study there is clear evidence that postviewing experimental groups out-performed postviewing control groups, although not differing on pretest scores.

Finally, the format of the program also seemed to be important when considering how children process televised information. Learning appeared more likely when the visual and oral message were successfully combined, and concepts were repeated in various ways. Elements of surprise and incongruity, as well as viewer identification also appeared to enhance learning.

Overall, then, this chapter has shown that children appreciate television science programs for what they can offer but as they get older they do not avail themselves of these programs as often as they might. When they choose to expose themselves to such programs they can learn from them — both superficially and at a deeper level.

However, the extent to which they benefit from viewing is very much a function of what they bring to that viewing in terms of preexisting knowledge and cognitive skills, combined with the way in which the information is presented.

6 Multitopic Science Magazine Shows: Evaluation, Comprehension, and Cognitive Impact

Continuing the investigation of children's comprehension of and learning from science programs, a further experiment was run with three different programs, intended for either a child audience or a family audience. The first study had shown that children can learn from science programs covering a single topic or theme. Comprehension of program content and knowledge uptake from these programs, however, do not occur universally or at the same level for all viewers. Some children understand and learn more than others. Furthermore, there seem to be certain key variables that are powerfully connected with learning from such programs.

Children who already have a well-developed and relevant background knowledge are better equipped to learn from science programs. This factor is most important of all. Next to that, age is a significant factor, with older children generally performing better than younger children. The importance of background knowledge in learning from factual television programs has been reliably demonstrated among adult viewers in previous research on information retention from broadcast news (Findahl & Hoijer, 1985; Larsen, 1981). Further, it has been shown that detailed information processing from televised texts comprised of factual content is more effectively carried out when audience members already have a degree of familiarity with the material being presented (see Gunter, 1987a).

A second experiment on learning from science programs was thus run to examine in more detail the factors related to effective information uptake by children. We were interested in whether level of background knowledge was a consistent predictor of learning performance and program comprehension. In addition to audience factors, however, we wished to discover the part program variables play in affecting comprehension and learning of program content. Extensive research with broadcast news has demonstrated that production factors in televised news bulletins, for example, can have profound effects on information retention (Gunter, 1987a), and we have indicated that the same effects may have been at play in chapter 5.

Therefore, this second science program study, investigated children's comprehension and learning from programs that differed in format from those used in the first study. In this case, the three programs sampled were all characterized by a magazine style offering a range of topics instead of concentrating only on one topic.

By including a wider range of age groups and programs it was hoped that interesting features of the previous experiment could be further investigated. To facilitate this, the test programs once again represented both adult-orientated and children-orientated offerings, as in chapter 5.

Although the main objective in this experiment was to better understand the factors that had proved significant under various analyses in the previous study, and to ascertain their reliability, we were also concerned to look again at factors that had previously proved marginal or even noncontributory to the appreciation and learnability of factual television programs.

It was hoped that by running basically the same experimental design, but employing more diverse groups and programs, the robustness and generalizability of the findings of the previous study would be demonstrated.

METHOD

The general methodology followed similar lines to that of chapter 5 in that a prescreening questionnaire testing relevant areas of general and scientific knowledge was followed 7 days later by two posttest questionnaires testing both program-related attitudes, and comprehension and science knowledge gain, these posttests being presented immediately after viewing one of three science programs. The prescreening questionnaire was the same as that used in the previous experiment (to establish comparability of groups across experiments) except that the program-related questions now referred to the programs that were to be viewed in the current experiment. These program-specific questions were repeated in the posttest questionnaire in order to obtain a direct measure of knowledge gain as a result of watching specific, topic-relevant, television programs.

The posttest questionnaires, as before, sought to investigate four basic areas of the children's learning from and appreciation of both the specific program they had been presented with and of science programs in general. To this end, the posttest questionnaires again contained both open-ended and multiple-choice questions (for the recall and comprehension part of the experiment) and statements that the children were asked to agree or disagree with (for the evaluation part of the experiment).

As before, information on demographic, viewing, and reading habits was obtained during the postquestionnaire phase of the experiment.

Three programs were analyzed and provided test material for this experiment:

1. "Owl TV": a new nature program aimed at the 5- to 11-year-old age range.
2. "Know How": a science program aimed at the 8- to 13-year-old age range.
3. "Tomorrow's World": an adult science program that investigates new technology.

All three programs had one main feature in common, that is, they adopted a magazine format and offered a variety of brief items on a range of topics. Details of these topics are outlined in chapter 2. However, as the number of items varied between programs, both "Tomorrow's World" and "Owl TV" were edited down to only four items so as to provide a suitable comparison to "Know How." There remained, however, sufficient variation in content, style, and speed of presentation in the three programs to provide a suitable range of material for testing purposes.

Taking part in both the pretest and the posttest phases of the experiment were 290 children, of whom 52% were boys and 48% were girls; 56% had English as a first language and 44% had English as a second language. In terms of ages, there were four age groups: 8- to 9-year-olds ($n = 74$); 10- to 11-year-olds ($n = 77$); 12- to 13-year-olds ($n = 73$); and 14- to 15-year-olds ($n = 66$).

Subjective Impressions of Science Programs

As in the previous experiments, we began by examining the children's evaluative comments about science programs in general and then about the particular program shown to them. These attitudes were measured using 5-point, agree–disagree scales.

Attitudes to Science Programs in General

As Table 6.1 shows, the majority of children agreed that science programs in general had merit—in the sense that they could help viewers learn new things, they discuss things viewers should know about, and that they made viewers think. In addition, only a minority agreed that they

TABLE 6.1
General Opinions About Science Programs

	"Owl TV" %	"Tomorrow's World" %	"Know How" %	Average %
Programs like these help you learn new things	82	92	92	89
Programs like these tell you about things you might need to know about	79	87	93	86
Programs like these make you think	71	90	83	81
It's easier to learn from TV than from books	54	56	63	58
There should be more programs like these on TV	44	50	64	53
I try to watch a lot of these kind of programs	38	49	53	47
Programs like this should be put on BBC2 or Channel 4	28	41	50	40
I usually switch over or go out of the room when these kind of programs are on	39	31	29	33
I often talk about these kind of programs with family/friends	22	41	26	30
There are too many information programs on TV nowadays	27	29	31	29
Programs like this should only be shown as school programs in school	26	21	32	26
These kind of programs go on too long	16	31	24	24

Note. Percentages are aggregated with children who agreed or agreed strongly with each statement

would either switch off or leave the room if these type of programs were on. Similarly, only a minority agreed that there were too many informational programs on television nowadays, or that they were too long.

However, in line with the results discussed in chapter 5, fewer than half our sample agreed that they watched a lot of science-type programs, and only about one quarter of all children said that they talked about such programs with family and friends.

The number of children who believed that it was easier to learn from television than from books showed a decline compared to the number who agreed with this statement in the previous experiment.

There were few systematic age or gender differences in general attitudes toward science programs on television. Girls were less likely than boys to agree that they tried to watch a lot of these kind of programs (39% vs. 54%), which was a bigger difference than in the previous experiment, or that they often talked about such programs with friends (23% vs. 36%), again, a bigger discrepancy than previously. Girls were also less likely than boys to say that there should be more science programs on television (45% vs. 60%), which is very different from the previous experiment where they did not differ, and were somewhat more likely to agree with the view that there were too many information programs on TV nowadays (35% vs. 24%), whereas they did not differ before. The oldest children (14–15 years) were also far less likely to agree with the latter opinion than were the younger groups (17% vs. 36%), which departs from the result of the previous experiment where they did not differ. In addition, this oldest group was much less likely than the younger group to agree that science programs are too lengthy (6% vs. 29%), which reverses the previous experiment's findings.

Attitudes to Test Programs

After viewing the test program that had been shown to their group, the children received a battery of 20 attitude statements that probed their subjective impressions of it. These attitudes were divided into five categories: general views about such programs, views about presenters, views about presentation style, views about special effects, and the perceived entertainment value of the program.

General Aspect. Looking at each of the three test programs in general terms, there was, among the children who watched them, a pervading view in respect of all three that they could learn a lot about science from these programs. This confirms the positive views held of such programs exhibited in the previous chapter. This opinion was widespread among all age groups and among both boys and girls. It was widely felt that helping people to know about science in this way was a good idea, although this view was not so prevalent within one group of children who had watched "Know How." In contradistinction to findings in the previous chapter the children had less positive and more mixed feelings about whether there should be more programs like each of these on television and on whether any of these programs qualified as the best science program on television. The two made-for-children programs, "Owl TV" and "Know How," were not widely regarded as the best of their genre, whereas the family audience show "Tomorrow's World" was much more extensively endorsed (see Table 6.2)

Tastes showed some variation with the age and gender of the children as they had done in chapter 5. Hence "Owl TV" and "Know How" were more often endorsed as the best science programs on television by the youngest children, ages 8–9 (27% and 42%, respectively) than by older children (10% and 20%, respectively). Boys (67%) were much more likely than girls (32%)

TABLE 6.2
Attitudes to General Aspects of Programs

	"Owl TV" %	"Tomorrow's World" %	"Know How" %	Average %
I feel I could learn a lot about science from this program	70	78	77	75
Helping people to know about science is a good idea	87	84	26	66
There should be more programs like this on TV	38	50	62	50
This is the best science program on TV	15	50	26	30

Note: Percentages are aggregated over children who agreed or agreed strongly with each statement

to want more programs like "Tomorrow's World." In respect to the latter program, boys (63%) were also more likely than girls (36%) to say it was the best science program on television.

Attitudes to Presenters. As in the previous study there was a generally positive view about the clarity with which the presenters of the three programs presented science. Nevertheless, more than half the children recognized that there were occasions when the presenters used words that they had difficulty understanding. This was a much higher proportion than in the previous study and may reflect the nature of the programs used here. There was a degree of skepticism about the expertise of the presenters themselves, with nearly one in two children perceiving presenters as nonexpert in science. There was, in addition, a note of concern among a substantial minority of children that the presenters tried to convey too much information. There was no widespread feeling that the female presenters, who figured prominently, were any better than the male at explaining things (see Table 6.3).

There were differences of opinion concerning presenters, however, between the test program groups, just as we had found previously. Here "Owl TV" received markedly lower ratings compared with the other two programs on most presenter-related attitudes. Although its language was least often likely to cause the children problems and its presenters were not perceived to overload the audience with information, there were some question marks about presenter clarity and expertise.

It was on the question of expert status of presenters that children of different ages exhibited discrepant opinions. For "Owl TV," for instance, preteenage children (8–11 years) were less likely than teenagers (12–15 years) to perceive the show's presenters as nonexperts (32% vs. 62%). An interesting reversal occurred for "Know How" and "Tomorrow's World,"

TABLE 6.3
Attitudes to Presenters

	"Owl TV" %	"Tomorrow's World" %	"Know How" %	Average %
The presenters always explain things clearly	52	74	68	65
Sometimes the presenters use words that are difficult to understand	36	63	66	55
It is obvious that the presenters themselves are not experts	52	45	43	47
The presenters try to tell you too much at once	36	51	44	44
The women presenters are betters at explaining things than the men	27	13	33	24

Percentages are aggregated over children who agreed or agreed strongly with early statements

however, where preteenagers were generally more skeptical than were teenagers (53% vs. 35%) about presenter expertise.

Boys and girls differed in their opinions most strongly where "Tomorrow's World" was concerned. Boys were more often positive than were girls about presenter clarity (81% vs. 54%), and were less likely to criticize this program's presenter for trying to tell the audience too much (37% vs. 50%) or using difficult words (19% vs. 46%).

Attitudes to Presentation Style.   Each test program was characterized by presenting a number of different topics every week. This feature distinguished these science programs from the two single topic shows studied in the previous chapter. One issue addressed in the present study, therefore, was whether the children liked the idea of a program that covered a number of topics. In general it was found that a majority of the children saw certain advantages in this type of presentation, although many also felt that a single topic might be better. This ambiguity reflects the same division of opinion we found in the previous study where we asked the children whether presenting only one topic was desirable. There was no widespread confusion caused by the presentation styles of any of these programs (however see Table 6.4). Generally, the oldest age group clearly appreciated the range of topics covered each week by "Tomorrow's World." There was a suggestion that females would prefer only one topic per week for both "Tomorrow's World" and "Know How," but not for "Owl TV."

Overall, the possibility that covering more than one topic per week could lead to confusion was overwhelmingly rejected, with the most noticeable decline in agreement being for "Tomorrow's World" children as a function of age (62%, 50%, 43%, 23%). Also noticeable in the "Tomorrow's World"

TABLE 6.4
Attitudes to Presentation Style of Programs

	"Owl TV" %	"Tomorrow's World" %	"Know How" %	Average %
Lots of different topics each week means you can learn more things	54	67	72	64
It would be better if it only had one topic per week	52	64	39	52
Sometimes it is too technical	17	38	60	38
Telling you lots of different things each week is confusing	31	39	39	36
It is often too difficult for people of my age to follow	14	27	49	30

Note. Percentages are aggregated over children who agreed or agreed strongly with each statement

group was the large difference in agreement with this statement as a function of gender. Females much more than males felt that more than one topic per program did lead to confusion (60% vs. 28%).

The general absence of agreement with one-topic programs being better was complemented by the general presence of agreement with the statement that presentation of a lot of topics increased the amount learned. Although the majority agreement to this assertion was not great it was consistent.

Difficulties and Age-Related Program.   In the present specific program-related questionnaire we embedded two statements that would give us insight into whether children of different ages found programs either made or not made for their age group differentially accessible and appealing. These two questions involved the assertion that the programs the children had just seen were "too technical" or were "difficult for people my age to follow" (see Table 6.4).

Everyone found "Owl TV" very easy to follow. Some difficulty was experienced with "Know How" but most felt they could follow it fairly well. Most children found some difficulty with "Tomorrow's World" (clearly an adult program). Most also felt that they could not fully follow this program, save for the oldest age group. This inability to follow "Tomorrow's World" was most acutely felt by females (70% vs. 28%) and, interestingly, by children with English as a first language, compared to those with English as a second language (57% vs. 36%).

Special Effects.   Following up on some spontaneous comments made by children in the previous study we took the opportunity in this study to ask the children if they agreed or disagreed with certain assertions concerning the presentation of information on television that capitalized on its unique medium. It was found that using close-ups was greatly appreciated by all but especially the two older groups (91% and 90%, respectively), and by females (87% vs. 70%). Likewise, a sizeable minority, if not a majority, agreed that the use of large-scale models could supplement the presentation of the real thing and more so with the youngest children (68%). This ability to utilize visualization beyond even the power of the human eye was a technique that, when exploited by television, was appreciated by viewers.

Entertainment Value of Test Programs. Most children (57%) agreed with statements that asserted that the program they had viewed could be made better if it were more entertaining, humorous, or amusing. However, the agreement with this statement was somewhat age-dependent. Thus, although the youngest group agreed 63% of the time, the older children agreed with the statement only 44% of the time. These levels of agreement just hint at the possibility that even with informational programs it is felt that the amusing/entertaining/humorous quality of television should be present. This suggests that children are rather unwilling to accept that something that is interesting need not necessarily be amusing/ entertaining/humorous, and none the worse for not having any of these latter three qualities. Conversely, there is nothing that says learning should be dull, boring, and unentertaining.

Viewing Habits and Attitudes to Science Programs

In chapter 5 we looked at previous viewing habits and their relation to information processing and knowledge gain. Although we do the same in this chapter we also took the opportunity to look at these in relation to attitudes toward observed programs.

Thus, the next set of analyses sought any relationships between attitudes toward the three test programs and children's reported television viewing habits. In particular, we were interested in any additional variations associated with prior experience with science programs in general and the test programs more specifically. Attitudes were examined in terms of whether the children had seen the specific program before (seen before), were heavy or light viewers of the program series they had been presented with (test program) or were heavy of light viewers of science programs in general (science viewing).

On the question of whether there should be more programs on television like the ones they had seen, those children who were experienced with such programs were more positively disposed to agree than those children not so experienced. Children who had experienced the viewing of either "Tomorrow's World" or "Know How" were much more in agreement with this sentiment than those children who had viewed "Owl TV." Thus, "Owl TV" was perceived to be the least personally relevant or informative of the three programs, on this reading.

As we saw earlier, the majority of children felt that they could learn from such programs and that helping people to understand science was a desirable objective, and these views were held irrespective of their viewing habits. Where such previous viewing experience did make a difference, it was seen that heavier viewing was associated with more positive attitudes.

Endorsing a program as the best science program on television was linked to regularity of viewing each television series, with heavier viewers in each case holding the more positive opinions. Reported viewing of science programs in general was less consistently connected with attitudes toward each test program (see Table 6.5).

TABLE 6.5
General Attitudes Toward Test Programs and Prior Viewing Experiences

| | | Prior Viewing Experience | | | | | |
| | | Seen Test Edition Before | | Test Program Series Viewing | | Science Program Viewing | |
Statement(s)	Program Viewed	Yes %	No %	Heavy %	Light %	Heavy %	Light %
I feel I could learn a lot about science from this program	"Owl"	69	67	83	65	59	72
	"TW"	70	80	91	67	85	73
	"KH"	77	78	83	76	85	73
Helping people to know about science is a good idea	"Owl"	75	87	83	86	91	82
	"TW"	83	84	86	82	88	81
	"KH"	92	91	96	90	93	90
There should be more programs like this on TV	"Owl"	38	37	50	37	44	33
	"TW"	70	41	71	29	62	41
	"KH"	77	58	81	56	73	57
"Owl"/"TW"/"KH" is the best science program on TV	"Owl"	19	13	42	10	15	13
	"TW"	65	43	74	28	74	34
	"KH"	39	21	35	23	28	24

"Owl" = "Owl TV"
"TW" = "Tomorrow's World"
"KH" = "Know How"

Attitudes to Presenters

Overall, children tended to agreed positively with the statement that presenters always explain things clearly. Having previously viewed the specific program that we presented during the experiment, or being a heavy viewer of that program in general, or of science programs in general, merely served to lead to more agreement.

In accord with this, most children irrespective of previous viewing experiences, chose to disagree with the statement that presenters tend to try and tell too much and very few children indeed agreed with the sentiment that the women presenters were better than the men presenters. Only when "Owl TV" was being considered did this proposition gain any degree of support, and then only from children who had seen the specific program before or were heavy viewers of the program. Interestingly, for "Tomorrow's World," whereas only 9% of those who had seen the specific program before agreed with the proposition, 41% who had not seen it (and thus had no general knowledge of the program to draw on) agreed that the woman was the best presenter. This specific contrast (seen before for "Tomorrow's World") may, however, simply be an artifact of the specific program presented during the experiment and not too much should be read into this finding.

On the question of whether presenters were not really experts, disagreement, although prevalent, was neither uniform nor overwhelming. In fact, for "Owl TV" agreement with the sentiment expressed in the statement best characterizes the data, with strongest agreement coming from those children who had seen the specific program before, who watched the program regularly, and/or were heavy viewers of science programs in general.

When it came to the ease or difficulty of vocabulary it can be seen that for "Tomorrow's World" and "Know How," both fairly complex programs, previous experience of the program type or of science programs in general made a difference. Those children with little or no experience of such programs agreed more with the statement that sometimes the vocabulary was difficult. Interestingly, quite the opposite effect was found for those who watched "Owl TV" These findings are presented in Table 6.6.

When we compare attitudes to programs across chapter 5 (where we did not "factor" these attitudes by previous viewing habits) and the present chapter (where we did break down attitudes by previous viewing profiles) it can be seen that although such finer grained analysis throws into relief certain specific mediating influences of previous viewing, the general conclusion to be drawn is that global evaluations of science programs are not terribly sensitive to particular viewing histories. Rather, appreciation of the potential value of such television fare is present in the majority of children for reasons other than mere television exposure.

TABLE 6.6
Attitudes Toward Presenters and Prior Viewing Experiences

Statement(s)	Program Viewed	Prior Viewing Experience					
		Seen Test Edition Before		Test Program Series Viewing		Science Program Viewing	
		Yes %	No %	Heavy %	Light %	Heavy %	Light %
The presenters in "Owl"/ "TW"/"KH" always explain things clearly	"Owl"	56	47	67	46	56	44
	"TW"	83	61	76	59	77	61
	"KH"	69	76	78	73	80	71
Sometimes the presenters use words that are difficult to understand	"Owl"	56	29	75	28	29	36
	"TW"	52	71	62	71	59	71
	"KH"	50	67	48	67	45	74
It is obvious that the presenters themselves are not real experts	"Owl"	63	51	75	49	68	44
	"TW"	26	49	41	45	35	48
	"KH"	39	47	46	45	50	41
The presenters in "Owl"/ "TW"/"KH" try to tell you too much at once	"Owl"	38	37	42	36	50	30
	"TW"	44	44	31	55	29	53
	"KH"	46	52	36	54	39	58
The women presenters in "Owl"/"TW"/"KH" are better at explaining things than men	"Owl"	38	24	42	24	18	31
	"TW"	9	41	29	37	24	39
	"KH"	8	13	17	10	18	8

Underlying global evaluation of specific programs there are, possibly, specific aspects of those programs that particularly attract or repel children. We sought these out, looking at them in terms of viewing factors, and they are detailed in Table 6.7.

On the assertion that covering more than one topic per week was confusing, more agreement with this view was found among those children who had light involvement with science programs. Thus, those who were presented with "Tomorrow's World" and "Know How," but who had little or no experience of the specific program, the series from which it came or science programs in general, were much more likely to agree with the statement than those who were heavier viewers. This suggests that exposure

TABLE 6.7
Attitudes Toward Presentation Style and Prior Viewing Experience

		Prior Viewing Experience					
		Seen Test Edition Before		Test Program Series Viewing		Science Program Viewing	
	Program	Yes	No	Heavy	Light	Heavy	Light
Statement(s)	Viewed	%	%	%	%	%	%
Lots of different topics each week means you can learn more things	"Owl"	50	57	59	55	62	53
	"TW"	83	61	79	57	79	59
	"KH"	65	68	83	63	75	63
"Owl"/TW/KH would be better if it only had one topic per week	"Owl"	50	53	67	51	56	51
	"TW"	30	47	31	53	24	54
	"KH"	65	63	48	68	48	74
Telling you lots of different things each week is confusing	"Owl"	31	30	33	30	27	33
	"TW"	26	51	33	55	38	49
	"KH"	42	36	22	42	25	45

to a complex program like "Tomorrow's World" can develop mental sets that make the uptake of disparate material easier.

Light viewing of the series from which the test program came and light viewing of science programs in general was linked to wider support for one-topic only programs among two groups out of three (viewers of "Know How" and "Tomorrow's World"). The same respondents also reported being confused by programs containing lots of different topics each week. Regular viewers of these two series were much less likely to complain about their multitopic magazine format.

PROGRAM COMPREHENSION

Having established the evaluations, perceptions, and opinions that the children held of the three science program they had viewed, we were then interested in establishing whether they had in fact learned from them. As before, we tested both memory and comprehension of program content, by using prompted written recall of details presented in the programs and testing ability to problem solve or go beyond the information presented by asking children to apply the information communicated. Both open-ended and multiple-choice question formats were utilized. As before, we were concerned to establish a base-line knowledge level before exposure to the programs, and to utilize questions that were known to be related to issues to be covered directly in the television programs. By this manipulation we could assess knowledge growth in addition to simple recall and comprehension of facts presented.

Overall Level of Comprehension and Recall

Collapsing across age groups, gender, language ability, and programs, the children scored a creditable 60.2% correct recall overall. This was slightly lower than in the previous experiment but allowing for different program material and different age groups within the two experiments the present score was directly comparable to the 64.5% found previously. Comprehension scores were also slightly lower than previously, currently 55% compared to 63%. Once again, however, this variability is within the bounds of comparability given the different manipulations between the two experiments.

In terms of the children's general knowledge before the experiment started, the overall performance level was 46%. Given the graded nature of this test and the fact that we expected, from pilot work, that the children should score between 20% and 80% depending on their age, this level of performance was predictable.

As would be expected from the previous study, however, there were wide variations in all aspects of performance as a function of a number of demographic and background experience factors. It is to these more focused breakdowns that we now turn.

Demographic Factors and Learning
From Television

We were interested to find out whether the results observed previously in learning from science programs would be repeated with different samples and programs.

Age.   In the last chapter we found that age was a major contributor of variance in terms of both program comprehension and recall. Table 6.8 presents percentage recall, comprehension, and general knowledge as a function of this factor for each program group in the current experiment.

As can be seen from this table, the general knowledge that the children brought with them was almost a linear function of age. When we look at

TABLE 6.8
Mean Percentage General Knowledge, Recall, and Comprehension

| | | | Posttest | | | | | |
| | | | Recall | | | Comprehension | | |
Program Viewed	Age	Pretest General Knowledge %	Mean Total %	OE %	MC %	Mean Total %	OE %	MC %
"Owl TV"	8–9	29	59	42	75	70	58	81
	10–11	44	63	50	74	70	67	73
	12–13	58	67	58	75	66	59	73
	14–15	68	72	56	88	82	76	88
"Tomorrow's World"	8–9	24	35	22	48	25	18	32
	10–11	40	41	29	52	42	32	52
	12–13	55	52	40	63	46	33	58
	14–15	71	64	56	72	61	53	68
"Know How"	8–9	26	57	48	66	37	20	54
	10–11	38	67	58	76	43	22	64
	12–13	39	65	61	68	49	32	65
	14–15	58	80	75	84	70	59	80

posttest recall and comprehension the age effect was less obvious but still present, for example, on comparing the youngest and the oldest groups. The age effect was least clearly present under multiple-choice type questioning, whether in the recall or comprehension domains, thus replicating the findings in chapter 5. The family science program ("Tomorrow's World") was the one program that still showed most clearly this age-related difference even under MC questioning.

On posttest total recall, age was a significant factor for both "Tomorrow's World" [$F (3,89) = 17.51, p < .001$] and for "Know How" [$F (3,98) = 4.64, p < .004$]. However for "Owl TV" age was not a significant factor, despite the numerical differences present. Total comprehension scores were also related to age, with this being a statistically significant factor in respect of all three programmes ("Owl TV," $p < .001$; "Tomorrow's World," $p < .001$; "Know How," $p < .001$).

Overall then, as in the previous study, age can be seen to be an important factor in information acquisition and utilization. As would be anticipated, age was also a significant contributor to General Knowledge level ($p < .001$) for all three program groups.

Gender. In line with the previous experiment, the differences between males and females were marginal at best except for "Tomorrow's World," which tends to be a technological, hard science-based program. Thus, "Owl TV" and "Know How" were equally well recalled and comprehended by both boys and girls. With "Tomorrow's World," however, boys outper-formed girls on comprehension [$F(1,91) = 10.41, p < .001$], and on recall [$F(1,91) = 8.65, p < .004$].

In terms of general knowledge, boys were better than girls only in the "Owl TV" group ($p < .02$). This result is interesting in that it is one of the few cases where general knowledge does not predict information pick-up because although boys surpassed girls on "Tomorrow's World" posttests of recall and comprehension they did not exhibit statistically different pretest general knowledge levels.

Language Ability.   Previous research (e.g., Gunter, 1988) revealed that adults found that the language used in science programs frequently led to confusion. It was relevant, therefore, to ask if ESL children would be disadvantaged in learning from science programs. The results here showed very few significant differences in program recall or understanding as a function of language ability, which mirrors the findings of the preceding chapter. Where statistical differences were observed they favored children without English as a first language. In general, posttest comprehension performance was not related to whether or not children had English as a first language, whereas it was in the previous experiment, with children having English as a first language doing better. In recall, only "Tomorrow's World" performance was related to this factor [$F(1,91) = 5.46, p < .02$], with ESL children doing better. This last result is opposite to that found in chapter 5. Comparing across experiments, however, it seems to be complexity of program rather than linguistic facility that is driving these apparent linguistic effects: Where programs were less complex in the previous or the present experiment children with differing linguistic backgrounds were indistinguishable in terms of information processing.

Viewing Habits and Recall and Comprehension

People watch television primarily to relax and to be entertained. This is true even with factual programs. Nevertheless, audiences do turn to television for information, although they often mislead themselves in terms of their beliefs concerning how much they actually learn from it. Effective recall from informational programs may require a special mental set not usually employed in front of the small screen (e.g., Saloman, 1979). Repetitions may help, however, and the more viewers view certain programs the more they may get out of them. Thus, repetitions or regular viewing of informational programs could produce increased knowledge levels, at least in principle. To the extent that an individual already has a good knowledge base, the amount gained from any one exposure to an informational program is likely to be enhanced (Gunter, 1987a).

It was arguments such as these—however tenuously held—that caused us to look at children's performance on recall and comprehension as a function of a number of related background viewing patterns, both in the previous study and again in the present one. In particular, we were interested to find out if the children had ever seen the test program before on television, if they were regular viewers of the series from which it was taken, and if they were regular viewers of science programs.

Seen Particular Program Before.   Comprehension results were negatively related to having seen the program previously for "Owl TV" [$F(1,93)$ = 16.12, $p < .001$), whereas for recall, having seen the program before was, once again, related to worse performance for "Owl TV" [$F(1,93)$ = 8.45, $p < .005$], but to better performance for "Tomorrow's World" [$F(1,91)$ = 5.10, $p < .03$].

These results indicated that there was little benefit for current performance of having seen a program before (within the last year). Further, it seems that whether the children benefited or not from having viewed previously depended on the particular program under consideration. This finding replicates that found in the previous chapter where only the more difficult of two single-topic science programs exhibited a positive influence of having been viewed before, whereas the easier program actually showed a negative influence of having been viewed before. This replication rules out the sampling artifact explanation we entertained for this finding in chapter 5.

Frequency of Viewing the TV Series.   Although it does not seem to be the case, generally, that watching specific programs confers advantages in information pick-up, nonetheless it could be that watching a number of programs from the same series could develop familiarity with presentational styles and format that could confer advantages in learning from them. We looked at this possibility by dividing each program viewing group into four: "watch it nearly every time," "watch it most of the time," "watch it occasionally," and "never watch it," and looking at their recall and comprehension scores as a function of their classification.

Effects of this variable were essentially nonexistent with only comprehension performance for "Owl TV" being related to frequency of viewing the series [$F(3,91)$ = 4.52, $p < .005$]. Once again, the effect of frequency of viewing in this case was negative. This general null effect of previous viewing of the program series and the specific negative effect of such viewing of "simple" science programs was also found in chapter 5.

Viewing Science Programs in General.   As a last attempt to investigate previous viewing behavior as an influence on current information pick-up, we looked at recall and comprehension as a function of whether the children were heavy or light viewers of science programs in general. In chapter 5 we had found that weight of viewing of science programs had no overall effect on either recall or comprehension of the more complex of two programs and a weakly significant and negative effect on OE recall and comprehension of the simpler program we presented. In the present experiment this effect was even weaker: Previous heavy or light viewing of science programs in general had no effect whatever on recall or comprehension of any of the three programs we presented.

Prior Reading Habits and Television Learning

We obtained some suggestive evidence in the previous experiment from our analysis of variance and regression analyses that the children's reported reading habits were associated with good recall and comprehension of viewed programs. In the current experiment this association emerged again and is presented in Table 6.9.

Children who reportedly read a daily newspaper scored better on both recall and comprehension than did children who claimed never to read a paper. Was this relationship a direct one or was it mediated by general knowledge that, as can be seen from the table, was directly correlated with newsprint reading; or are both these factors merely identifying those children who are more intellectually able in the first place and therefore more proficient in processing information generally?

Exploring this relationship further, newspaper reading was broken down into types of paper read, distinguishing "down-market tabloid" reading from "middle-of-the-road tabloid" reading. If it was newspaper reading per se that was contributing to information pick-up from television programs then it should not matter what the children read. If, however, knowledge

TABLE 6.9
Mean Percentage General Knowledge, Recall, and Comprehension as a
Function of Reading

			Posttest					
		Posttest General Knowledge %	Recall			Comprehension		
Program Viewed	Frequency of Reading		Total %	OE %	MC %	Total %	OE %	MC %
"Owl TV"	Nearly every day	59	67	59	75	70	64	76
	Never	36	59	41	76	66	56	75
"Tomorrow's World"	Nearly every day	54	55	44	65	47	39	55
	Never	27	35	24	45	35	26	44
'Know How"	Nearly every day	45	70	62	78	52	36	64
	Never	22	51	44	58	33	14	52

Note: Scores show percentages of correct responses

level was the important factor then middle-of-the-road tabloids would, because of their depth of news coverage, be expected to provide more of this and we should find information pick-up to be greater with children who claimed to read such papers than among those who claimed to read the down-market variety. A glance at Table 6.10 indicates that the latter prediction is upheld.

Although the present study supports the somewhat isolated and localized finding of reading's impact on information pick-up from science programs in the previous study, the current data also serves to elucidate those findings. In the present study, the data suggest that reading behavior is something over and above mere background general knowledge. A glance at "Owl TV" in Table 6.10 shows that although general knowledge is associated with higher comprehension scoring, it is not for recall. Here then the children's reading habits may truly be having an effect. For the other two programs the variables of general knowledge and nature of material read are confounded in ways that do not allow unequivocal conclusion to be drawn concerning what is causing better recall and comprehension performance: reading or general knowledge level.

TABLE 6.10
Mean Percentage General Knowledge, Recall, and Comprehension as a
Function of Type of Paper Read

Program Viewed	Nature of Paper Read	Pretest General Knowledge %	Posttest					
			Recall			Comprehension		
			Total %	OE %	MC %	Total %	OE %	MC %
"Owl TV"	Down-market tabloid	52	64	55	72	72	65	78
	Middle-of-road tabloid	48	69	56	82	68	61	74
"Tomorrow's World"	Down-market tabloid	45	47	35	59	39	29	49
	Middle-of-road tabloid	58	56	43	68	53	48	58
"Know How"	Down-market tabloid	40	69	63	75	51	36	66
	Middle-of-road tabloid	57	78	71	85	64	47	80

Note: Scores show percentages of correct responses

KNOWLEDGE GROWTH

So far in this chapter we have concentrated on children's memory and comprehension of facts and principles contained in a science program they had just viewed. We also wanted to establish unambiguously that any learning and comprehension that occurred stemmed from the viewed material and not from some pre-experimental source. To this end we deliberately placed identical questions in both the pretest and posttest phases that were directly related to the contents of the presented television program. To the extent that children could not answer these specific questions in the pretest, but could do so in the posttest we would have evidence of learning from the test programs.

As before, knowledge growth was examined in relation to various demographic, viewing, and reading factors. A number of two-way ANOVAs were computed to measure the significance of knowledge growth contingent upon viewing different test programs among boys and girls in different age bands, and with differing English language abilities and viewing and reading habits.

Age Differences. Table 6.11 presents the mean recall scores (out of 6) for identical pre- and posttest items directly addressed by the different programs as a function of the age of the children.

For all three programs, the patterns of results were similar. Age and test were both significant effects ($ps < .001$), whereas in none of the cases was the age by test interaction significant (all $Fs < 1$). This indicates that for all programs, knowledge growth occurred between pre- and posttest, and that the amount of growth did not fluctuate significantly as a function of

TABLE 6.11
Mean Pre- and Posttest Scores as a Function of Age and Program Viewed

Program Viewed	Age	Pretest	Posttest	
				Average
"Owl TV"	8–9	1.32	3.32	2.32
	10–11	2.20	3.84	3.02
	12–13	2.93	4.39	3.66
	14–15	3.95	5.60	4.78
	Average	2.60	4.29	
"Tomorrow's World"	8–9	.00	2.73	1.37
	10–11	.29	2.92	1.61
	12–13	.91	3.52	2.22
	14–15	2.50	5.09	3.80
	Average	0.93	3.57	
"Know How"	8–9	1.00	2.50	1.75
	10–11	1.71	3.32	2.52
	12–13	1.71	3.92	3.23
	14–15	3.38	5.29	4.34
	Average	1.95	3.76	

age: The relative standing of the different age groups was maintained at posttest, merely being at a higher level.

These data powerfully confirm the similar findings we obtained in chapter 5. In the light of this replication, very strong evidence exists that children of various ages can learn scientific facts and principles from prime-time television science programs however they are presented—be it single topic or magazinelike format.

Gender Differences.   Table 6.12 reveals that although for "Know How," gender did not seem to make a difference to scoring, it did for the other two programs, with boys scoring better than girls. This is a finding at variance with the overall results of the previous experiment, although even there we found certain localized gender effects. Here, however, gender effects seem much more powerful.

Test (knowledge growth) was significant in all three program groups (all ps $< .001$). Gender was found to be significant in "Owl TV" [$F(1,93) = 10.22, p < .002$] and "Tomorrow's World" [$F(1,91) = 5.70, p < .02$] but not for "Know How" [$F(1,100) = 1.63, p < .05$].

A significant gender X test interaction appeared in the "Owl TV" sample ($p < .02$) and "Tomorrow's World" ($p < .01$). As can be seen from Table 6.12, these interactions are best explained by the fact that females improved much more than did males from pretest to posttest.

TABLE 6.12
Mean Pre- and Posttest Scoring for Males and Females as a Function of Programs Viewed

Program Viewed	Gender	Pretest	Posttest	Average
"Owl TV"	Male	3.16	4.51	3.84
	Female	1.78	3.90	2.84
	Average	2.47	4.21	
"Tomorrow's World"	Male	1.16	3.88	2.52
	Female	0.54	3.20	1.87
	Average	0.85	3.54	
"Know How"	Male	2.37	3.84	3.11
	Female	1.80	3.56	2.68
	Average	2.09	3.70	

Language Fluency Difference.   Table 6.13 reveals that, like gender fluency in English was sporadically related to differences in knowledge growth across certain of the test programs but not for others.

TABLE 6.13
Mean Scores for Pre- and Posttest as a function of Fluency in English and
Program Viewed

Program Viewed	Language Facility	Pretest	Posttest	
				Average
"Owl TV"	Second language	3.17	4.86	4.02
	First language	2.32	3.98	3.15
	Average	2.75	4.42	
"Tomorrow's World"	Second language	1.50	4.14	2.82
	First language	0.54	3.25	1.90
	Average	1.02	3.70	
"Know How"	Second language	2.35	3.82	3.09
	First language	1.79	3.57	2.68
	Average	2.07	3.70	

Test as a factor was significant in every program case (all $ps < .001$). Fluency in English was significant for "Owl TV" [$F(1,93) = 6.44$, $p < .01$] and "Tomorrow's World" [$F(1, 91) = 10.22$, $p < .002$], but not for "Know How." In both "Owl TV" and "Tomorrow's World" ESL children scored better. There were no significant fluency in English test interactions.

In contradistinction to the previous study then, the present set of findings suggest that linguistic fluency may be a consideration when predicting learning from science programs on television. However, the fact that ESL children did better than children with English as a first language may suggest that motivational dispositions rather than language facility are the real explanation for these findings. Our evaluation data give some support to this possibility.

Viewing Experience

Having already seen the specific program used in the experiment was not related, to a significant extent, to knowledge gain.

There was, however, some indication of a possible effect of regularly watching the television series from which the test program came in the case of "Tomorrow's World" and "Know How," but such prior viewing was significant only in the case of "Know How" [$F(1,100) = 5.00$, $p < 0.03$].

Reported high levels of science program viewing in general, was not a great predictor of test performance. Only in the case of "Owl TV" did a result of any significance occur, where heavy reported viewing of science-type programs was related to higher scoring on science general knowledge questions [$F(1,93) = 6.98$, $p < 0.01$]. These somewhat fragile and particular associations are reminiscent of those found in the previous chapter.

From these results, certain clear patterns are discernible. Every analysis indicates that exposure to a relevant television program can produce clearly identified short-term knowledge growth, and these learning effects are both large and statistically reliable. The other clear finding is the absence of any ubiquitous interactions between this learning and the numerous demographic and viewing background factors we chose to look at. Thus, whether the children had seen the program before or not, watched the series or not, or were heavy or light viewers of science programs in general did not influence whether they learned or not from the program they were exposed to. Whatever their status in terms of these viewing habits they all learned from the program at about the same level.

We did in fact go on to perform higher order ANOVAs but these results merely served to consolidate the findings of the two-way analyses. This was shown by the near-complete absence of first-order and second-order interactions that would have served to indicate that the learning from the program they viewed was in fact modifiable by certain of the demographic and viewing factors operating together. The clear absence of any indication of this in the more complex analyses merely serves to underscore the chief finding of this section—children of varying status, background, and experience can learn from programs they are exposed to.

FURTHER ANALYSIS OF RECALL AND COMPREHENSION

So far in this chapter we have discussed children's subjective evaluations of science programs separately from their learning from and comprehension of such programs. To what extent, however, are these two set of responses interrelated? Do the attitudes the children have toward programs have any influence on their learning from these programs? This section begins to tease out these possible relationships.

Attitudes and Their Relation to Learning

As in the previous experiment we were concerned to ascertain whether our children's responses to attitudinal statements about science programs in general had some internal coherence or structure. We assessed this possibility by means of factor analysis. We found that the children's attitudinal responses clustered into groupings that we labeled as Factor 1: program perception/attraction, Factor 2: program utility; and Factor 3: home-school comparison. These factors replicated those found in the previous experiment. In the current experiment we wished to go a little further and find out if these additional factors had predictive validity. That is, could we predict total, open-ended and multiple-choice responding in recall and comprehension on the bases of these factors? To answer this question we employed multiple regression techniques. However, as we see here, the answers we got were rather equivocal.

In addition to program-related attitudes, we were also interested to find out if our children's learning from television science programs was influenced by having studied "scientific" topics at school. We have already confirmed that preexisting knowledge (as assessed by a general knowledge questionnaire) was related to performance on postviewing questionnaires. To what extent would having studied science "topics" in school predict knowledge gain from watching science programs on television? In this context the children were asked if they had ever studied any of the following in school: (a) the human body, (b) insects, (c) electricity, (d) government or trade unions, (e) dinosaurs, (f) Third World countries, (g) mammals, (h) pollution, (i) television, and (j) car manufacture.

In addition to looking at each of these areas of study individually as predictors of learning we also factor analyzed the children's responses to highlight any structural groupings in their reported subjects of study. Four such groupings appeared. Factor 1: Study areas involving the human body, mammals, and insects, which we labeled *biology*; Factor 2: study areas involving Third World countries, pollution, and government and trade unions, which we labeled *politics and science*; Factor 3: study areas including electricity, television, and car manufacture, which we labeled *electronics*; and Factor 4: the study area involving dinosaurs.

These study factors were then looked at for their ability to predict performance in OE and MC responding of the children following their viewing of a science program. Once again, multiple regression was the preferred mode of analysis to give us answers to these questions.

Open-Ended Question Answering

Although none of the programme attitude factors predicted performance for "Know How," Factor 3 (home–school comparison) predicted scoring for "Owl TV" [$F(3,91) = 4.903$, $p < .03$] and Factor 1 (program perception) and Factor 2 (program utility) predicted "Tomorrow's World" scoring [$F(3,89) = 20.874$, $p < .001$ and $F(3,89) = 3.992$, $p < .05$, respectively].

When we looked at study factors, again the results were mixed: for "Owl TV" none of the four factors predicted OE performance. For "Know How," Factor 4 (dinosaurs) predicted scoring [$F(4,97) = 9.901$, $p < .002$], whereas for "Tomorrow's World" Factor 2 (politics and science) predicted performance [$F(4,88) = 18.884$, $p < .001$).

Multiple-Choice Question Answering

None of the program attitude factors predicted performance for "Owl TV" but Factor 1 (program perception) predicted performance of "Tomorrow's World" $[F(3,89) = 15.896, p < .001]$, and, in conjunction with Factor 2 (program utility), both predicted multiple-choice answering for "Know How" $[F(3,98) = 4.567, p < .03$ and $F(3,98) = 6.050, p < .01$, respectively].

Study factors seemed to be slightly more nascent with Factor 4 (dinosaurs) predicting scoring for "Know How" $[F(4,97) = 10.706, p < .001]$, and in conjunction with Factor 3 (electronics), "Owl TV" $[F(4,90) = 4.725, p < .03$ and $F(4,90) = 5.203, p < .02$, respectively]. Study Factor 2 (politics and science) predicted performance only for "Tomorrow's World" $[F(4,88) = 28.948, p < .001]$.

Particular Program Attitudes and Studied Areas

Having established that the factor structures underlying both program attitudes and school-based studies had some power to predict how the children would perform in open-ended and multiple-choice environments following the viewing of a science program, we then asked if particular program attitudes or subjects studied could predict outcomes of learning from television. To effect this analysis we treated each program attitude statement or subject studied at school as a distinct variable and looked to see if it uniquely contributed to science knowledge performance.

Open-Ended Responding

When we employed all 12 program attitude statements as independent variables and observed their influence on the dependent variable of open-ended answers to our science questions, the influence was found to be marginal at best. Thus, for "Know How" only responses involving either "switching off the television and/or leaving the room" predicted performance $[F(12,89) = 5.915, p < .01]$ and the relationship was positive. That is, to the extent that children said that they did not switch off/leave, then learning was demonstrated. For "Owl TV" the only program attitude that predicted performance was whether children thought it was "easier to learn from television than from books" $[F(12,82) = 4.763, p < .05]$. For "Tomorrow's World," once again, only one program attitude appeared as a significant contributor to the variance in scoring. Whether children felt that "such programs should be put on BBC2/Channel 4" or not predicted performance $[F(12,80) = 6.016, p < .01]$.

In terms of the subject matter studied at school we found that, for "Owl

TV," only having studied "television" predicted, negatively, OE scoring [$F(10,84) = 5.959$, $p < .01$], whereas for "Tomorrow's World" two studied areas seemed important, "pollution" [$F(10,82) = 8.485$, $p < .01$] and "car manufacture" [$F(10,82) = 4.978$, $p < .025$]. With "Know How," recall and comprehension performance was influenced by having studied "electronics" [$F(10,91) = 16.290$, $p < .001$], "insects" [$F(10,91) = 4.660$, $p < .03$), and "the human body" [$F(10,91) = 4.036$, $p < .05$].

Multiple-Choice Responding

For "Tomorrow's World" no attitude whatever predicted science knowledge measured by MC questions. For "Owl TV" only attitudes concerned with ease of learning from television predicted this performance [$F(12,82) = 4.763$, $p < .03$] and for "Know How" only switching off/leaving the room was predictive, in a positive way, of MC question answering [$F(12,89) = 8.907$, $p < .005$].

Subjects reportedly studied by children at school proved to be only a little more powerful as predictors of performance. Thus, although only one subject area predicted performance for "Tomorrow's World," "pollution" [$F = (10,82)$ 5.240, $p < .025$], for both "Owl TV" and "Know How," two of the 10 study areas were significant predictors: for "Owl TV" having studied "electronics" [$F(10,84) = 5.241$, $p < .025$] and "television" [$F(10,84) = 3.891$, $p < .05$] (negative effect) were influential, whereas for "Know How," having studied "electronics" [$F(10,91) = 15.762$, $p < .001$] and "the human body" [$F(10,91) = 6.003$, $p < .05$] were predictive of MC question answering.

Further Predictors of Performance

Having looked closely at two specific aspects of our database, we were concerned now to cast the net more widely and probe, in a principled way, what other variables, which we had been interested in, were related to memory and comprehension of test program content.

Demographics, Viewing, Reading, and General Knowledge

We selected a group of variables that either proved to be powerfully associated with different scoring profiles in our ANOVA analysis (e.g., general knowledge, age); that emerged in earlier analyses to be a variable of some interest (e.g., daily and Sunday paper reading); or that seemed intuitively to be possibly related to learning from a program just viewed, but that, so far, had proved of little importance (e.g., seen the program before, level of program enjoyment). In addition to these variables, the gender of the children was also included. This produced a list of 10 potential predictors of memory and comprehension. These variables were submitted to multiple regression analysis with OE and MC scores as the dependent variables of interest.

The regression analyses for OE scoring are given in Table 6.14 and for MC answering in Table 6.15, in both cases broken down by program viewed.

As can be seen from Table 6.14, general knowledge was the chief predictor in OE recall for all three programs, and indeed the only variable of importance for both "Know How" and "Tomorrow's World." For "Owl TV," however, having seen the program before and giving it a high enjoyment score also had a positive effect on performance.

In terms of MC answering, Table 6.15 indicates that general knowledge once again is the only variable to be a significant influence in all three programming groups. For "Know How" the regression equation was also influenced, negatively, by the enjoyment score given (out of 10). For "Owl TV" it can be seen that MC scoring was influenced by the general knowledge the children brought to the testing, whether they had seen the program edition before and the enjoyment score given. This time, however, the enjoyment score influence was positive. Reading a Sunday paper and age were negatively associated with MC performance for this program group.

TABLE 6.14
Multiple Regression (Enter) for "Tomorrow's World," "Owl TV," and "Know How" Open-Ended Question Performance

Variables	"Tomorrow's World"			"Owl TV"			"Know How"		
	Beta	F	Sig.	Beta	F	Sig.	Beta	F	Sig.
Seen program before	.009	0.13	.909	.270	10.420	.002	.099	1.825	.179
Read a Sunday paper	−.021	.060	.808	−.013	.012	.914	.366	.210	.655
Gender	−.276	12.010	.001	−.054	.384	.537	.031	.183	.669
Score for program out of 10	−.039	.192	.662	.249	7.788	.007	−.088	1.393	.241
Age	.130	1.251	.267	−.029	.068	.795	.142	2.723	.102
Read a daily paper	.011	.019	.892	−.001	.000	.992	.036	.198	.657
General knowledge	.567	20.897	.000	.598	27.298	.000	.676	60.670	.000
	$R^2 = .562$			$R^2 = .425$			$R^2 = .546$		
	Adj $R^2 = .527$			Adj $R^2 = .379$			Adj $R^2 = .512$		

TABLE 6.15
Multiple Regression for "Tomorrow's World," "Owl TV," and "Know How"
(Enter): Multiple-Choice Performance

Variables	"Tomorrow's World"			"Owl TV"			"Know How"		
	Beta	F	Sig.	Beta	F	Sig.	Beta	F	Sig.
Seen program before	.016	.043	.836	.237	7.376	.008	0.015	.046	.831
Read a Sunday paper	.082	.869	.354	− .325	6.976	.009	.098	1.439	.233
Gender	− .043	.281	.597	− .053	.340	.561	− .053	.340	.561
Score for program out of 10	.059	.435	.511	.207	4.922	.029	− .298	16.078	.000
Age	.166	1.991	.162	− .258	5.070	.0269	− .030	.123	.727
Read a daily paper	− .046	.280	.598	.330	7.605	.007	− .086	1.148	.286
General knowledge	.589	21.912	.000	.572	22.955	.000	.640	55.282	.000
	R^2 = .550			R^2 = .375			R^2 = .552		
	Adj R^2 = .512			Adj ^{2} = .325			Adj ^{2} = .519		

Program Format and Learning

This study focused on programs that employed a magazine format rather than presenting only one topic and devoting the whole program to it, as was the case in the experiment reported in chapter 5. Magazine format programs present a series of topics, one after the other, on the assumption that this creates variety and serves to maintain children's interest. There are, however, a number of potential risks in presenting a series of topics rather than just one. For example, Gunter et al. (1980) showed that, in a series of loosely related news items, late items were more poorly recalled than earlier ones. The explanation offered for this finding was that earlier items somehow "interfered" with the uptake of later items.

Another possibility is that although both early and later items in a topic series may be well recalled, because they are at the start and end of the program respectively, and thus have perceptual saliency, the middle items may be poorly recalled because they do not have such saliency (the so-called serial position effect). This effect, although its explanation is somewhat obscure, is readily demonstrable in a wide variety of verbal contexts. If either of these two effects were found to be operating in the present programs, then it would suggest that a magazine format might invite information losses disproportionately more often from certain sections of a program, despite the possible creation of variety.

Table 6.16 reveals some primacy and recency effects in the case of two

TABLE 6.16
Recall of the Four Items Contained Within Each Program as a Function of Age

Age	"Owl TV"				"Tomorrow's World"				"Know How"			
	First Item	Second Item	Third Item	Fourth Item	First Item	Second Item	Third Item	Fourth Item	First Item	Second Item	Third Item	Fourth Item
8–9	7.91	5.18	6.05	5.82	4.92	1.33	1.38	3.19	4.35	3.38	4.31	5.73
10–11	7.24	6.24	6.52	5.68	5.83	2.92	2.33	4.42	5.00	4.93	4.18	6.71
12–13	7.71	6.79	5.89	6.07	6.67	2.71	3.90	5.05	5.33	4.83	4.17	7.33
14–15	6.90	7.60	7.50	7.60	7.45	4.32	5.23	7.27	7.21	7.13	6.71	8.17
Mean	7.44	6.45	6.45	6.29	6.22	2.82	3.21	4.98	5.47	5.07	4.84	6.99

Note. Maximum score per cell = 12

programs—"Tomorrow's World" and "Know How." In the case of the remaining program—"Owl TV"—there was a progressive decline in content recall for the three youngest age groups, and a reversal of this pattern among 14- to 15-year-olds. The serial learning curve was most pronounced in relation to recall of material from "Tomorrow's World."

The fact that "Tomorrow's World" is an adult-based program whereas both "Owl TV" and "Know How" are targeted at younger audiences may suggest that if a serial position effect does occur it may be especially pronounced with difficult items. It may also be, of course, that poor recall of these particular items is purely a function of item difficulty or the way in which it was presented, irrespective of where they appear in the series of items. If this were so then poor learning of specific topics in a magazine format program would not be so much a function of an item's positioning as of the topic itself, and magazine format programs would then seem to benefit from the variety they introduce while suffering none of the possible dangers inherent in that structure. Table 6.17 attempts to disentangle these two possibilities—item difficulty versus serial position—by listing the 12 items presented in the three programs viewed, having had these items rated as "easy" or "difficult" by 15 children unrelated to the current or previous experiments.

Unlike the previous experiment, the presentation format of specific information produced varied responses in terms of recall and comprehen-

TABLE 6.17
Quality of Recall and Item Position and Rating

Mean Recall	Item	Program (Item Place)	Rating (by 15 Children 9–11 Years)
2.82	Shock absorbtion	"TW" (item 2)	simple
3.21	Nerve cell regeneration	"TW" (3)	difficult
4.84	Hyperspace hotel	"KH" (3)	diff/easy
4.98	Plastic cars	"TW" (4)	difficult
5.07	Video discs	"KH" (2)	difficult
5.47	Suspension	"KH" (1)	difficult
6.22	Records	"TW" (1)	easy
6.29	Dinosaurs	"Owl" (4)	easy
6.45	Crabs	"Owl" (3)	difficult
6.45	Elephants	"Owl" (2)	easy
6.99	Gravity	"KH" (4)	easy
7.44	Wallabies	"Owl" (1)	easy

Sequence of Items

	1	2	3	4
"TW"	Record repair	Shock abs.	Nerve cell regen.	Plastic cars
"KH"	Suspension	Video discs	Hyperspace	Gravity
"Owl"	Wallabies	Elephants	Crabs	Dinosaurs

sion. Whether information was presented orally, visually, or by a combination of the two, our sample sometimes obtained a correct response, other times they did not. However, the magazine format, unlike the programs in the previous experiment did not allow for concepts to be reinforced via a range of presentation factors or repeated experiments. Magazine programs convey a lot of information very quickly, making it almost impossible to identify any effect occurring from the way in which individual items were presented, other than those already identified with.

Another way of evaluating, somewhat crudely, the magazine format as a style of information presentation is to compare the overall recall and comprehension scores found in the present and the previous chapter where program format was deliberately varied. When we do this we find that comprehension differed by only 10% between the two studies and recall by only 4.5%. Allowing for different programs, different subjects, and age groups these figures indicate that there is little difference between multitopic and single-topic informational program formats in the quality of learning they can produce. In the former, breadth of learning has been demonstrated; in the latter, depth of learning.

DISCUSSION

This chapter reported a second experiment on children's attitudes toward and comprehension of informational programs concerned with science. The present study was a larger experiment than the previous one in that it involved the presentation of three, rather than two programs, and looked at four, rather than two age groups. The science programs used in this study were different from those used in the previous one in that they dealt with a number of distinct topics as opposed to devoting the whole of each edition to the examination of a single topic or theme. This second experiment enabled us to extend the findings of the previous study; to look again at which factors were most significantly related to program learning and, generally, to check on the robustness and generalizability of the earlier study's findings.

Broadly, the qualitative aspects of the previous findings were found again here. The children felt that they could learn from informational programs such as the ones with which they were presented, and from science programs in general, and they felt that there should be more programs of this type on prime-time television. They held a positive attitude toward prime-time science programs with which they were familiar and felt that such programs generally covered topics of interest to them. They enjoyed and appreciated the special effects that television could provide, and valued those programs that presented more than one topic per episode. These positive perceptions tended to be heightened by particular program or general science program loyalty. The more children reportedly watched the specific programs presented to them in the experiment, or other science programs on television, the more positive they were about such programs.

The overall enjoyment level for these programs was high and comparable to that observed in the previous chapter. Once again, background viewing habits were seen to have a moderating effect. Those children who viewed such programs regularly espoused higher enjoyment scores than those children who viewed science programs only infrequently. Interestingly, those children who claimed to be regular watchers of science on television found less difficulty with the vocabulary and technical issues raised in the test programs used in this study than did children who claimed to be relatively irregular science viewers. Thus, familiarity may breed appreciation and a capability to learn more effectively from televised science.

Although the children displayed a favorable reaction to science programs, nonetheless, and in line with the previous chapter's findings, their involvement levels with such programs did not invariably show signs of commitment. There was no widespread tendency actively to avoid science programs, but nor was there an overwhelming inclination deliberately to select to watch these programs, and few of the children reportedly discussed the content of science programs or their implications with friends or family. In this experiment boys claimed to discuss these programs more than did girls, and the older age groups reportedly discussed them more than did the younger age groups.

Although children perceived the value and benefit of science programs, they did not automatically avail themselves of these television offerings. Suggestively, in earlier qualitative research with children ages 8–15, we found that not one child had been encouraged by a teacher to watch a science program on television at home (Gunter et al., 1991).

When we look at the children's ability to learn from televised science many of the results reported in this chapter support those discussed in chapter 5. In terms of the overall level of comprehension and recall exhibited by our current sample we are left in little doubt that children can learn from informational programs, even when they do not deliberately set out to learn from them. This is an important consideration because these were not "memory experiments" with a primed learning set. Rather, children were "set" to watch programs in a relaxed atmosphere with no instructions as to what they would be expected to do once they had finished viewing. If the children had been told to "pay close attention to the content because you will be asked questions on that content" then there is every possibility that both memory and comprehension scores might have been higher.

In the event, under these non primed conditions, the children correctly recalled 60% and correctly understood 53% of the test programs. Allowing for differences between the children, in particular their age ranges, and between the type of programs presented, these figures are sufficiently close to those reported in chapter 5 to allow us to conclude that learning from science programs does, most certainly, take place under relatively relaxed learning conditions, at least in the short term.

These global figures, however, conceal significant age differences. As in the previous chapter, we found, once again, that older children generally scored much higher than younger children. What is of additional interest is that age was highly correlated with the general knowledge factor. The effect of this correlation is to leave uncertain the true explanation of age differences in recall and comprehension. In other words, being older may mean that you have more knowledge or it may mean that you have better developed information-processing skills or metacognition that, in turn, confers an advantage in any information-processing task — such as learning the informational content from television science programs. We began to unpick this relationship through multiple regression analysis. Here, it was clear that the chief contributor to variation in both OE and MC recall and recognition was general knowledge. Only when general knowledge was removed from the analysis did age emerge as a significant influence. We conclude then that it is not accumulated years (age) but rather accumulated knowledge and possibly developed information-processing skills that predict the amount of novel learning that will be exhibited in a television viewing situation.

As in chapter 5, children's gender and language ability had particular, local effects but could not be construed as major influences on learning in the same way as age or general knowledge could.

We looked again at previous reported viewing habits as a possible influence on the uptake of information from the test programs. Here it appears that whether it is beneficial or not to have viewed a particular program before depends on the nature of the program. Where the program has relatively simplistic content (e.g., "Owl TV"), previous viewing may not be beneficial. When the program is complex and targeted principally at older viewers (e.g., "Tomorrow's World"), then having previously watched that program does appear to enable children to take more from it. Of course, complex programs may require complex information-processing skills and the required cognitive skill level may be cultivated through previous exposure to the actual program. That these information-processing skills may be highly specific is shown by the absence of general effects of either watching the *series* regularly or watching science programs generally on specific program learning. This notion of developmental improvement in children's ability to learn from television is consonant with research elsewhere, which has indicated that children must learn the symbol systems of different media through experience in order to be able to acquire information from media more effectively. Experience with media symbol systems enables children to acquire the requisite intellectual skills that promote more effective learning of media content (Salomon, 1979).

The results presented in this chapter elaborate on those findings in chapter 5 that suggested that reading behavior may be associated with learning from the visual (or audiovisual) medium. The current experiment shows clearly that children who claimed to read newspapers perform better than those children who do not read. In addition, those children who claimed to read the better quality tabloids perform better than those children who reportedly read poorer quality tabloids. Once again this suggests a knowledge effect rather than a reading effect per se. Under regression analysis this "reading" factor appeared as a significant predictor of posttest OE and MC recall and comprehension performance, under certain conditions, although the actual amount of variability actually contributed is modest.

Knowledge growth, as conceptually distinct from immediate memory for program content, was clearly demonstrated, thus replicating a major concern of this whole project. We measured this growth by focusing specifically on key items (questions) that were included in both the previewing and the postviewing tests, and that were addressed in the specific television programs that the children saw. To the extent that the children demonstrated improved scoring on these key items in the posttest relative to their performance in the pretest (test effects) we have a fairly pure measure of the influence of television in generating knowledge growth.

The evidence is clear and compelling. There were significant differences between posttest and pretest scores in every analysis we performed. Additionally, these improvements were not conditional on any demographic, previous viewing habit, or reading behavior dimension. The presence of this test effect in every analysis, and the almost total absence of any interaction effects with other variables, renders this a very "clean" result and thus affords a strong conclusion. Television that involves informational material can produce learning of various kinds in children who are not "set" to deliberately learn from it at least in the short term. The corollary may be that if they were so set the learning that took place may be greater still.

Having performed standard analyses on our data to detect differences between programs, groups, and various other variables of interest, we moved on to multivariate analysis that acknowledges the fact that many of the variables that we were examining are in fact related or correlated with one other. Such tests allowed us to ask in what measure the overall effects obtained were due to the specific variable we were interested in. Factor analysis as a research tool allows a mass of data to be systemized and structured according to a number of statistical principles. This often allows clearer perceptions of what one's data are actually saying. Factor analysis and multiple regression can also be used in tandem to render data maximally informative. We employed this opportunity in the current research by structuring the responses of our children to the 12 agree–disagree statements that addressed the issue of their attitudes to science programs in general, and then used these structured groupings that exhibited a "family resemblance" in terms of correlation as possible predictors of variance in OE and MC recall and comprehension performance.

The groupings we obtained under factor analysis agreed with those found previously and reported in chapter 5. These factors were most usefully labeled, *program perception attraction, program utility*, and *home–school comparison*. We also factor analyzed certain school subjects that the children had studied, which produced four groupings, or factors, best referred to as "biology," "politics and science," "electronics," and "dinosaurs."

Having established these factor structurings for both program attitudes and school-based learning we went on to look at their ability to predict OE and MC performance. However, the findings were mixed, with program attitude factors being most predictive for OE recall from the most complex program ("Tomorrow's World"), but not at all predictive of OE recall from "Know How," a moderately complex program. In a similar fashion, school study factors did not predict OE question performance at all consistently: Different factors predicted performance on different programs differentially and usually in isolation.

Multiple-choice performance was likewise underpredicted by the program attitude and school study factors that we had isolated. However, the program attitude factors of "perception" and "utility" powerfully predicted "Know How" performance, and "program perception" on its own predicted recall performance on "Tomorrow's World." "Electronics" and "politics and science" were the most consistent predictors of MC question performance across our programs when we looked at the school subjects studied.

Having looked at the possible predictive power of factors that underlay program attitudes and school-based study we moved on to look at whether each individual program attitude or distinct school subject had an influence on overall scoring performance. In the event only a few attitudes proved important: for OE scoring, not switching off the television when informational programs came on was associated with good performance in "Know How," whereas "Tomorrow's World" performance was partially "explained" by the attitude children had to the channel placing of informational programs. The involvement indicated by whether or not children would switch off, or over, was implicated in MC performance, but only for "Know How."

In terms of the specific topics children had studied in school, recall from "Tomorrow's World" was predicted partially by children having studied "pollution" and "car manufacture," whereas for "Know How" having studied "electronics" and "the human body" best predicted memory performance following the viewing of this program. The topics of "pollution," "electronics," and "the human body" appeared again as fairly important predictors of memory performance when we looked at MC recall and comprehension.

Because one of the objectives of this present experiment was to seek the robustness of the findings of the previous experiment, we analyzed the data very much with an eye to the way we had analyzed it before. As a result of this objective we went on to select, first, a group of variables that had proved to be powerfully associated with different scoring profiles either in the first or the present experiment, second, variables that had proved noncontributory in either experiment or, finally, variables that had behaved differently across the two experiments. These various variables were selected from among those we have been labeling demographic, viewing, reading, and general knowledge variables. These selected variables were then subjected to multiple regression to ascertain their independent and joint contribution to the OE and MC performances that we were interested in.

In concert with the previous experiment, general knowledge was the one variable that appeared ubiquitously as a powerful predictor. In this experiment, however, for certain programs, variables that had either not appeared in the previous experiment or had proved not to be of consistent importance began to show through. Thus, for "Owl TV" in addition to general knowledge, having seen the program before and giving it a high enjoyment score contributed to the open-ended performance observed. When we considered MC performance, although general knowledge was the chief contributory variable, enjoyment score again predicted, negatively, MC recall and comprehension for "Know How," but positively for "Owl TV." In addition, in terms of "Owl TV" a third variable of importance in predicting this group's score was seen to be whether the children had seen the program before.

In summary, then, this chapter supports and extends the findings reported in the previous chapter. Children appreciate informational television and can clearly see its relevance and importance. However, the children do not always seek out such programs. If they do choose to watch them then there can be little doubt that they can learn facts and principles from them. The nature and amount of what is learned, however, is a complex function of certain demographic factors, previous viewing, and reading habits, the web of attitudes, beliefs, and values that the children hold about television and the knowledge and cognitive skills that they bring to bear on their viewing.

7 Children's Perceptions of and Learning From TV Entertainment (Quiz) Programs

Quiz and game shows are without a doubt one of the most popular forms of entertainment programming on television today. They attract large audiences among young and old alike and feature among the best-liked programs (Gunter, 1986).

Such shows come in a variety of forms. The games played, the types of contestants featured, the prizes offered, and the seriousness versus the light-heartedness of these programs can vary a great deal. Some shows feature celebrity contestants only, others are played by ordinary members of the public, whereas a small number team up celebrities and the public. Some shows offer big star prizes for winners, whereas others offer only points. Some shows involve a certain amount of skill or put the knowledge of contestants to the test. Others rely mainly on chance and good luck. Some are played by teams, whereas others pit individuals against each other.

Which among these shows and particular features appeal most and least to children? Are there special ingredients of quiz shows that really attract younger viewers to make such light entertainment regular or even compulsive viewing? What is it that they like or dislike about them? This phase of the project set out to answer some of these questions.

Another issue addressed was the fundamental question posed in chapter 1 about children's use of television: Do they control the set or does it control them? Children's relative "activity" or "passivity" in their time spent with television can be assessed in a variety of ways. At the level of their behavioral involvement with television is the question of whether they watch programs selectively. At the level of their intellectual involvement

165

with television, we can ask how much effort do children invest in trying to follow and understand programs. The degree of attention children pay to programs may be controlled both by their personal level of interest or enjoyment and by particular features of the programs themselves. What then is the nature of children's watching of television quiz shows?

This volume has focused on children's learning from television programs. The programs studied contained material on which children's content recall and comprehension could be readily tested. In addition, both drama and factual (science) programs used in this research carried messages about aspects of the world whose impact upon children's general knowledge and social beliefs could be measured. Having represented two of the three broad program strands of television introduced at the beginning of this book, we now turn to the third — (light) entertainment.

Entertainment programs, according to the classification system we have chosen to adopt, include comedy, variety, talk, and quiz and game shows. In continuing the theme of children's learning from television, and more especially, television's impact upon children's general knowledge, we needed to select a category of entertainment programming that contained appropriately testable material. We chose quiz shows because they comprise question-and-answer formats featuring general knowledge questions. This "informational" content could, we reasoned, be conveyed to the audience and enhance viewers' knowledge on those subjects dealt with in the quiz. There were further questions concerning audience understanding of the way the game in the quiz show was played that we also wished to explore. The degree of cognitive involvement in quiz shows would be operationally defined in terms of viewers' subjective responses and objectively measured performance in tests of information recall.

As further background, we also looked at children's behavioral activity or passivity toward such programs. We asked whether they chose to watch specific quiz programs or whether they simply watched them because they happened to come on while they were watching television.

Based on extended interviews with children (Gunter et al., 1991) the anticipation was that we would find both active and passive watching, but with the former behavior exceeding the latter. That is, passive watching by children of TV quiz and game shows was not seen to be typical on the basis of earlier testimony we had obtained from them. Rather, quiz shows either have some special function for children or they contain particular features that appeal strongly to children's tastes. The current research sought to identify what these features were. As an example, children's attention to television programs is known to be controlled by special sound and visual effects (D. R. Anderson & Lorch, 1983). A child looking away from the screen may still be monitoring it by listening to what is going on in a program. A sound effect or somebody saying something significant can draw the child's eyes back to the screen again. Continued visual attention may then depend on what is happening visually in a program as well as on what is being said.

Some quiz shows try to be visually interesting and stimulating by employing technical gimmicks and gadgets, such as computers and computer graphics and stimulations. Do shows that contain such visual accessories hold children's attention? The current research set out to investigate this.

Another sign of active viewing that we found (Gunter et al., 1991) was that the children's experience and enjoyment of quizzes resided partly in the intellectual challenge that such shows provided. Among the several functions recognized by the children we spoke to was that quizzes provided a source of learning. Additionally, children liked to try to answer the questions themselves and saw them as a test of their own general knowledge, or as a source of competition with contestants or family members.

This anecdotal evidence of a learning function of a program directly construed by the program makers as an entertainment program relates to the manifest and latent functions of programs addressed in chapter 1. This phase of the project directly set out to investigate this issue of programming effect. As such, then, knowledge gain was investigated in terms of the children's ability to obtain information from quizzes that they were instructed to watch but with no indication that their memory for answers to questions would be tested at a later date. In other words, as near normal viewing as possible was sought.

Over and above the investigation of what children like, how they select the programs they watch and on what grounds, and their ability to understand the rules of various quizzes, and to learn from them, we were interested in how the children evaluated the rewarding of effort or noneffort in such shows. It became clear to us in our conversations with children of various ages that they had fairly strong views on whether contestants should be rewarded — quite extravagantly in certain cases — for minimal effort. There was a suggestion, from our older respondents, that they were concerned about the "greed" factor that they believed motivated certain contestants to appear on quiz shows. Here then, once again, an entertainment show or genre was precipitating cognitive activity that appeared to have little to do, prima facie, with the manifest function of the program. We were thus interested to look more closely at perceptions of the "prize" element of, and the motives for being contestants in, quiz shows.

METHOD

As in previous parts of the project a pre- and posttest design was employed whereby 221 boys ($n = 118$) and girls ($n = 103$) ages 9-10 ($n = 78$), 11-12

($n = 75$), and 13–14 ($n = 68$) were tested in a number of areas 7 days before being presented with one of three quiz programs ("Knock Knock," "Blockbusters," "Every Second Counts"), and then being tested again on issues related to the programs they had just seen. In terms of ethnic composition, using as a criterion of allocation English as a first language, there were 163 who fell into this category, and 58 who did not have English as their first language.

In the pretest we were interested to ascertain the general knowledge level of our children by means of a questionnaire, whereas in the posttest we emphasized—as before—OE and MC recall and comprehension questionnaires to ascertain learning of information given in the program, understanding of the rules of the game, and awareness of contestant characteristics.

In addition, information was obtained from the children about their television viewing habits, and liking, appreciation, evaluation, and attitudes toward the programs were sought, which served as additional dependent and independent variables of interest.

Taking account of children's opinions about entertainment programming and responses to content in the qualitative research phase and viewing figures for individual programs, three quiz shows ("Blockbusters," "Every Second Counts," and "Knock Knock") were selected as material for testing. All three of these seemed popular with children, although age appeared to be an important variable when determining the extent of popularity. All three shows had one thing in common, that is, they required contestants to answer a selection of general knowledge questions. Beyond this, however, there were marked differences in the form of presentation, the types of contestants, and the difficulty level of questions in all three programs (chapter 2 has already provided a detailed descriptive account of each of these programs).

All three programs were analyzed in depth and formed the basis of the main posttest questionnaire, and furnished specific questions for the pretest general knowledge questionnaire.

This instrument was devised to act as a pretest of knowledge and a baseline for knowledge growth for each program with the content of questions varied according to the program being tested. Difficulty levels of questions ranged from very easy to quite hard, with approximately 50% of the questions derived from the to-be-presented material, and it was anticipated that few children would be able to score much more than 80% on the overall questionnaire. Questions were presented in both an OE and MC format. At this stage, subjects were also asked about the extent to which they viewed different quiz programs and their likelihood of participation in other forms of general knowledge "testing" (e.g., crossword puzzles, board games, and so on).

As with the science and drama experiments, the postscreening tests took place 7 days after completing the prescreening test. The same children (within their year group) were presented with a full screening of the selected programs (either "Blockbusters," "Every Second Counts," or "Knock Knock") and were then asked to complete a structured questionnaire immediately afterward.

The questionnaires, containing a mixture of OE, MC, and precoded items related to program content and format, sought to measure children's recall of information, comprehension of the "rules of the game," knowledge growth, and reasons for watching quiz shows. Specific attitudes toward the different programs were also examined.

RESULTS

Reasons for Liking Quiz Shows

We were keen to find out why children watched quiz shows. We gave the children the chance to check one or more of six possible reasons we knew they usually cited for such viewing (Gunter et al., 1991). The percentages of children selecting each of these reasons is presented in Table 7.1.

As can be seen in the table, the children clearly indicated that the chief motivation for watching quiz shows was to try to answer the questions themselves, and this held true for both gender as well as across all three age groups. "To compete with the family" was also rated as a major factor for watching quiz shows. Between 50% and 60% of respondents gave this as a reason and thus testified to the fact that television viewing can be a source of family interaction.

TABLE 7.1
Reasons for Watching Quiz Shows as a Function of Age and Gender
($N = 221$)

	Age				Gender	
	All	*9–10*	*11–12*	*13–14*	*Male*	*Female*
Reasons for Watching	%	%	%	%	%	%
To try to answer questions	85	84	86	90	87	83
To compete with family	63	63	69	57	61	64
To see what prizes are	52	59	52	49	51	53
To learn new things	59	66	60	50	61	56
To find out who wins	54	71	43	47	53	55
To see presenter(s)	16	22	15	12	21	11

Another category gaining near-universal agreement, but this time as being of low attraction value, was "to see the presenter." All age groups and both language-ability groups rated this equally as of low priority. Although males and females also tended to agree that presenters were not important in encouraging viewing of quizzes there was a slight tendency for boys to opt for this as a reason for viewing more than girls.

The high degree of positive agreement across ages for trying to answer questions was not present for the other possible reasons for watching such shows. Thus "to see what the prizes are" was attractive to 9- to 10-year-olds, but less for older children and generally was less widespread than the elements of competing against contestants or other family members.

"To learn new things" and "to find out who wins" were fairly widely endorsed, although not on the same scale and were given about equal weight by each age and gender grouping.

Attitudes Toward Quiz Programs

General Attitudes

Before reporting the agreement or disagreement of children to a set of attitude statements purportedly made about the specific quiz program they had just watched, we take a look at their reactions to statements about quiz programs in general. We did this via an 18-item questionnaire. We were further interested in their opinions as a function of a number of demographic factors that we have attempted to track throughout this program of research.

The Prize Element.   There was little evidence that children think prizes should be of more value than they are—although there was a suggestion that with increased age more children do agree with this opinion (see Table 7.2). Again there was little agreement that exposure to the winning of prizes would lead to greed on the part of the young viewer, although younger children felt this was a possibility a little more strongly than did older children. Somewhat paradoxically, although children of all ages expressed no strong agreement that prizes should be much more expensive, they did not agree that there should be a limit on how much prizes should be worth.

No strong agreement was observed for the assertion that money rather than prizes should be awarded to successful contestants. This may reflect the fact that money ceilings would be known beforehand, whereas prizes always have the element of surprise, which children of all ages like.

Boys agreed more than did girls with the assertion that prizes should be more expensive, and that seeing people win prizes could render the viewers greedy. There were few systematic differences between genders on the issue

TABLE 7.2
Opinions About Prizes in Quiz Shows as a Function of Age and
Gender (*N* = 221)

Statements	Age				Gender	
	All %	*9–10* %	*11–12* %	*13–14* %	*Male* %	*Female* %
The prizes on quiz shows should be much more expensive	48	44	45	62	55	41
There should be a limit as to how much prizes in quiz shows are worth	37	42	30	37	38	36
I prefer quiz shows where people win money instead of prizes	36	42	33	35	43	27
Seeing people win big prizes on TV makes viewers greedy	31	39	33	22	31	25

of upper limits on the value of prizes or whether money or prizes was the better reward.

Content Element of Quiz Shows. When we looked at the children's agreement patterns within statements that can be classified as content-relevant we discovered a few interesting differences. These are presented in Table 7.3.

Children of all ages exhibited a preference for a game show format over straight "quiz" shows. There was a slight preference for shows in which group or team spirit was to the fore rather than individual competition. There was a strong agreement that quiz shows involving children of the same age as the viewers would be liked, but with a gradual tapering off of this preference with increasing age.

The item concerning guessing versus knowing produced a heterogeneous pattern of agreement and disagreement. Averaging over the three test programs there was just a very slight tendency for older children compared to younger children to prefer quiz shows where participants need to know the answer rather than guess at it.

Gender preferences for content features were marginal in the majority of cases. Differences were quite small and unsystematic over the three groups. The biggest differences occurred on the question concerning guessing versus knowing, with girls agreeing much more with the statement, and team versus individual competition, where boys much preferred team-based competition compared to the girls.

TABLE 7.3
Opinions About the Content of Quiz Shows as a Function of Age and
Gender (*N* = 221)

Statement	Age				Gender	
	All %	*9–10* %	*11–12* %	*13–14* %	*Male* %	*Female* %
There should be more quiz shows that have contestants the same age as me	68	73	73	53	65	70
I prefer shows where people have to do things instead of answer questions	59	70	63	51	64	59
I prefer quiz shows where you can guess the right answer rather than having to know what it is	57	65	58	51	55	59
I prefer shows where contestants are part of a team instead of on their own	53	57	48	56	55	51

Involvement With Quiz Shows.   Seven items in our questionnaire dealt with children's degree of involvement with quiz programs. Their responses to these items are summarized in Table 7.4.

Children stated that they rarely talked about quiz shows with others, and the little they did, decreased with age. All ages widely agreed that it was possible to learn from such programs, but fewer than half claimed to watch a lot of these shows. Averaged across the three quiz shows, even fewer children agreed that watching quiz shows helps you to relax; relaxation being one of the chief motivations for watching television (e.g., Greenberg, 1974). This, however, may follow from the fact that in watching quiz shows viewers can get involved in what is happening and thus become quite excited about the game being played (e.g., the vast majority of all age groups said they often identified with one person whom they wanted to win). Although reportedly not choosing to watch quiz shows all the time, when they did watch, most children of all ages agreed that they try to answer the questions.

Once again, there were few gender differences. What boys agreed and disagreed with, so too did the girls. On learning new things from quiz shows more boys than girls in one of our viewing groups agreed that you could learn from quiz shows, but this was reversed in one of the other two groups and in the third, differences were neither systematic nor substantial.

TABLE 7.4

Opinions Relating to Personal Involvement with Quiz Programs, as a Function of Age and Gender (N = 221)

	Age				Gender	
Statement	All %	9-10 %	11-12 %	13-4 %	Male %	Female %
I often want one particular person to win	81	85	78	82	78	83
I always join in and try to answer the questions	73	76	80	71	77	72
Quiz shows can help you learn new things	71	72	77	64	72	69
I would like to go on a quiz show	54	60	73	46	56	52
Watching quiz shows makes you feel relaxed	38	51	32	33	38	38
I try to watch a lot of quiz shows	37	38	43	32	41	33
I often talk about quiz shows with my family	24	29	25	18	27	21

Presenters, Contestants, and Amount of Quiz Shows on Television. We were also interested to find out if demographic factors influenced agreement with statements concerned with presenters, contestants, and amounts of quiz programs on television. Only a minority of children (38%) agreed with the assertion that there were too many quiz programs on television. This implies that they would like to see even more perhaps. Boys (45%), however, agreed in greater numbers than girls (31%) that there were too many, suggesting that they did not like such programs as much as the girls. This view also became more widespread with increasing age (9-10s: 32%; 11-12s: 45%; 13-14s: 49%).

Children did not agree that the contestants on quiz programs were very like people they knew. This suggests that young viewers found it difficult to identify with them.

Presenters can make or break a program. How were quiz hosts or presenters evaluated? One question we asked on this matter was whether presenters sometimes try to be too funny. Clear homogeneity of opinion was found here. Children of all ages widely agreed (75% on average across the three quiz shows) that presenters can often try to be too funny. Boys and girls agreed equally strongly on this question and age made little difference to opinions. From these data, then, presenters should not strain to be overly funny or too prominent. The focus should be placed on the contestants and the game/quiz, not the presenter.

Program-Specific Attitudes

Having looked at general reasons for liking of quiz shows, we then turned to what the children thought about each of the three test programs they were shown. That is, what did they think they could get out of such programs and what did such programs have to offer them?

In this phase of the study, we presented 20 attitude statements that were grouped into programme, content, presenter, contestant, and personal reference statements. Responses to items were given along 5-point, agree-disagree scales. Children's opinions relating to each of these aspects of the test programs, are examined in the following sections of this chapter.

General Program Evaluations

The children were given three general attitude statements relating to the three test quiz shows. These statements invited the children to say how much they agreed or disagreed that each show was "a fun program to watch," "the best show on TV," and something they "try to watch every time it is on." The results are summarized in Table 7.5, which shows the prevalence of agreement with each statement in respect of each quiz program.

A clear pattern of age differences in response emerged that reflected, in two cases, the designated target age group for the program. "Knock Knock," which is made for pre-teenage children, was widely regarded as fun to watch up to the age of 12. During the early teens, the show's popularity clearly waned. Even among the younger two age groups, however, it was not widely endorsed as the best show on TV, although this was true also of the other two quiz shows.

TABLE 7.5
Children's General Evaluations of Each Quiz Show

Statement		All %	9–10 %	11–12 %	13–14 %
Is a fun program					
to watch	"KK"	66	82	84	32
	"BB"	56	30	71	68
	"ESC"	68	78	64	62
I try to watch it					
every time it is on	"KK"	35	46	50	8
	"BB"	25	18	43	14
	"ESC"	38	57	23	24
Is the best show					
on TV	"KK"	20	23	25	12
	"BB"	20	12	29	18
	"ESC"	25	39	18	19

"KK" = "Knock Knock." "BB" = "Blockbusters." "ESC" = "Every Second Counts."

With "Blockbusters," which is aimed at the teenage audience, general evaluations were highest among the 11- to 14-year-olds, and especially among the 11- to 12-year-olds. Finally "Every Second Counts," a program made for all ages and shown during prime-time rather than children's viewing time, was widely endorsed by all children as fun to watch. It was much more likely to be endorsed by the 9- to 10-year-olds than by older children as the best program on TV or as something they tried to watch every time it was on.

Opinions About Presenters

Most of the children (especially the 11- to 12-year-olds) agreed that presenters spent a little too much time talking to contestants. The oldest children (13–14) tended not to agree with this, perhaps reflecting their growing social awareness and decreasing ego centrism. Most children felt that presenters were good at explaining the rules, and at putting contestants at their ease, but less strongly in the latter case.

Only with "Every Second Counts" (hosted by Paul Daniels) did children think presenters ate into program time too much by telling jokes. Although this reflects actual program content, it may also indicate that the jokes told by the compere in this family show may be above the heads of the younger viewers and thus not appreciated by them. On the whole, however, presenters seemed to be acceptable to our children in their key roles, for the three programs viewed (see Table 7.6).

TABLE 7.6
Opinions about Quiz Show Presenters

Statement		All %	9–10 %	11–12 %	13–14 %
Always explains the rules clearly	"KK"	57	59	75	36
	"BB"	52	61	71	24
	"ESC"	73	78	64	76
Wastes too much time talking to contestants	"KK"	50	50	56	44
	"BB"	54	55	62	46
	"ESC"	65	65	73	57
Good at helping contestants to relax	"KK"	46	50	56	32
	"BB"	64	52	81	59
	"ESC"	71	83	64	67
Spends too much time telling jokes	"KK"	29	36	22	28
	"BB"	28	42	24	18
	"ESC"	54	61	68	33

Involvement With Quiz Shows

We next turned our attention to children's degree of involvement with quiz shows. Did they identify with the contestant who competed in these programs? Would they like to appear on a quiz show themselves? Did they find any benefits from watching TV quiz shows in terms of what could be learned from them?

The children obviously did not think that the contestants they watched on their quiz shows were drawn from people like them or children they knew and, except for the 9- to 10-year-olds who were referring to "Knock Knock," they did not particularly see themselves as wishing to be a contestant. Across our three groups, only "Blockbusters" as a quiz show seemed to be perceived as requiring brains. The noticeable exception to this is the youngest age group (for whom "Knock Knock" is targeted), who thought you had to be clever to go on all three programs.

All children, except the oldest children under the youngest programme condition ("Knock Knock"), agreed that viewers could learn from quiz programs. This indicates that the children were responding to the particular attitude statement we had presented them with, rather than to some general, global, or diffuse schema of quiz programs that, at this stage, we were not addressing (see Table 7.7).

TABLE 7.7
Involvement With Quiz Shows

		All %	9–10 %	11–12 %	13–14 %
Can help you to learn new things	"KK"	57	64	75	32
	"BB"	84	79	86	86
	"ESC"	69	91	59	57
I would like to go on myself	"KK"	48	73	47	24
	"BB"	34	24	52	27
	"ESC"	48	52	41	52
Contestants are just like people I know	"KK"	35	27	50	28
	"BB"	18	21	19	14
	"ESC"	26	30	14	33
You have to be clever to answer the questions	"KK"	21	50	9	4
	"BB"	59	73	48	55
	"ESC"	28	52	23	10

Attitudes Toward Attributes of TV Quiz Shows

Children were invited to give their views about a range of attributes of TV quiz shows, relating to the way the games in each show were played, the difficulty they had following the rules and scoring procedures, and the prizes that could be won. As Table 7.8 shows, there were differences between programs as well as between age groups in the extent to which each opinion was agreed with.

TABLE 7.8
Attitudes Toward Attributes of TV Quiz Shows

Statement		All %	9–10 %	11–12 %	13–14 %
There should be better prizes for the losers	"KK"	71	64	72	76
	"BB"	69	64	81	64
	"ESC"	61	52	59	71
The final is always exciting	"KK"	62	68	75	44
	"BB"	84	79	95	77
	"ESC"	53	96	50	57
They always have good prizes	"KK"	59	64	69	44
	"BB"	57	85	86	77
	"ESC"	66	87	68	43
Would be better if answer in team rather than on own	"KK"	56	64	53	52
	"BB"	31	27	38	27
	"ESC"	50	70	41	38
Would be better if contestants played games instead of just answering questions	"KK"	46	46	47	44
	"BB"	48	61	33	50
	"ESC"	48	65	46	33
The scoring is far too complicated	"KK"	30	50	16	24
	"BB"	24	21	19	32
	"ESC"	22	35	18	14
The questions are often too difficult for the contestants	"KK"	28	41	22	20
	"BB"	28	24	33	27
	"ESC"	36	57	32	19
The rules are difficult to follow	"KK"	26	55	16	8
	"BB"	21	30	24	9
	"ESC"	15	26	5	14
The questions are often too difficult for me	"KK"	16	23	16	8
	"BB"	55	67	57	41
	"ESC"	23	30	9	29

Note. Percentages are of those who agreed with each attitude statement.

Between-show differences are most immediately noticeable in terms of the rank order of opinions. There were, as can be seen, occasionally substantial differences between quiz shows in the extent to which particular opinions obtained agreement from children.

On the issue of question difficulty, two angles were explored: difficulty of questions for the children themselves, and children's perceptions of question difficulty for the contestants. Generally, there was no widespread impression that the questions in these three quiz shows were difficult, except in the case of "Blockbusters," where the children themselves were concerned. More than half felt that the questions on "Blockbusters" were often too difficult for them. This opinion was considerably, and not surprisingly, much more widespread among the youngest children.

Although there was general satisfaction in all age groups with the nature of the prizes offered across programs, there was a high level of agreement that losers should get better prizes than they do at the moment.

No children, save for the youngest group who viewed "Knock Knock," had difficulty with either the rules or the scoring of any of the three shows. Interestingly, although "Knock Knock" is aimed at the youngest group, it was precisely this group that agreed most with the assertion that rules were difficult to follow and, in fact, they were quite complex relative to the other quizzes.

Generally speaking, the children were evenly split between wishing for a little more game showlike content or not so wishing. Although Only for the youngest age group (9–10) in the "Every Second Counts" and "Blockbusters" conditions did the majority actually agree with this assertion, the minority agreeing with it was substantial.

All three programs seemed to be succeeding in producing shows that built to a dramatic climax. A glance at Table 7.8, however, indicates that greatest appreciation of this feature varied for each program as a function of age. Thus, the oldest children who viewed "Knock Knock" did not agree that the final was always exciting. The 9- to 10-year-olds, much more than the 11- to 12- or 13- to 14-year-olds, did agree with the assertion for "Every Second Counts," whereas for "Blockbusters" the 10- to 12-year-olds agreed much more than the youngest and the oldest groups that the ending is always exciting.

Taken as a whole then these attitudes indicate that the format and content of the three programs chosen for examination were more appreciated than not appreciated, and were evaluated positively rather than negatively.

Specific Information Pick-Up

Having obtained subjective reactions of children to the three quiz shows, the next part of the analysis examined comprehension and recall of their contents. We were interested to know how much specific information concerning quiz content, rules, and answers the children could demonstrate under OE and MC questioning. Performance on these measures was investigated over the children as a whole, and in relation to their age, gender, fluency level in English, and viewing experiences.

Memory and comprehension levels varied across the three quiz shows. In terms of general content, children exhibited a correct retention rate of 63% for "Knock Knock" (designed for preteens), 78% for "Blockbusters" (designed for teenagers), and 84% for "Every Second Counts" (designed for adults).

Turning to rules of the game, levels of understanding across all children were best for "Blockbusters" (82%), followed by "Knock Knock" (79%), and finally by "Every Second Counts" (74%). Remembering of specific information contained in quiz items was best for "Knock Knock" (73%), followed by "Blockbusters" (67%), and finally by "Every Second Counts"(60%). In general, responses to MC questions produced better performance levels than cued recall to OE questions (see Table 7.9).

TABLE 7.9

Percentage Correct Memory Scores for Aspects of Program Content as a Function of Age and Test

Program Viewed	Age	Open-Ended Questions			Multiple-Choice Questions		
		General Content	Rules of Game	Quiz Items	General Content	Rules of Game	Quiz Items
"Knock Knock"	9–10	46[a]	98[b]	61[c]	88[d]	68[e]	60[f]
	11–12	57	88	79	69	65	69
	13–14	55	78	94	62	74	76
		—	—	—	—	—	—
		53	88	78	73	69	68
"Every Second Counts"	9–10	69[g]	57[h]	42[i]	87[j]	57[k]	44[l]
	11–12	82	76	70	83	82	60
	13–14	89	81	67	90	90	73
		—	—	—	—	—	—
		80	71	60	87	76	59
"Blockbusters"	9–10	67[g]	87[h]	43[i]	75[j]	81[m]	62[n]
	11–12	69	83	59	95	81	82
	13–14	64	82	68	87	78	84
		—	—	—	—	—	—
		67	84	57	86	80	76

Maximum scores possible: [a]Max = 8 [d]Max = 3 [g]Max = 4 [j]Max = 5 [m]Max = 2
[b]Max = 4 [e]Max = 6 [h]Max = 6 [k]Max = 1 [n]Max = 9
[c]Max = 12 [f]Max = 7 [i]Max = 14 [l]Max = 10

Age

In line with the previous experiments we were interested to find out if age would prove to be a significant factor in the obtaining of information from entertainment type programs, and whether the type of information picked up (general content, rules of the game, and answers to quiz items) would differ as a function of this factor.

Age differences in rates of correct recall and recognition of quiz program content were clearly apparent in respect of all three aspects of content and for each quiz program. However, age differences were not always in the same direction. The general trend, as illustrated in Table 7.9, was for older children to perform better than younger children. This pattern was reversed on a number of measures in relation to the program designed for preteen children ("Knock Knock"). Although older children performed better on cued recall of general program content, they were surpassed by younger children on correct responses to OE questions about rules of the game and quiz items. Older children performed better in the latter two respects with MC questions. It seems likely, therefore, that those children in the target age group for this program were more familiar with the way this particular television quiz was played and were better able to remember what happened with minimal cueing. Older children, who were less likely to watch this program, had less general familiarity with it but with more detailed prompting were able to recount what it contained. The degree of statistical significance to these results was tested via a series of analyses of variance, which were computed on the mean scores shown in Table 7.10.

One-way ANOVAs for "Knock Knock" revealed that age was a significant factor in OE rules of game recall [$F = (2,76) = 4.05, p < .02$] and quiz items [$F(2,76) = 13.37, p < .001$], and for MC recall of quiz items [$F(2,76) = 3.98, p < .02$]. Although both OE and MC means were in the direction that would have been predicted from previous studies in this project — the older children scoring better — for rules of the game, under OE recall, this age trend was reversed. In addition to this reversal, three other conditions showed no significant effect whatsoever of age. This pattern of findings for "Knock Knock" clearly goes against previous findings.

When we look at "Every Second Counts" the age trend was more pronounced and in line with previous results. For "Every Second Counts," age was a significant factor for both OE and MC rules of the game recall (both $ps < .001$) and for quiz items (both $ps < .02$). However, although age was significant for OE recall of general content [$F(2,63) = 4.78, p < .01$] it was not under MC recall of this category of material.

The "Blockbuster" means show a pattern closer to "Knock Knock" than "Every Second Counts," with only one category of knowledge being significantly influenced by age under both OE and MC recall — quiz items

TABLE 7.10

Mean Memory Scores for Aspects of Program Content as a Function of Age and Test

		Open-Ended Questions			Multiple-Choice Questions		
Program Viewed	Age	General Content	Rules of Game	Quiz Items	General Content	Rules of Game	Quiz Items
"Knock Knock"	9–10	3.68[a]	3.91[b]	7.36[c]	2.64[d]	4.05[e]	4.23[f]
	11–12	4.53	3.50	9.47	2.75	3.91	4.84
	13–14	4.40	3.12	11.28	2.48	4.44	5.32
"Every Second Counts"	9–10	2.74[g]	3.39[h]	5.87[i]	4.35[j]	0.57[k]	4.39[l]
	11–12	3.27	4.55	9.82	4.14	0.82	6.00
	13–14	3.57	4.86	9.43	4.52	0.90	7.29
"Blockbusters"	9–10	2.67[g]	5.21[h]	6.06[i]	3.76[j]	1.61[m]	5.58[n]
	11–12	2.76	4.95	8.19	4.76	1.62	7.38
	13–14	2.59	4.90	9.45	4.36	1.55	7.59

Maximum scores possible: [a]Max = 8   [d]Max = 3   [g]Max = 4   [j]Max = 5   [m]Max = 2
[b]Max = 4   [e]Max = 6   [h]Max = 6   [k]Max = 1   [n]Max = 9
[c]Max = 12   [f]Max = 7   [i]Max = 14   [l]Max = 10

(both ps $< .001$). The only other age effect was found for MC recall of general content [$F (2,73) = 11.10$, $p < .001$].

Two points can be made about this age effect. First, the effect was much less ubiquitous than it was in the science program phase of this project. Second, where age did appear as a significant factor, it was not a linear effect but a much more steplike one, with the major age difference occurring between the ages of 9–10 and 11–12. It is hard to escape the conclusion that the type of knowledge communicated by quiz shows is different from that found in information programs, and that the former type of knowledge is much less dependent on age-related knowledge structures and disciplined learning.

In addition, it seems that although "quiz items" scoring produced the expected age effect, knowledge of the other types of content—rules of the game and general content—were not so age dependent. Thus, recall of general content, such as who won what, for "Knock Knock" was equally good, under both OE and MC questioning, for all age groups. For "Every Second Counts," MC questioning exhibited no difference in recall as a function of age nor did OE questioning for "Blockbusters." This pattern of age-unrelated recall seems to indicate that children of all ages were sufficiently interested in the outcomes of the various quizzes they watched to remember winners, losers, prizes, and consolations.

With performance on rules of the game, "Knock Knock" and "Block-busters" subjects did not differ as a function of age under MC questioning. Under OE questioning, the youngest children actually scored higher than the oldest children for both "Knock Knock" (significantly) and "Blockbusters" (nonsignificantly). For "Every Second Counts," the usual age effect was present. Once again, this pattern of results suggests that interest and motivation to understand what a program was about, and how it should be played, may be related to the perceived age appropriateness of the program.

The overall pattern of significant and nonsignificant differences within and between programs suggests that the actual nature of the program, whether game show based or pure quiz, and whether "easy" or "difficult" in terms of questions, are important to memory and comprehension. Despite all that, memory for what happened to the contestants and how the game or quiz was actually played will be well recalled by children of any age if they are keen to watch. That is, motivation and interest rather than cognitive ability predicts what children will take away from watching. It is only where the knowledge being tested consists of what could be called "general knowledge" (i.e., quiz questions and answers) that cognitive ability rather than any motivational attribute of the viewer comes to the fore. These findings taken as a whole are interesting because the three programs viewed differed greatly in their presentation. "Knock Knock" was produced for children, had children as contestants, and involved much running about. "Every Second Counts" was a family-based program involving adults as contestants and was basically quite stationary and involved fairly simple questions mostly involving a right or wrong answer and thus, by chance, one could be right half of the time. "Blockbusters" was produced for older children, involved quite complex cued questions where the first letter of the answer was given, and the setting was very static and predictable. Despite all these differences, children of all ages easily understood the rules of the game and remembered well who won what and how much was won. Only with recall of the answers given in the programs did age effects appear in line with the objective difficulty of the questions.

General Content and Rules of the Game—A Closer Look

Quiz shows have been attacked for being merely a form of celebration of consumption, glorifying consumer goods (e.g., Goodwin & Whannel, 1990). Our own qualitative and quantitative research cited in this book also show that children are interested in the prizes awarded in game and quiz shows. But is their viewing governed solely by avarice or at least vicarious avarice?

When we look at "Knock Knock," a child's program with minimal prizes, we find that recall to questions that asked "What did Monica win?" "What was the amount won by Monica overall?" and "What prizes did the first-round losers get?" were 85%, 90%, and 92%, respectively. This does suggest that prizes are a key attraction for viewers. However, when we asked "What career did Monica wish to pursue?" no less than 91% of our respondents recalled this correctly. Thus, although memory for prize-related general content is high, it is no higher than for nonprize-related general content. In addition, the highest percentage correct recall — 100% — was for a quiz item concerning the name of a television program that had nothing to do with money.

With "Every Second Counts," which is an adult quiz show with expensive prizes (consumables and holidays), 92% of the children recalled the first of many prizes won in the quiz, 89% remembered where the holiday was that was won, and 86% could correctly recall what the losers took home. Once again, however, 91% of our respondents also remembered which company one of the contestants worked for—a piece of information completely unrelated to the winning of prizes. The highest recall score in "Every Second Counts," as with "Knock Knock" was on a "quiz item" and not on a prize-related general content question.

This, by now familiar, pattern was repeated with our third quiz show—"Blockbusters." This quiz show is targeted to older adolescents and the prizes involve expensive consumables, training courses, and worldwide travel. In the episode shown to the children, a contestant named Graham was the reigning champion. His previous winnings were recounted in the show. Some 61% of our respondents could recall what they were; 90% remembered what he won in his last "Gold Run" that took place in the middle of the transmission. A new champion performed his first Gold Run near the end of the transmission and 92% remembered what he won for completing it successfully. In addition, 99% could recall what losers take away as consolation prizes and 72% remembered what one contestant said about her sister and 68% remembered why the host asked one of the contestants to "show his muscles." These last general content recalls show excellent memory for events that occurred in the quiz that were not concerned with winning expensive prizes.

Further evidence that the focus on prize winning is only one of the many foci of attention in viewers of quiz shows is the fact that 96% of candidates who had not seen "Blockbusters" before could recall exactly the number of seconds that a contestant has to complete the Gold Run (i.e., answer a series of questions whose answers were cued by initial letters, successful completion involving getting from one side of the quiz board to the other).

This last finding takes us into rules of the game memory. If quizzes have attraction for children purely because of their prize element then the rules of the game become largely incidental and an obstacle to be endured on the way to seeing who wins what. If, on the other hand, children are actively involved in quiz shows and form allegiances with contestants or are in competition with them then the rules of engagement become important. If this is the case then our children should show good recall of the rules.

In "Knock Knock," somewhat paradoxically given it is targeted on the young age group of viewers (8–10 years), the rules are quite complex involving contestants being placed in a "skip" (or sin bin) for wrong answers, traffic lights that signal whether contestants can proceed or not onto the next stage of the game, and so on. Despite this, recall of such rules ranged from 61% (for "what is the purpose of the parking meter?") to 89% (for "how many points do contestants start the second round with?"). For "Every Second Counts," recall ranged from 53% (for "How many seconds can you win in the first round?") to 86% (for "How many seconds are awarded in the general round?"). "Blockbusters" exhibited a range of rule recall from 67% correct recall for "the number of games that have to be won before you can do a Gold Run?" to 96% correct recall of the time constraints operating in such a Gold Run.

There seems little evidence in these figures that children do not set out to understand how games are played or quizzes are negotiated. If prize winning were the sole reason for watching quiz shows there seems no reason to devote cognitive effort to understand what has to be done to win those prizes. The fact that rules are well understood clearly indicates that children are getting more out of quiz and game shows than vicarious pleasure in acquisitive behavior. In the light of these performance levels on all content, rule, and quiz-item recall, unrelated to prize winning, children in this study would seem to be telling the truth when they aver that the prize element of game and quiz shows is not their chief motive for viewing such programs.

Gender of Respondents

Gender was not a significant factor for any of the programs nor was it a significant factor in obtaining any of the different types of knowledge or information communicated by the different programs.

Fluency in English

As can be seen from Table 7.11, fluency in English was at best a weak effect. This was a significant factor in "Knock Knock" for OE recall of quiz items [$F(1,77) = 15.12$, $p < .001$], with children who had English as a first language performing better. Fluency in English was also a significant effect in MC recall for general content [$F(1,76) = 4.61$, $p < .04$], but this time ESL children did better.

With "Every Second Counts," fluency in English was again significant in OE recall of quiz items [$F(1,64) = 7.83$, $p < .01$] again with English as a first language children performing better. With this program, however, this quiz-item recall superiority also held for MC [$F(1,64) = 4.41$, $p < .04$].

With "Blockbusters," children with English as a first language did better

TABLE 7.11
Memory for Aspects of Program Content as a Function of Language Ability

Program Viewed	Fluency in English	Multiple-Choice Questions			Open-Ended Questions		
		General Content	Rules of Game	Quiz Items	General Content	Rules of Game	Quiz Items
"Knock Knock"	English as second language	3.60[a]	3.70[b]	7.40[c]	2.85[d]	4.25[e]	4.35[f]
	English as first language	4.47	3.42	10.15	2.56	4.07	4.98
"Every Second Counts"	English as second language	3.17[g]	3.50[h]	6.08[i]	4.58[j]	0.58[k]	4.75[l]
	English as first language	3.19	4.41	8.81	4.28	0.80	6.09
"Blockbusters"	English as second language	2.50[g]	4.69	7.77[i]	4.27[j]	1.38[m]	7.00[n]
	English as first language	2.76	5.24	7.50	4.18	1.70	6.48

Maximum scores possible: [a]Max = 8 [d]Max = 3 [g]Max = 4 [j]Max = 5 [m]Max = 2
[b]Max = 4 [e]Max = 6 [h]Max = 6 [k]Max = 1 [n]Max = 9
[c]Max = 12 [f]Max = 7 [i]Max = 14 [l]Max = 10

than children without English as a first language only on MC recall of the rules of the game [$F(1,74) = 5.11, p < .03$]. Language ability did not appear as a significant effect in any other condition.

Overall then, language ability proved to be a weak effect in information acquisition from entertainment (quiz) programs. Where it did appear English as first language children performed marginally better.

Previous Viewing Experience

Children have their favorite programs and it would be logical to assume that more attention will be paid to a favored program and further, that the greater the attention paid to a program the more its messages and content should be absorbed. To look at this hypothesis we had children rate the program they had seen out of 10 and then used this rating to divide viewers into those who had high, medium, and low appreciation and then looked at recall as a function of this. However, out of 18 possible cases only in 3 were different appreciation levels found to be associated with significantly different recall levels.

For "Every Second Counts," there was an inverse linear relationship between appreciation and recall of quiz items. Thus, for OE recall, those children who had lowest appreciation scores scored highest, those with medium appreciation scored slightly less, and those who had the highest appreciation scored lowest [$F(2,63) = 4.06, p < .02$] with the means, out of a possible 14 being 10.60, 8.40, and 7.35, respectively. This inverse linear relationship held for MC recall of quiz items also [$F(2,63) = 3.46, p < .04$] with the means, out of 10, being ordered 6.70, 6.23, and 5.08, respectively.

"Blockbusters" produced one result (out of 6) in which appreciation was a significant influence. Again, this was for MC recall of quiz items but this time the relationship was curvilinear [$F(2,73) = 3.50, p < 0.04$], with the means out of 9, being: low appreciation, 5.59; medium appreciation, 7.21; high appreciation, 6.80.

Clearly then, appreciation is a poor predictor of information pick-up from entertainment programs. Where it is associated with such activity the relationship is complex.

Given that certain quiz and game shows can be quite complex affairs, we were interested to know if heavy viewing of such programs in general would make understanding of a specific quiz game easier. If it did we should find that heavy viewers of such genres should score well, especially in terms of the rules of the game. However, when we looked at this factor across the three programs, of the 18 conditions, and the 6 specific conditions involving rules, in only one case was weight of quiz viewing found to be important. Interestingly, this isolated finding was in the rules of the game category under OE recall for "Knock Knock" [$F(1,77) = 10.41, p < .002$], where medium to heavy quiz viewers outperformed light viewers.

General Information Absorption

Having looked at specific recall of different aspects of knowledge gain across the three types of program, as a function of several factors, the overall importance of these factors can be gauged by looking at them in terms of total recall. These totals, as a function of the factors of interest, are presented in Table 7.12.

As one would expect, when discrete scores were collapsed into an omnibus total mean score, many effects disappear. From the Table 7.12 it can be seen that age alone endured as a reliable factor for all three

TABLE 7.12
Summary: Factors Related to Memory for Quiz Show Content

		Program Viewed		
Factors		"Knock Knock"	"Blockbusters"	"Every Second Counts"
Age	9–10	25.86**	24.88*	21.65*
	11–12	29.00	29.67	29.00
	13–14	31.04	30.45	30.86
Gender	Male	28.82	27.85	26.85
	Female	28.73	27.78	27.32
Fluency in English	English as a second language	26.15***	27.62	23.08***
	English as a first language	29.66	27.92	27.91
Ever seen episode?	Yes	27.74	27.36	28.74***
	No	29.59	27.92	25.22
Interest in quiz activity	Low	28.33	26.64	27.38
	High	29.09	28.39	26.71
Quiz favorites	Theme	34.20	30.60	21.00
	Game	28.16	27.42	27.29
	Quiz	29.17	27.96	29.00
Weight of quiz viewing	Medium/heavy	29.38	26.63	26.21
	Light	28.31	28.41	27.50
Appreciation of test program	High	27.57	28.66***	24.77
	Medium	29.09	28.92	28.30
	Low	30.57	24.66	30.00
Weight of viewing test program	Medium/heavy	28.37	27.13	26.56
	Light	29.25	28.26	27.53

Note. Maximum score possible = 40
*p < .001. **p < .01. ***p < .05.

programs. Language ability appeared as an important consideration in "Knock Knock" and "Every Second Counts," with children who had English as a first language performing better overall. Having seen the specific program episode before only had an effect with "Every Second Counts," and that effect was positive. Finally, appreciation of the program only had an influence for "Blockbusters," with high and medium appreciation scores being associated with high recall scores.

Learning From Quiz Shows

Following the same line of investigation as that used with the drama and science program studies, the next step in the analysis of children's responses to quiz shows was to examine any growth in their knowledge, contingent upon watching these programs. Knowledge growth was assessed by the difference in pre- and postviewing scores on those items that referred specifically to subject matter that appeared in the quiz shows and to which the children were exposed.

A series of two-way analyses of variance enabled us to compare test performance in relation to a range of factors including the children's age, gender, language ability, previous viewing experiences, familiarity with the programs, and program edition appreciation. These analyses were computed on each program separately.

Age. Age differences were found to be among the most significant of all. Mean scores on knowledge items during pre- and posttests for all three quiz show groups are presented in Table 7.13. For the "Knock Knock" group, both age [$F(3,76) = 13.90, p < .001$] and test [$F(1,76) = 158.85, p < .001$] were significant. From the table it can be seen that the older children performed better than the younger children and that posttest scores

TABLE 7.13
Age Differences in Knowledge of Program-Related Material Before and After Watching TV Quiz Shows

Program Viewed	Age	Pretest	Posttest
"Knock Knock"	9–10	5.05	8.68
	11–12	7.47	11.25
	13–14	8.52	13.20
"Every Second Counts"	9–10	4.65	7.48
	11–12	5.86	11.18
	13–14	5.19	11.29
"Blockbusters"	9–10	2.09	6.15
	11–12	3.00	9.00
	13–14	3.00	10.00

were much higher than the pretest scores. There was no interaction between age and test.

For "Every Second Counts," the two main effects and the interaction between age and test were all significant [Age: $F(2,63) = 10.52$, $p < .001$; Test: $F(1,63) = 200.79$, $p < .001$; Age x Test: $F(2,63) = 8.79$, $p < .001$].

As with "Knock Knock," the older children performed better than the younger children, and the posttest scoring was higher than the pretest scoring for "Every Second Counts." However, the presence of a significant interaction indicates qualification of these main effects. This interaction is best explained by the fact that the two older age groups exhibited better knowledge gain than the youngest age group. This faster growth from pre- to posttest for the two older age groups relative to the youngest group is again observed in "Blockbusters." Although both age [$F(2,73) = 12.69$, $p < .001$] and test [$F(1,73) = 216.39$, $p < .001$] were significant main effects, they are qualified by the significant age x test interaction [$F(2,63) = 9.34$, $p < .025$].

Gender Effects.   Although the differences between pre- and posttest scoring were significant for "Knock Knock" [$F(1,77) = 159.90$, $p < .001$], "Every Second Counts" [$F(1,64) = 150.43$, $p < .001$], and for "Blockbusters" [$F(1,74) = 182.19$, $p < .001$], gender was a nonsignificant factor in all three program groups. In addition, there was no significant interaction between gender and test performance in respect of any of the three quiz programs analyzed.

Fluency in English Effects.   Children for whom English was either their first language or second language were compared on their pretest and posttest knowledge scores. The mean scores are presented in Table 7.14.

Once again there were significant differences between tests, reiterating results reported earlier. Fluency in English ability, however, was a significant factor only for the "Knock Knock" group [$F(1,77) = 10.96$, $p < .001$] and for "Every Second Counts" [$F(1,64) = 5.51$, $p < .02$]. Fluency in English was unrelated to knowledge level among the "Blockbuster" group. In the two cases where language ability did appear as a main effect, children with English as a first language did better than ESL children. In no case, however, did language ability interact with test score producing differential knowledge growth pre- and postviewing.

Preferred Quiz Show Type.   The preferences that children had for specific types of quiz programs had some interesting, albeit marginally, significant effects upon knowledge level and growth.[1] Mean scores for

---

[1]A word of caution is in order here because some of the cell sizes in this analysis were small.

TABLE 7.14

Fluency in English Differences in Knowledge of Program-Related Material
Before and After Watching TV Quiz Shows

Program Viewed	Fluency in English	Pretest	Posttest
"Knock Knock"	English as second language	5.50	8.85
	English as first language	7.58	11.93
"Every Second Counts"	English as second language	4.50	8.00
	English as first language	5.39	10.35
"Blockbusters"	English as second language	2.81	8.58
	English as first language	2.50	7.78

pre- and posttests for each quiz show group are shown in Table 7.15 as a function of the nature of children's preferences.

Taken at face value, analyses of these means indicated that test was significant in all three program cases (all $ps < .001$). Further significant effects were found for the "Knock Knock" and "Every Second Counts" groups. For "Knock Knock," preference was found to be a significant factor [$F (2,76) = 3.34$, $p < .05$], with a preference for "theme" eventuating in much better recall than a preference for game or quiz formats. For "Every Second Counts," preference and test interacted [$F(2,63) = 3.15$, $p < .05$], best explained by the fact the children who preferred either game or quiz format produced much better knowledge gain scores (pre- to posttest score differences) than did those children who preferred theme.

In general, however, the stability of these scores is questionable given the

TABLE 7.15

Preferred Quiz Type and Pretest Versus Posttest General Knowledge of
Quiz-Related Material

Program Viewed	Type Preference	Pretest	Posttest	Number Preferring
"Knock Knock"	Theme	10.60	14.20	(5)
	Game	7.00	10.93	(56)
	Quiz	6.56	11.00	(18)
"Every Second Counts"	Theme	5.17	7.00	(6)
	Game	5.13	10.13	(48)
	Quiz	5.67	10.58	(12)
"Blockbusters"	Theme	3.20	9.40	(5)
	Game	2.73	7.71	(45)
	Quiz	2.27	8.38	(26)

low number of children who preferred theme in all three program types. Thus, the conclusions that may be drawn must be accepted to be provisional and subject to revision.

Program Appreciation Effects

We were also interested to see whether the extent to which a child appreciated a program would influence his or her knowledge growth concerning that program. The relevant mean scores are presented in Table 7.16, where it can be seen that for certain programs, preference did seem to make a difference, but not in the way expected.

Analyses revealed that for all three program groups, test was a significant factor (all $ps <.001$). For both "Knock Knock" [$F(2,76) = 7.08$, $p<.002$] and for "For Every Second Counts" [$F(2,63) = 3.64$, $p<.03$] but not for "Blockbusters," appreciation was negatively associated with recall. Thus, as appreciation of the program increased, recall of program-related material decreased. This factor did not enter into any significant interactions with test, thus indicating its robustness. A cautionary note should perhaps again be entered concerning the robustness of these findings because of the unequal cell sizes, especially for those categories of low appreciation in "Knock Knock" and "Every Second Counts," relative to the other two categories of appreciation.

Knowledge Gain — A Closer Look

What we hope has been conveyed by the previous sections is that there is clear evidence that children can learn incidentally from watching game and quiz shows. What may not be so clearly communicated is the magnitude of

TABLE 7.16
Program Appreciation and Pretest Versus Posttest General Knowledge of Quiz-Related Material

Program Viewed	Appreciation Level	Pretest	Posttest
"Knock Knock"	Low	9.29	13.07
	Medium	7.47	11.53
	High	5.88	9.97
"Every Second Counts"	Low	5.80	12.10
	Medium	5.27	10.23
	High	4.96	8.73
"Blockbusters"	Low	2.47	6.47
	Medium	2.63	8.67
	High	2.66	8.40

gain that we observed. It may be speculated that if an educational method was developed that could produce the gain scores that we obtained there it would be heralded as a major educational breakthrough!

What is also very interesting is that the magnitude of gain occurred across different program formats. Thus, in "Knock Knock" question answering occurs almost as an incidental requirement to contestants frenetically getting to knock on a door through which celebrities would appear. The game element swamps the questioning element to a large extent, at least perceptually. In "Every Second Counts" the questions are more clearly foregrounded but are used mainly as a vehicle for the presenter to raise laughs, at least in the early rounds. Only in the last round are questions foregrounded but even here they are "perceptually" swamped by a focus on lights that have to be put out within a time period that is clearly displayed and presented in a countdown format. Tension, anxiety, and excitement govern this phase of "Every Second Counts" for viewers, rather than cool analytic processing of the answers being given in rapid succession. "Blockbusters" is altogether different. Here the question-and-answer aspect is paramount. Nothing else is happening, and the quiz board only changes as a result of correct responses. Because there is a time constraint imposed on answering, viewers are actually focused on the answer to be given and are thus waiting eagerly for it. Even in the Gold Run, which is time constrained, viewers hear the answer before the board changes and thus have a chance to work out if it is right or wrong.

Despite all these very different contexts for the giving of answers what surprised us was that the magnitude of gain was fairly similar whatever the program viewed. Thus, for "Knock Knock" the average gain from pre- to posttest was 35% and the biggest gain was from a pretest score of 11% to a 70% correct posttest to the question "What color is the ribbon on a medal that is the symbol of the highest order of bravery?". The average gain in "Every Second Counts" was 34% with the biggest gain being from 29% in pretest to 83% in posttest to the question "In which sport would you compete for the Rowse Cup?". For "Blockbusters," the mean percentage gain was 40%, with the biggest pretest–posttest difference being 77% to the question "How many teams take part in the Home Counties Rugby Union Championships?".

These findings for quiz shows are reminiscent of the pattern of learning we observed for information (science) programs in chapters 5 and 6 where, despite large program format differences—single topic versus magazine format—the patterns of knowledge acquisition were broadly the same. In this chapter, quizzes that ranged from adult- to child-focused; from frenetic to staid; and, from formats that rendered questions and answers almost obscure to those that placed them totally central to the program, all were capable of generating information pick-up and knowledge growth, and in similar proportions.

Clearly, then, quizzes have attributes that have, until now, been largely unanticipated and have, therefore, remained largely untapped.

DISCUSSION

Television quiz shows are a popular program format with children. However, it would be wrong to treat all quiz shows in the same light. The research reported in this chapter clearly showed that children during their teenage and preteenage years hold varied opinions about the genre in general that become more focused when they are pressed for their views about specific quiz shows.

The appeal of the genre stems centrally from an active involvement and participation in the games played in these programs. Children say that they enjoy trying to answer the questions themselves and compete both with the contestants on screen and with other members of their family. There are allegiances formed with on-screen competitors and involvement can be generated through identifying with contestants and willing them to win. This, however, is not such a strong motive for watching. Seeing people win prizes is named as important by some children but although presented as the main goal in many quiz shows on television, this element is less significant than enjoyment of the game itself in relation to the overall appeal of a show.

Children thus report getting involved in quiz shows by vicariously taking part at home. This was more important than identification with contestants; children did not widely perceive quiz show contestants to be like people they knew.

After examining general attitudes about quiz shows, we explored children's opinions about the specific programs shown to them in the study. To recap, these three shows could be differentiated in terms of the age group at which they were directed. "Knock Knock" was aimed at young children in the 9–14 age range; "Blockbusters" was designed for the mid- to late-teen audience; and "Every Second Counts" was a prime-time show for the entire family.

General attitudes revealed that a majority of children enjoyed these programs but only a minority reported any degree of regularity or loyalty in their viewing of them. There were marked age differences in enjoyment of "Knock Knock" and "Blockbusters" that reflected the target markets at which they were aimed. The family show, "Every Second Counts," was enjoyed widely by all age groups, although most especially by the youngest children (ages 9–10). Further questioning explored opinions about specific features of these shows.

Presenters were generally praised for explaining the rules of the game clearly and helping to put contestants at ease. However, they were criticized by many children for talking too much to contestants. Involvement with quiz shows was characterized principally in the case of all three shows used in this study, by a feeling among the children that such programs can help you learn new things. This was felt to be especially the case with the teenage show "Blockbusters," which was perhaps the most difficult of the three in terms of questions contestants had to answer. This was further reflected in the finding that a majority of children who watched an edition of "Blockbusters" said that contestants have to be clever to answer the questions. Only minorities of those children who watched the other two shows agreed with the same opinion. Thus, although there were certain common elements to the three quiz shows, children did distinguish between them on other attributes.

There were also age-related differences in opinion about these shows. "Knock Knock" appealed much more to 9- to 10-year-olds than to older children, and these younger children were also far and away the most likely to think that its questions were difficult. This is not surprising given the fact that "Knock Knock" is specifically made for younger children. All children felt that "Blockbusters" had an educational function, whereas the youngest children most often found its questions to be difficult. "Every Second Counts" was felt to help viewers learn new things most often by 9- to 10-year-olds, who also felt that contestants had to be clever to answer the questions. Older children, however, did not generally perceive this show to pose any serious difficulties with its questions.

Profiles of opinion about attributes that were central to children's enjoyment of quiz shows varied across the three test programs. These results indicated that children obtain different kinds of gratification from different quiz shows, quite apart from those broad factors that characterize their overriding appeal to young audiences. Although all three shows were generally found to be easy to follow, differences in opinion occurred in respect of the perceived value of prizes to winners and losers, and in regard to the degree of excitement generated by the climax to each program.

Turning from what children claimed to get out of quiz shows to what they actually remembered from the test programs, the findings showed that children of all ages performed reasonably well in remembering aspects of the general content of each program and very well in terms of their understanding of how the game is played in each case. Memory for information picked up from quiz show questions was poorer, but was nevertheless respectable. Older children performed significantly better than younger children throughout. Gender of respondents made no difference to their memory and comprehension performance, but language ability had a weak effect. Children whose first language was English exhibited better memory for general content and quiz items than did those for whom English was their second language, among the group who watched the children's quiz show "Knock Knock."

Viewing experience with quiz shows and appreciation of these shows showed some relationship with memory for program content. These relationships were, however, by no means consistent across the test programs. For "Every Second Counts" for instance, children who exhibited the highest appreciation scores had the poorest memory for quiz items. Among the "Blockbusters" group the relationship between appreciation and recall of content was curvilinear. Those children showing moderate levels of appreciation performed better on memory for quiz content than did low or high appreciation scorers.

Reported weight of viewing of quiz shows was connected significantly with program-content recall only among those children who watched "Knock Knock." This show, readers will remember, had the youngest target audience of the three. Here, medium to heavy reported viewers of quiz shows outperformed light reported viewers.

There was, finally, some evidence of children being able to learn from quiz shows. In previewing and postviewing tests of general knowledge on items that featured as questions in the shows, performance improved after viewing compared with before watching each show. There was also a significant interaction of this effect with age for all three test program groups. In the case of two shows, "Knock Knock" and "Every Second Counts," older children outperformed younger children. In the case of "Blockbusters," however, younger children, surprisingly, benefited more from watching the show.

There was further evidence that children's degree of preference for different forms of quiz shows as well as their general appreciation of the three shows, were related to general knowledge growth as a function of viewing. Among "Knock Knock" viewers, a preference for theme shows enhanced general knowledge growth, whereas for viewers of "Every Second Counts," a preference for game or quiz formats enhanced general knowledge growth after viewing the show. In the case of general appreciation of the shows, in two cases ("Knock Knock" and "Every Second Counts") higher appreciation was linked with lower knowledge growth.

In summary, even entertainment-oriented programs such as television quiz shows, often regarded as the lowest common denominator programming by critics, are capable of imparting not only enjoyment, but also knowledge to children. Children get actively involved in such shows at an emotional and a cognitive level, they find such programs challenging, and can acquire new information and knowledge from them.

Theoretical Explanations of Memory for Quiz Shows

Unlike police dramas or science programs that present information that can be related to preexisting knowledge structures and schemas, quiz shows seem to deal with pieces of information that have no necessary connection with anything that came immediately before or after their presentation. How, then, can we begin to explain the relatively good memory shown by children for this type of information?

A clue may be provided by one of the motivations given by children for watching quiz shows — to compete against the contestants. This means that when watching quiz shows, but not when watching science or drama programs, children may be engaged in explicit generation of answers. This, after all, is the only way they could beat the contestant, by getting their answers out faster.

This fact takes quiz shows into the realm of learning by doing, an acknowledged effective way of acquiring knowledge. Slamecka and Graf (1978) designed a laboratory procedure for studying the effects on memory of generation of to-be-remembered material. They compared two conditions. The first involved a subject merely reading an answer to a question. The second condition involved the subject generating the (same) answer to the question. They found in a later memory test for these answers, that the "generate" subjects did much better at recalling the answers that did the "read-only" group. Slamecka and Graf called this the *generation effect*.

Now one of the most striking aspects of the generation effect is its broad generality. It seems to work under a great many conditions and with many different types of material (e.g., Greene, 1989, 1992).

However, there would seem to be a problem when we try to apply this theory of generation to quiz show memory because although the children may wish to beat the contestants it may be that they cannot produce a correct response (because they do not know it) and thus they are not, in fact, generating an answer. However, precisely this situation has been found in the laboratory. Slamecka and Fevreiski (1983) examined the situation where situations were deliberately set up to ensure generation attempts failed to produce an answer and the answer was eventually presented by the experimenter. On later recall tests of all the answers, those answers that had been successfully generated and those that had been attempted but failed, and had eventually been supplied by the experimenter, were all better recalled than the same answers recalled by another group who had merely read all the answers.

Thus, somewhat paradoxically, subjects do not have to actually generate an answer to bring about a generation effect. Rather, the effect is found as long as the subject tries to generate an item.

There is, however, one further problem with applying the generation effect literature to our current quiz performance. This is that when researchers have actually looked directly for a generation effect with general knowledge information items (e.g., "What is the capital of Finland?") they have not always found such an effect. Thus, although Blaxton (1989) did obtain such an effect, Carroll and Nelson (1993) did not. These latter researchers in fact conducted no fewer than seven experiments with a testing delay of 1 week and found the generation effect in only one of the experiments. Until further work is done on real-world knowledge and testing at ecologically valid intervals, as in learning for school-based tests, over an extended time scale, our application of the generation effect to explain our good quiz memory will have to remain tentative.

A number of theoretical accounts have been offered for the generation effect. One account can be called the *effort hypothesis*. This states that the more effort that is expended in trying to generate an answer the better memory will be for that answer, whether generated or eventually given. Now effort cannot be an explanation because it is only a description. One must go beyond this description to explain why effort influences memory. It is known that effort at generation only has an influence on memory if the to-be-generated answer is sensible and related to the semantic memory of the generator (i.e., the generated word has meaning). For example, the generation effect does not appear when the to-be-generated item is a nonsense word. Now given that generation of a nonsense word is likely to be as effortful as generating a sensible (real) word and perhaps more so, this finding shows effort per se cannot be the explanation of good memory for generated or attempted-generation words or knowledge items. Thus, effort cannot be responsible for the generation effect (Greene, 1988, 1992).

In addition, effort accounts of the generation effect can only be plausible if there is convincing evidence that effort inevitably influences memory. But as Mitchell and Hunt (1989) argued, "changes in cognitive effort are not sufficient to produce changes in memory" (p. 343). Indeed, given our experimental paradigm throughout the book, it could be argued that we have been looking at incidental memory every bit as much as intentional, effortful, memory. Yet good recall has been obtained across programming genres.

An alternative to the effort account of the generation effect — or rather a refinement of it — is the rehearsal account. Rehearsal as an account of memory has a long and distinguished pedigree. Up until about 1972, memory was held to be a direct function of the amount of rehearsal given to an item. When children generate their answers they tend to repeat them while waiting for the contestant to respond. This repetition would be classically defined as rehearsal. Note, however, that attempted generation that did not result in an answer would be hard pressed to fall within this definition of rehearsal. Thus, rehearsal as an account of our quiz results is not without its problems. In the event it is unlikely that rehearsal can explain the quiz generation effects. This is suggested by Watkins and Sechler (1988), who examined incidental memory for read and generated items. Because subjects were led to believe that their memories would not be tested, they had no reason to engage in rehearsal of read or generated items. Nonetheless, the generation effect still appeared. Indeed, the generation effect in this incidental set-up was larger than it is often found to be in intentional generation type experiments. Thus, presence of a generation effect when subjects were not employing rehearsal strategies is inconsistent with Slamecka and Katsaiti's (1987) rehearsal account of the generation effect.

The currently favored explanation of the generation effect is some variant of a multiprocess theory (Burns, 1990; Greene, 1992; Hirshman & Bjork, 1988). Thus, McDaniel, Waddill, and Einstein (1988) offered a three-process theory of generation effects whereby the act of generation produces, first, increased processing of the answer generated, second, increased strengthening of the link between the eliciting question and the generated answer, and, third, increased processing of the set of generated answers. Thus item—relational—and whole-context information processing is increased by generation effort. Although this degree of complexity of multiprocess theories of generation effects gives a feeling of over elaborativeness and vagueness, and appears difficult to disprove, it is likely that because of its ubiquitous nature any explanation that is remotely adequate will have to have something like this level of complexity.

Of late, some order has been brought into the theoretical speculation around the generation effect that sits easily with the overall tenor of this book. Fiedler, Lachnit, Fay, and Krug (1992) compared four accounts of the effect. First, the selective displaced rehearsal account of Slamecka and Katsaiti (1987), which was outlined earlier. Second, the degree of elaboration hypothesis of Graf (1980) and McElroy and Slamecka (1982), which states that although attempting to generate an answer the person must search in the "semantic neighborhood" of the target item and thus creates more semantic associations than would be the case if the answer was merely supplied with no need to attempt a generation. The third account investigated was that suggested by Hirshman and Bjork (1988) and Nairne and Widner (1987), which reflects the encoding-specificity interpretation of memory formulated by Tulving and Thompson (1973). This account suggests that generating an answer during learning (encoding) is more like giving an answer at testing (when once again the person has to try to come up with an answer) than is being supplied with an answer at encoding but then having to supply an answer at testing. The last account investigated was the mobilization of cognitive resources hypothesis. This argues that genuine motivational factors are involved in the generation effect. Generation activities mobilize additional cognitive resources that eventuate in better memory. Thus, this account explains the generation effect as a motivational one brought about by the learner recruiting more cognitive capacity under generation conditions than he or she recruits when merely receiving answers.

Fiedler et al. (1992) concluded, on the basis of several experiments, in favor of the mobilization of cognitive resources account and said, "the contribution of motivational factors to the generation effect should not be neglected" (p. 170).

This last study serves to demonstrate that despite the difficulty of explaining the effect, nonetheless the effect does indicate how specific processes — such as memory — cannot be considered apart from the subject's mental attitude to, involvement with, and active processing of the medium. If the viewers were not keen to "beat the contestants" then they would not be motivated to generate answers (or be vigilant as to the answers they could not generate) and hence would not learn from quiz shows. This chapter clearly shows that discrete information can be learned from prime-time entertainment shows that have information "giving" only as a minor part of their production.

As we see in the next chapter, where we develop a model of cognitive impact, "abilities to process" may be present in a viewer but unless and until they are triggered by "motivations to process" they will not be engaged and hence will not allow the viewed program to have impact. Once again, we stress that it is very much the viewer, rather than the program, that mediates impact.

8 Interpreting the Cognitive Impact of Television

This book has discussed a series of research studies designed to investigate children's learning from television. A guiding assumption for this investigation was a theoretical view of children's involvement with television that laid stress on an active, cognitive, information-processing notion of learning. This perspective assumed that children's cognitive learning from television could be influenced by their own predispositions, background knowledge and attitudes, cognitive developmental level, and language ability. In addition, it was reasoned that there might be program attributes that could effect learning.

This stress on what the child brings to the viewing situation was thought to be important for at least two reasons. First, if we could establish what their preexisting knowledge, beliefs, opinions, or attitudes were, we could then explore the extent to which they could be augmented, changed, or shaped by the content of the television programs the children watched.

Research elsewhere had emphasized the role of existing knowledge in understanding and organizing new information (Brown, Bransford, Ferrara, & Campione, 1983). With regard to television programs, real-life experience with or knowledge about the types of people and situations depicted should help viewers to understand program content (Hoffner & Cantor, 1991).

Second, it is likely that the influence television has is dependent on the information or kinds of enjoyment children take from it. If they fail to absorb its contents to any great extent, it is unlikely that television will effect any significant changes in children's knowledge, beliefs, or attitudes. But, as we have argued, what children take from television may be critically dependant on what they bring to the viewing situation. In other words, a knowledge of the viewer's background experiential status is necessary both to understand the possible impact of television and how that impact is mediated.

A number of earlier studies have indicated that familiarity with the roles, events, and situations depicted in television programs can affect viewers' comprehension of television portrayals (W. Collins, 1984; W. Collins & Wellman, 1982; W. Collins & Zimmermann, 1975; Newcomb & Collins, 1979).

The current research examined cognitive-level learning (i.e., knowledge gain, belief/attitude change, program content retention, and comprehension) from three program genres. Learning from television as such has generally been measured in relation to factual programs that contain explicit information content. A substantial body of research literature exists on this type of learning from television, especially with regard to learning from news programs (e.g., Gunter, 1987a; Robinson & Levy, 1986). Extending this dominant trend, this new series of studies with children also explored memory and comprehension of "factual" information content from two other primarily entertainment-oriented genres—drama and light entertainment in the form of quiz shows.

This chapter reviews the main findings for each genre and discusses them in the context of other relevant research and theory. In so doing, it attempts to identify important themes and lessons to emerge from this research as a whole.

 The key themes are threefold: (a) the extent to which children remember and comprehend the contents of programs they have watched; (b) the impact of programs on related areas of knowledge, attitudes, and beliefs; and (c) the role of mediating variables such as age, gender, language ability, and television viewing habits upon learning from programs.

MEMORY AND COMPREHENSION OF PROGRAMS

We can begin by reviewing what this research revealed about children's retention and comprehension of television program content. The studies reported in this book explored children's cognitive information processing from three broad program types: drama, factual, and entertainment. Drama was represented by two British-made police drama series. The factual category focused on five science programs, three of which were made especially for children and two of which were aimed at the general family audience. The entertainment category comprised three television quiz shows, one aimed at preteens, the second one at teenagers, and the third at the adult audience. It may be helpful to readers if we review the results for each program genre and then pull together the threads of these separate findings into a coherent statement about children's memory and comprehension of television programs.

Drama

Children's impressions of the two drama programs used in this research provided a measure of subjective comprehension that accompanied more objective measures of program content retention. These sets of measures focused specifically on the perceived realism of each program and children's ability to follow the story line.

Children's perceptions of those aspects of the real world dealt with by two British-made police dramas were measured in terms of the children's impressions of the realism of the settings, characters, and events portrayed.

Asked about police dramas in general, children perceived a degree of realism in the characters portrayed and the problems featured in contemporary television drama of this sort. The degree of perceived realism was weaker among older children. This trend was mirrored by a decrease in "involvement" with such programs in the sense of believing that such shows could teach valuable social lessons, make you think, and evoke empathetic feelings.

When the "reality" issue was raised in terms of the specific program the children had been shown, they felt that although the crimes dealt with tended to reflect the crimes real-life police deal with, the "clear-up" rate and the roles portrayed were felt to be unrealistic.

Subtle differences appeared between the two program-viewing groups with respect to specific attributes of each program's portrayals. These differences indicated how important it is to explore children's reality perceptions in respect of specific aspects of actual programs. Although broad distinctions across program genres in terms of their relative realism can provide some indication of how children respond to television, such simplistic measures fail to reveal deeper and more complex perceptual distinctions that children make about specific program content realism.

Following Story Lines. In terms of factual understanding, it was clear that our respondents were able to follow the story line of the episodes from the two British-made police drama series, although such understanding clearly increased with age. The children in the current research understood both explicitly presented material and inferential material only implied in story lines. There was little evidence here, then, for the view expressed by Sheppard (1990) that the greatest part of adult-oriented television viewed by children goes "over their heads." Although respondents here were slightly older than those of Sheppard, it is the case that in the "Juliet Bravo" group the children ages 9–10 actually outperformed the 11- to 12-year-olds, at least on certain measures of comprehension.

Factual (Science) Programs

Cognitive information gain might not be automatically expected from viewing of television drama, which is regarded by broadcasters and audiences as primarily an entertainment-oriented genre. With factual programs, however, there is an implicit assumption that viewers will learn something. The current research chose to investigate science programs as an exemplar of television's factual output. These posed an interesting type of televised subject matter for a number of reasons. First, a number of science programs were available for study on mainstream television at the time of the research. Second, these programs exhibited interesting variations in terms of intended audience (children or adults) and presentation format (matter-of-fact presentation, semi-dramatical reconstructions entirely studio-based, use of film reports, etc). Third, they varied in terms of content variety (single theme or multitopic). A further reason was a general concern, debated publicly, about poor general levels of science knowledge and the role mass media could play in making people more science aware.

Subjective Impressions.   We found that children of all ages appreciated that science programs on television are desirable and beneficial. They felt that such programs could communicate important information that they should be aware of. They further felt that prime-time slots were appropriate locations for such programs and that they should not be ghettoized on minority channels or only presented in schools programs. These positive perceptions held firm across the different program formats examined in this research, although the absolute level of appreciation did vary from one test program to another as a function of certain content and format differences and as a result of particular program loyalty or of being a frequent viewer of science programs in general.

Although it was found that children's perception and evaluation of informational television were very positive, both of the studies involving such programs raised issues of the children's involvement with them. Although the children did not report actively trying to avoid science programs, only about half of them went out of their way to watch these programs. In addition, few of the children reported discussing the content of science programs or their implications with friends or family members. Somewhat perplexingly, boys appeared to discuss the programs more than girls in one experiment but less in the other. Similarly, although the older age groups reportedly discussed televised science more than the younger age group in the second experiment, they discussed it less than the younger viewers in the first experiment. The clearest trend, present in both of the science program experiments, was that as children got older their involvement with science programming became less, and this held true for both boys and girls.

Objectively Measured Learning. A very clear finding was that children can learn from science programs—at least in the short term. Our research went beyond mere recall of facts given out explicitly in the programs to the testing of the children's comprehension of the program material. We also utilized different types of questioning that, at least potentially, would allow different statements to be made about how memory was organized and accessed after program viewing. Under relatively relaxed viewing conditions, and collapsing across different age ranges (7–15 years of age) and program format and complexity, the children were able to recall about 60% and comprehend over 50% of the test material.

In the first science program study, the children correctly recalled about two thirds (65%) of program content, scoring significantly better, however, on the children's science program (76%) compared with the adult science program (54%). Comprehension, overall, averaged 63% with relatively little difference between the two programs (65% vs. 61%). In the second science study, overall correct recall was 60% and overall comprehension was 53%. There were, once again, significant differences in rates of correct recall and comprehension of program content. Science programs made especially for child audiences produced better retention and understanding of information than did the prime-time program made for adult audiences.

Children recalled correctly about two thirds of program content from the children's science programs, "Owl TV" (65%) and "Know How" (67%), compared to less than half of the adult's science program "Tomorrow's World" (48%). Respective comprehension levels for these programs were 72%, 50%, and 44%.

The second study examined magazine programs that covered a number of different topics. Serial position effects were found in relation to item recall. In the case of two programs ("Tomorrow's World" and "Know How"), there were primacy and recency effects, whereas with the third program ("Owl TV") there was a clear primacy effect and a progressive decline in content recall across all successive items. Serial learning curves as observed with the first two programs, have been reported in relation to recall of broadcast news items (Gunter, 1979, 1980; Tannenbaum, 1954). Continued decrement of memory performance has also been shown to occur across successive news items (Gunter et al., 1980, 1981). The latter have been explained in terms of proactive interference whereby encoding, storage, and retrieval of one item or cluster of items, can impede cognitive information processing of subsequent items, particularly if all items deal with the same or similar subject matter.

Entertainment (Quiz) Programs

In line with our assumption that all television programs are multidimensional in terms of the nature of the messages they convey, and commensurate with our desire to explore children's cognitive learning from a variety of television programs, the last part of this research involved a light entertainment genre—the quiz or game show. Television quiz shows are a popular program form with children of all ages (Gunter et al., 1991).

We presented different groups of children with three different programs from the genre. "Knock Knock" was aimed at children in the 9–14 age range and involved elements of the game show in addition to the more straightforward question-and-answer quiz format. The second quiz program we used, "Blockbusters," was designed for the mid- to late-teen audience, and was the quintessential quiz show. Contestants sat behind a desk and answered questions fired by a quiz master, with the intention of beating their opponents to the "buzzer." The third quiz program presented was a prime-time show for the entire family. This show, "Every Second Counts," was more light-hearted than "Blockbusters" but had as a central format husband-and-wife teams competing against each other to gain points that would eventually lead to the couple with the greatest number of points playing for the "star prize."

Subjective Opinions About Quiz Shows. The children held varying opinions about quiz and game shows. Their chief reported motive for viewing was active involvement and participation in the games played in these types of programs. Children enjoyed trying to answer the questions themselves and competing with coviewing family members. In some cases they enjoyed identifying with and thus supporting particular contestants, but in other cases the children felt many of the contestants on television quizzes were "not like me."

An interesting topic was that of the prizes that could be won on quiz shows. Although the nature and value of the prize was a motivator to view for some, for others it played a subsidiary role in attracting viewers.

When we specifically addressed our questions to the programs that we had presented to the children, it appeared that only a minority had any degree of regularity or loyalty in viewing these programs. Clearly, we had not chosen the most popular examples of the genre. As would be expected, there were marked age differences in enjoyment of "Knock Knock" and "Blockbusters" that reflected the target audience at which they were aimed.

The family show, "Every Second Counts," however, was generally liked by all.

Although there were common elements to all of the three television quiz shows we presented, children distinguished between them on a number of attributes. Profiles of opinions about attributes that were central to children's enjoyment of quiz shows varied across the three test programs. These results indicated that children obtained different kinds of gratification from different quiz shows, quite apart from those broad factors that characterize their overriding appeal to young audiences. Although all three shows were generally found to be easy to follow, differences of opinion occurred in respect of the difficulty of questions, the perceived value of prizes to winners and losers, and in regard to the degree of excitement generated by the climax to each program.

Objective Learning From Quiz Shows.   Children of all ages performed reasonably well in the areas of remembering the general content of each program (e.g., who won what?), the rules of the game being played (e.g., how contestants achieved passage into the final round), and the answers given to the questions asked in the quiz element of each show. General content recall was best for the program targeted at adult audiences ("Every Second Counts"), but memory for rules of the game and quiz items was best for those programs aimed at younger audiences ("Blockbusters" and "Knock Knock").

IMPACT ON KNOWLEDGE, ATTITUDE, AND BELIEF

In addition to measuring children's immediate impressions, and memory and comprehension of programs just watched, this research also explored the impact of the programs on children's knowledge, attitudes, and beliefs. Postviewing performance on these measures was compared to previewing baselines, established 1 week earlier.

Drama

In relation to drama programs, we specifically wanted to know if young viewers' knowledge, attitudes, and beliefs about the police were in any way shaped or altered as a result of what they saw in the program shown to them. Comparing the responses given on pre- and postviewing occasions revealed that some perceptions and attitudes hardly changed at all, whereas others exhibited marked shifts. In addition, control groups, who did not see either program, also exhibited both shifts and stability in attitudes and opinions, but in slightly different ways.

We interpreted the experimental and control groups similarities and differences as reflecting the fact that in those aspects of social reality where firsthand experience was limited or nonexistent, children's beliefs, attitudes, and ideas were both unstable and malleable. Where exposure to mass media information relevant to these views is also minimal or reduced (as in the case of control groups in this study) those beliefs, attitudes, and ideas remain relatively unstable and subject to random fluctuations because they lack any firm anchor points.

Where exposure to relevant or related mass media information does occur, however, as by watching television programs, these relatively loosely held beliefs and ideas may be subject to change — stabilizing or altering — but in a principled way. This is illustrated in our research where beliefs and perceptions of the police held by children in the two viewing groups shifted in line with attributes and events depicted in the two programs, whereas those of the controls did not.

This suggests that television exposure has the ability to stabilize certain beliefs about aspects of the real world that are relatively firmly grounded (being based on many sources, perhaps including television), while being able to change those not so strongly held.

We have shown that, in fact, knowledge about jobs done by uniformed and plainclothed police officers did not exhibit marked changes after viewing, but such changes as there were showed an influence of age, victimization, and level of program comprehension.

Endorsement of different characteristics of policemen and policewomen again showed little change after viewing. However, the changes that were observed to occur were clearly related to dominant themes in the presented programs. For example, both controls and "The Bill" viewers shifted on a question relating to policewomen being fit, whereas the "Juliet Bravo" viewers exhibited no shift at all. The "Juliet Bravo" episode specifically addressed the fitness of a policewoman compared to the unfitness of several policemen. This is perhaps an example of what we indicated earlier concerning the possibility that in uncertain situations television content can serve to stabilize opinions already held. This stabilizing or consolidating effect of television can also be deduced in other aspects of our data concerning this issue. For example, we found a reduction in the number of factors found in a factor analysis of perceptions of policemen and policewomen following viewing of the drama programs compared with the number of factors that had emerged before viewing.

The data reported here are consistent with the cognitive model of construct accessibility. Certain constructs can be rendered more readily accessible from memory if they are supported or "reactivated" by incoming information. This priming process itself does not represent attitudinal or belief change, but is a cognitive activity that strengthens the body of knowledge and perceptions held about a particular entity (Higgins & King, 1981).

Another example of the possible consolidating or priming influence of television can be seen in the data concerning the perceived types of crime police have to deal with. Children in the control groups exhibited the greatest shifts in beliefs of all groups, whereas the main perceptual shift for the two viewing groups occurred in respect of two items that were prominent features of the plots in the presented programs — kidnapping and suicide.

We also looked at the influence of television on the opinions children held about the police. We found that children shown "Juliet Bravo" exhibited more shifts than those shown "The Bill" and quite a few of these shifts were program-linked. For example, children's impressions of policewomen improved substantially on a number of characteristics addressed by "Juliet Bravo" in which a police woman was in a position of authority. Policewomen were more often seen to be competent in catching criminals and as having a good chance of promotion after viewing this relevant episode. At the same time, there was a reduction in the number of children who believed that men were better at telling people what to do than women in the police. These findings, we believe, illustrate the potential of television drama to effect short-term shifts in children's opinions, where the latter have a specific and direct link with portrayals in the dramatic narrative.

It appears that selective priming of particular attributes of police officers occurred among children who watched one or other of the two television police drama episodes. One explanation of priming assumes that semantic memory, which contains the world knowledge of the individual, is an interlinked network consisting of nodes that represent constructs and links between the nodes that represent relations between constructs (J. Anderson, 1976; A. Collins & Loftus, 1975). When a node is activated during retrieval, the activation spreads instantaneously along the paths of the network to adjacent semantically related nodes. The more frequently a particular attribute of an object is activated, the more likely it is to be accessed from semantic memory in the future (Higgins, Bargh, & Lombardi, 1985).

An alternative explanation of how priming effects work is the storage bin model (Wyer & Srull, 1981, 1986). According to this model, long-term memory consists of a set of content specific bins. The constructs in each bin are stored on top of one another in the order in which they were previously primed.

The most recently primed construct is placed on top of the storage bin and is thus accessed first in the subsequent processing of information to which it is relevant. In the current experiment, recent exposure to a contemporary television police drama activated certain attributes of policemen and police women that colored children's perceptions of police officers, being more accessible immediately post viewing than they were prior to viewing. Constructs that are highly accessible from frequent or recent use will be accessed first in a task that requires individuals to match those constructs to a target stimulus. Thus, in responding to questions about the characteristics of police officers, the attributes portrayed in a recently watched contemporary television drama may, in the absence of alternative constructs, achieve prominence for child viewers, at least in the short term (see Bargh & Pietromonaco, 1982; James, 1986; Srull & Wyer, 1979).

Despite reports by some researchers that viewing habits are significantly related to what children take from television and thus the impact it has (Gerbner et al., 1979, 1980), we found that viewing patterns as reported by our respondents had only marginal links with their perceptions of crime and the police. In line with Pingree (1983), however, we did find that comprehension of program content mediated levels of knowledge gain about certain aspects of police work.

Just as contact with real police had been found to have little effect on story line comprehension, so too with impact. Such contact had little influence on changes in belief contingent upon viewing the police drama episodes.

In response to police drama episodes, therefore, the research served to reveal that children held varied beliefs about the police and their work in dealing with crime. Watching police drama episodes appeared to have some short-term effects on particular perceptions that concerned police characteristics that featured strongly in the programs. These priming effects were mediated by certain other factors, but it is clear that single episodes provided insufficient viewing experience to generate widespread and significant shifts in the children's real-world perceptions. Many of these perceptions appear to be unstable and, if anything, television programs that contain relevant context can act to stabilize them.

The fact that a single concentrated exposure to a police drama episode was capable of producing some short-term impact on the accessibility of certain constructs relating to police officers and the nature of police work, however, may mean that regular viewing of such programs could yield more lasting effects on children's perceptions of the police, particularly if there is an element of consistency in their portrayal across a television series. Further research on this topic might usefully examine the knowledge and attitude priming effects of exposure to varying numbers of episodes from a police television drama series.

Factual (Science) Programs

In both science experiments, knowledge growth from pretest levels to posttest levels was highly significant, and numerically substantial. Most interestingly, in terms of this last finding, exposure to television science programs seemed to contribute equally to all children, irrespective of their age. Because there were clear age differences in program retention, with older children scoring much higher than younger children initially, one might have expected the older children to gain more from program exposure but such was not the case; television programs seemed to be operating as a constant. That is, although initial and eventual levels of knowledge were always different, with eventual levels being higher than initial, younger and older viewers retained their relative differences. As we argue later, this is a finding of some importance.

Quiz Shows.

General knowledge questions were given to children before and after viewing three television quiz shows, based on questions used in those television quizzes. Significant improvements in knowledge scores were recorded after viewing a quiz show on those questions featured in the show. These results showed that children can and do learn from television even when information is contained in a primarily light entertainment context.

In expressing personal opinions about quiz shows, a great many of the children taking part in this study indicated that they believed that such programs can help viewers learn new things. This was a view held about quiz shows in general as well as about the specific shows used in this research. There was attitudinal evidence also that children can get involved with events in quiz shows, identify with contestants, and try to answer the questions themselves while viewing at home. This cognitively active involvement on the part of young viewers may create a psychological context in which learning can take place. Thus, subjective impressions of being able to learn from this form of television light entertainment were borne out by objective measures of knowledge gain.

In terms of knowledge growth, assessed by comparing postviewing scores on target items with previewing scores on these same items, children showed clear learning effects. The interesting finding was that this knowledge growth was fairly similar across all three quiz programs. Thus, it would seem to be the case that whether questions and their associated answers are backgrounded (as in "Knock Knock") or foregrounded as in "Blockbusters," children still "pick up" the answers and remember them, at least in the short term. This may support their contention that they really do watch quiz shows to learn new information and to compete with contestants and others. If they really watched for avaricious reasons then one would not predict good recall of answers given to questions that were swamped by gamelike hysterical activity and high-priced prizes.

MEDIATING VARIABLES

A variety of different kinds of background information were obtained from the children. This concerned their age, gender, and language ability. The latter variable was defined in terms of whether the child's first language was English or whether English, although fluent, was the child's second language. All children was asked about television viewing habits, both generally and in relation to the specific programs watched in these studies. Children were also differentiated in terms of relevant areas of background knowledge that might affect program comprehension. Children in the study with police drama programs were asked about the extent of their real-world contact with the police or crime, and those in one of the studies with science programs were asked about experience of relevant subjects at school. It was reasoned that any or all of these factors might be significant to cognitive learning from television.

Age

It is known that as children grow older they develop enhanced proficiency in television viewing. Greater sophistication in the reading of filmic codes and interpreting narrative structures leads to more effective information processing from programs and better all round levels of comprehension (Husson, 1982; Salomon, 1977). In addition to generic features that children can learn, there are idiosyncratic structural attributes of programs that relate to the way information in the program is organized. Such structures may be cognitively represented in the viewer's memory as a schema. Schemas facilitate information processing from stimulus materials by providing a framework within which new information can be ordered and by allowing inferences to be made where gaps in expected information exist (Taylor & Crocker, 1981).

The significance of well-developed program-related schemas may become increasingly important as content complexity increases (see Bryant & Rockwell, 1991). A relatively simple program may be easy to follow and understand anyway. A complex program may produce cognitive overload unless effective schemas are activated enabling greater ease of information organization. Experienced or regular viewers of such a program may be more likely to have developed program-related schemas that would enable them to process the factual information from that program more efficiently.

Age emerged as an important variable in distinguishing levels of performance on science program content retention and comprehension. However, age was highly correlated with general knowledge and, in fact, in multiple regression analyses, general knowledge swamped age as a predictor of most of the areas of measured performance. Only when general knowledge was removed from the analysis did age appear as a significant predictor of open-ended and multiple-choice recall and comprehension. Thus, it appears that it is not accumulated years (age), but rather accumulated knowledge and possibly developed information-processing skills that predict the amount of novel learning that will take place upon viewing a factual television program.

Turning to quiz shows, older children, in general, performed better than younger children, although not always. This age effect was clearly apparent in respect of remembering information based on questions and answers given in the quiz. Age differences were generally weaker, however, in relation to understanding how the game was played in the particular quiz show watched and general understanding of the quiz outcomes for particular contestants.

Gender and Language Ability

Although the children's gender and language facility had particular, local effects, such demographic variables could not be construed as major influences on learning from science-based informational television. Thus, we found that girls could learn science as well as boys, across the board, which contrasts with what might be predicted by notions of gender stereotyping in relation to science (e.g., Archer, 1992).

Again, children's gender and fluency in English made virtually no difference to their retention and comprehension of drama program material. Memory and comprehension of quiz show content, rules, or quiz-related general knowledge were also generally unrelated to the child's gender or first language, nor did they exhibit any relationship with differential rates of knowledge growth contingent upon viewing.

Viewing History

Past research on learning from television, whether from fictional or factual programs, has examined whether amounts of viewing are linked to television's impact upon knowledge, attitudes, and beliefs. The potential impact of televised fiction upon real-world perceptions was frequently measured in terms of relationships between global, self-report indicators of overall amount of television watched and beliefs about different aspects of social reality. This approach was used for many years in connection with establishing the influence of television upon real-world perceptions of crime and law enforcement (Gerbner & Gross, 1976; Gerbner et al., 1977, 1978, 1979, 1980). In relation to the impact of factual programs, links have been explored between reported amounts of television viewing and political awareness (Atkin & Gantz, 1978; Dominick, 1972; Furnham & Gunter, 1983) and knowledge of current news stories (Gunter, 1985, 1987a; Robinson & Levy, 1986). Some researchers have focused on links between relative amounts of viewing of particular program strands and knowledge and beliefs concerning program content-related topics or themes (Gunter & Wober, 1982, 1983; Wober & Gunter, 1988).

In the research reported in earlier chapters, previous viewing habits were measured once again. In addition to general viewing of television, measures were obtained from children of their claimed levels of viewing programs of the type on which they were tested as well as previous experience of the specific television series from which the test programs were taken.

For the two police drama programs, previous viewing habits were not associated with information acquisition or comprehension—whether expressed in terms of children's overall amount of television viewing, their viewing of the series from which the program shown to them had been drawn, having seen the actual program presented before, or their viewing of factual television crime programs, or U.S. or U.K. drama viewing. All these prior viewing habits failed to differentiate good and poor program comprehension.

In regard to science programs, it appeared that whether previous viewing and its nature made any difference to program comprehension or impact depended on the program. Minimally complex programs, such as those made for the youngest age groups, were equally well followed regardless of prior viewing habits.

However, where the program was more complex, because it was designed for older viewers (e.g., "Tomorrow's World"), it did seem as if previous viewing of that program conferred benefits on current viewing.

General reported amount of television viewing was unrelated to learning from quiz shows, but reported viewing of quiz shows was significantly associated with program content recall from the children's quiz show "Knock Knock." Here, medium to heavy viewers of quiz shows outperformed reportedly light quiz show viewers.

Other Variables

In addition to standard demographic variables and reported viewing experiences, a number of additional individual difference variables were measured and used to discriminate children who were good and poor performers in terms of program content retention and comprehension, and knowledge gain. These variables comprised existing relevant background general knowledge, world experiences, and program-related attitudes.

Previous research has found that common social knowledge about police, specific crimes, and the law can facilitate children's understanding of characters and events in a police drama. Children with more varied and detailed background knowledge were more sensitive to television portrayals that departed from common expectations of how people like that should behave. It is also known that the greater the degree of similarity between children's own social experiences and situation and the characters and settings in a television drama the greater the facilitation of young viewers' understanding of the program (Newcomb & Collins, 1979). In the current research, reported real-life contact with the police or crime was related, but only weakly, to learning from the two police drama episodes shown.

Real-life contact with police, likewise, had marginal and differential effects upon uptake of information. It was not significant with "The Bill" group for any measure of comprehension, and only for implicit information in the "Juliet Bravo" group. Here, however, contrary to the previously cited research showing a positive relationship between contact with the police and amount of information taken from a television presentation, the relationship was negative. That is, low real-life contact was associated with better comprehension in the "Juliet Bravo" viewers.

It would seem clear from this information that if contact with the police is to serve as a powerful mediator of program learning and comprehension then that contact must be either extensive (which, in this study, it was not) or extended in time, and be relevant and ego-involving.

On this last point, the other "reality-contact" measure of victimization proved to be more discriminating in relation to programme comprehension. This variable was significantly related to both total comprehension and explicit comprehension in "Juliet Bravo" and implicit comprehension in "The Bill" group. In both program groups, those respondents who reportedly had been victimized or knew of people who had been victims of criminal activity, scored higher on program comprehension. This must mean that to be a victim brought about contact with the police that was real and meaningful and that this meaningful experience became part of the person's personal autobiographical memory that was then available to be called upon when processing television portrayals of police and police work. Greater perceived consistency between certain television portrayals and real-life experiences of the same phenomena may have enhanced the accessibility of mental constructs representing those phenomena, through a process of priming. This may, in turn, have produced wider retention of other related aspects of each program (see Sanbonmatsu & Fazio, 1991).

Program-specific knowledge has been found to help viewers understand certain aspects of television programs such as characters' motives and behaviors (W. Collins & Wellmann, 1982; Livingstone, 1987, 1989). It might be anticipated, therefore, that regular viewers of a television series will be more familiar with its narrative structure and characterizations.

One other background factor that was associated with good comprehension was the level of knowledge that the children had about the respective roles of nonuniformed and uniformed police. For "The Bill" group, those who had high knowledge showed better comprehension of program content than those who had low knowledge. This agrees with the findings of Pingree

(1983), but remains suggestive rather than definitive because of the absence of such an association in our other program group ("Juliet Bravo"). Thus, background knowledge about the police emerged as a more significant predictor of program comprehension than familiarity with the program.

Level of relevant background general knowledge emerged as a key variable in relation to learning from science programs. This factor swamped all other demographic, reading, and viewing factors in predicting or explaining variance in recall and comprehension performance. This factor, more than any other, testifies to the fact that what a child takes away from a viewed program depend critically on what he brings to it.

Program-related attitudes were also related to cognitive learning, although they were not as significant as relevant general knowledge. Children's responses concerning attitudes toward science programs in general were factor analysed, and then looked at as possible predictors of open-ended and multiple-choice recall and comprehension performance. For both studies, three factors, which could best be labeled *program perception, program utility*, and *home–school comparison*, emerged.

Despite this stability of structure in children's attitudes to science programs, the factors were not strongly predictive of learning. They predicted open-ended scoring of the most complex programme produced for grown-ups ("Tomorrow's World"), but not for the less complex children's science program (i.e., "Know How").

Multiple-choice responding was also under predicted by program attitude factors. However "perception" and "utility" did predict, quite powerfully, performance on one children's science programme ("Know How"), whereas program perception on its own predicted learning from the adult science program ("Tomorrow's World").

Having looked at constellations of program attitudes that seemed to "hang together" as possible predictors of learning we then looked at each individual attitude to see if that predicted outcomes. In the event only a few individual attitudes proved important. An aversive attitude toward switching over or off when factual programs came on was associated with good open-ended and multiple-choice answering for one children's science program ("Know How"), whereas in the case of the adult science program ("Tomorrow's World"), open-ended responding was partially "explained" by the attitude children had to the scheduling of factual programs.

School Learning and Television Learning.   It would seem reasonable to assume that part of the general knowledge that children have is based on whether they have studied a topic at school. In addition, it is likely that children who have studied topics in school will be more motivated to view a program that contains these topic than will children who have no interest in or knowledge about the topic. On this assumption, we factor analyzed a number of subjects that our respondents said they had studied at school and then looked to see if these factor groupings predicted cognitive performance following the viewing of their particular program. Four groupings emerged under this analysis, best classified as *biology, politics and science, electronics*, and *dinosaurs*.

Unfortunately these factors did not predict open-ended answers at all consistently: Different factors predicted performance on different programs differentially and usually in isolation. In the light of this inconsistency we then looked at specific topics children had studied at school as predictors of recall and comprehension. Here the results were a little more principled. Memory and comprehension of "Tomorrow's World," a science program for adult audiences, was predicted partially by children having studied pollution and 'car manufacturing,' whereas for "Know How" having studied electronics and the human body best predicted performance following the viewing of this program. These topics of pollution, electronics, and the human body that were associated with open-ended recall, also appeared as important in multiple-choice responding. As chapter 2 points out, these topics were featured in the programs we had selected for presentation.

In summary, we have shown that children appreciate informational television and clearly perceived the functions such programs can perform. However, as they get older children develop a low-involvement relationship to such programs. This is unfortunate because the research has clearly shown that, at least in the short term, children can learn from the medium. The actual nature and amount of what is learned, however, is a complex web of certain demographic factors, previous viewing, and reading habits, and the attitudes, beliefs, and values that the children hold about informational television and that they bring with them to the viewing situation.

It was with quiz shows that we first came across evidence that children who began at different levels of knowledge gained differentially following exposure to a common television program. In the case of two shows, "Knock Knock" and "Every Second Counts," older children gained more than did younger (and initially less knowledgeable) subjects. In the case of "Blockbusters," however, younger children (again initially less knowledgeable) gained more as a result of watching this program. This first appearance of differential knowledge growth may be a function of the nature of the "knowledge" tested—in quizzes, essentially decontextualized items of information, whereas in science programs or drama episodes the knowledge is integrated chunks of contextualized factual (in the case of science) or social evidence (in the case of drama). It may be important also that only with quizzes but not with informational or drama programs did the age "break" appear around 10 years of age rather than 12, as was the case in the latter two program genres.

A Proposed Cognitive Processing Model of Television Effects

Reflecting on the mass of empirical data made available from this extended study, it becomes obvious that certain models and theories currently available in mass communication research gain support, whereas others fair less well.

The first point to note is that we have shown good memory for factual over and above thematic details of the programs shown.

This immediately causes problems for schema theory, a theory that, of late, has been hailed as playing "an important role in mass communication research" (Wicks, 1992, p.116). Now, although there can be little doubt that schemas, as cognitive structures abstracted from past experience (Fiske & Taylor, 1984), guide the processing of specific information, what the theory is uniformly bad at explaining is memory accuracy or good recall or recognition — precisely the performance we were so pleased to see in our subjects. Clearly, then, a comprehensive account of the cognitive processing and the cognitive effects of mass media reception must allow for structures over and above schema. Candidate mechanisms would be episodic, semantic, and procedural memories as suggested by Tulving (1985). The reason that episodic memory needs to be included is to account for the quiz show performance we observed. In quizzes, a random assortment of "facts" are addressed. What a contestant in the program must do, or a viewer of the program who is later asked the same question again, is to recollect a personally experienced event. It requires no structured knowledge embedding, just a memory trace that somewhere at some time they learned that, for example, WHO stands for World Health Organization.

Semantic memory also needs to be assumed because of our science program findings. Here we found that both facts given explicitly in the program and inferential reasoning around these facts could be exhibited. Science knowledge is not fragmented (like acronyms) but rather is conceptual, structured, and associated. Note that although schema theory is often loosely described by media theorists as concerning concepts, categories, and so on, this is not what schema, scripts, or frames are concerned with. These latter three notions are concerned with larger knowledge chunks such as "stories" (schema); visiting a restaurant (scripts), or a collection of semantic net nodes and slots that together describe a stereotyped object, act, or event (frame). All three are concerned with common sense knowledge or world knowledge, not logic or subset–superset hierarchies, which is the province of semantic memory.

The third type of memory that Tulving (1985) mentioned is procedural memory. In opposition to the previous types of memory we have been describing, which can all be called *declarative memory* (knowing that such and such is the case), procedural memory is concerned with knowing how to do such and such. This type of memory is concerned with the how of processing in contrast to the contents of processing. This type of memory is required to fully account for television processing given our ubiquitous finding of no interaction between age of viewer and test–retest performance. If one assumes unequal processing mechanisms or processes between age groups and the presentation of a common stimulus (a television program), one would have to posit better performance, eventually, for those viewers with the greater processing resources/mechanisms. However, if one posits comparable procedural memory (unconscious knowledge of and skills in processing a television program) and a common stimulus (television program), then one has to posit stable differences, both before and after viewing between groups who are shown to be initially different. It is the latter finding that frequently appeared in our data and failed to support the knowledge-gap hypothesis (see Gaziano, 1983).

To support this argument that our viewing groups, despite wide age ranges, had comparable procedural knowledge, it should be noted that research is beginning to appear that contradicts the received position that young children are lacking in certain cognitive ingredients when compared to older children. For example, work by Smith, Anderson, and Fischer (1985) and Pingree et al. (1984) has shown that preschool children can reproduce much more of a television story than had previously been thought possible, providing that appropriate retrieval techniques are employed and verbal responses are given less weight. In the field of script theory, also, Nelson (1986) and Hudson, Fivush, and Kuebli (1992) showed that very young children have general, well-organized knowledge about routine and recurring events, previously considered only to be available to much older children. Given that our viewers ranged from 7 to 15 years of age, the argument for comparable procedural memory for "how to process television, of whatever genre," should not be too difficult to accept.

The last issue we would take with using schema theory as either the only or the best account of cognitive television effects is that the uncritical adoption of the purely cognitive aspects of schema theory misses a huge area of performance also frequently missed by cognitive psychologists. Garramone (1992) argued that theorists such as Wicks (1992) employ a "cold" perspective whereby they seek to explain all television effects in purely cognitive information-processing terms without invoking such "hot" factors as motives, values, affect, or goals, and suggested that a merging of the uses-and-gratifications approach to mass communication with an information-processing approach is desirable. This would serve to orientate researchers to the fact that viewers are active, goal-seeking, and purposive (e.g., Hastie, 1981)

Our data clearly indicate that children decide whether or not to enter a particular television arena. Our previous work (Gunter et al., 1991) and the present findings show that children have likes and dislikes in terms of programming genres. Within genres, they again exhibit easily accessed hierarchies of predilections and pet peeves. Within a specific domain of a genre, for example, science programs within a factual programming genre, children of all ages clearly articulate likes and dislikes, positive and negative evaluations, presence or absence of follow-up activity, and both loyalty to and active avoidance of specific programs. Thus, any comprehensive model of cognitive processing must build in this level of analysis, because motivation and emotion is the fuel that drives the cognitive engine in processing television programs. However, as we have observed in the data, although important, such motivation is neither necessary nor sufficient to ensure cognitive impact of programs. This follows from the fact that, within our studies, many children performed very well on recall and recognition of program content despite explicitly stating that they chose not to watch such programs at home, and they were not given explicit memorization instructions in the experiments. Now, although it could be argued that it is naive of us to believe that the demand characteristics of the testing situation were not such as to cause children to develop a testing "set" it should be recalled that testing was done in a quiet area of school (not the university), that a week had elapsed between a paper-and-pencil pretest and the showing of the selected television programs, and the "instructions" to subjects were sufficiently bland as to leave open as possibilities many possible self-generated mental sets. Having said this, however, we would probably accept that testing fell somewhere between an "incidental" and an "intentional" learning paradigm, and the results must be couched and interpreted within this realization.

So far we have talked mainly of cognitive change (ability to recall new or previously unknown facts) as the index of cognitive impact of television viewing. A chief finding, however, in the drama section of the research, was the marked absence of significant change as between pre- and posttest. It may be legitimately argued that to look for change after only one exposure to a 30-minute police drama is to ignore the "drip" effect of mass media communication. However, what has to be accounted for is the different pattern of change and stability in the control and the experimental (exposure) groups. Whatever is true for the control group (within the bounds of random and experimental error) should also be true of the experimental groups if television could not be expected to have an effect as a result of only one short exposure. The patterns of the two groups however were different — and this is what needs to be explained.

The argument we advanced in the drama chapters was that where attitudes, beliefs, and opinions are unstable and malleable, exposure to relevant or related mass media information can cause alterations to these.

The alterations will either be toward stability or the refining of these attitudinal and knowledge structures. In the latter case, accretion, restructuring, or schema tuning (Rumelhart & Norman, 1978) can be observed. This is illustrated in our research where beliefs and perceptions of the police held by children in the two viewing groups shifted in line with attributes and events depicted in the two programs, whereas those of the controls did not.

Cognitive impact, then, must be considered to have at least two aspects. Television reception can produce a consolidation and reaffirmation of currently held beliefs or conversely it can cause preexisting knowledge to be changed: expanded (accretion), reorganized (restructuring), or adjusted (schema tuning).

The last issue that our research addresses is the active or passive nature of the child viewer. Hawkins and Pingree (1986) brought a degree of conceptual clarity to this topic by pointing out that talk of active viewers can denote, first, the locus of control in the communicative transaction as in D. R. Anderson and Lorch's (1983) active monitoring research. Second, the uses-and-gratification approach of Blumler (1979) and Levy and Windahl (1984) stresses that viewers approach television with various purposes and needs. A third approach to active viewers is the stress on comprehension strategies that lead to focusing on central rather than on peripheral story events (e.g., W. Collins, 1982). A fourth approach is that of Salomon (1983b) who argued that memory and understanding of a medium will be a direct functon of the amount of mental effort that a viewer actively decides to allocate to the viewing situation. Dervin (1982) approached the active viewer by stressing the subjectively defined and controlled construction of meaning from a text by a viewer.

Hawkins and Pingree (1986) suggested that a clear distinction should be drawn between the amount of cognitive effort applied when viewing a program, and the cognitive activities that are employed once the decision to attend actively has been made. They do, of course, accept that although conceptually distinct these two aspects are intimately intertwined in reality. Having distinguished between cognitive effort and cognitive activities, Hawkins and Pingree (1986) then listed a number of cognitive activities that underpin cognitive effects. These activities include segmenting programs into meaningful chunks of related actions and focusing on central meaning-bearing messages rather than peripheral, incidental plot material. A third cognitive activity is held to be reading formal features of the medium that involves applying learned or constructed interpretations to the formal features of television presentation. A fourth active cognitive activity is the drawing of inferences concerning the passage of time, character perspective and motivation, and causation and consequences on the bases of presented explicit content and format features. Although this is the cognitive activity held to be least available to young children, we have already had occasion when discussing procedural memory matters, to point out that if appropriate testing techniques are employed even preschoolers can be shown to draw inferences concerning missing events (e.g., Smith et al., 1985).

A sixth cognitive activity that Hawkins and Pingree (1986) stressed is the drawing on world knowledge, which often proceeds via scripts, frames, and schema. Drawing on these knowledge structures affords children frameworks for the embedding of new incoming information, mnemonic aids, and inferential resources. Somewhat contentiously, Hawkins and Pingree (1986) also argued that evaluating information and making connections are two further cognitive activities that are deployed. It is questionable if these latter two activities are separable from the superordinate "drawing upon world knowledge." However, as an activity, evaluating information does have implications for the impact of the meanings they construct in terms of the value and affect that are ascribed to them. By making connections, Hawkins and Pingree meant something more general, subjective, and less tied to regularities than the application of schemas. They see this activity as making comparisons between the current content of viewed programs and past real-life and television experience.

Although our research project took the "active viewer" as an orienting assumption and thus not as an hypothesis to be tested directly, a perusal of our findings does talk to this issue in modeling the impact process. Segmenting and focusing clearly occurred as demonstrated by the children's ability to retell story lines in the police dramas that faithfully reproduced the major story lines and causal sequences. Reading formal features was demonstrated by the ability to instantiate implicit events, actions, and motives that were communicated covertly by the programs viewed. Drawing inferences and drawing on world knowledge was clearly demonstrated in the drama and factual programming sections of this research and objectively indexed by our comprehension tests.

In factual programming this is most clearly seen by the massive effect of general knowledge on the dependent variables of interest. In the drama research, background experience both of television viewing and interaction with police was a marginal effect at best but some evidence did appear that, to the extent that the past experience was meaningful and ego-involving then that background knowledge was drawn on to evaluate and comprehend program issues.

The issue of the extent to which previous experience impacted on program evaluation relates to Hawkins and Pingree's (1986) "making connections." Here we found conflicting evidence. We found some evidence that children who had a good grasp of police crime characteristics and solution rates also exhibited good comprehension of the police drama programs they viewed. In factual programs (science) we again found some evidence that those children who valued such programs, did not actively avoid watching them, and had some experience of the domain within the genre produced better performance than children with less positive past experiences and perceptions. But it has to be admitted that in all these areas we also found some evidence of little or no connection between previous experience and current cognitive functioning. Thus, evidence for Hawkins and Pingree's (1986) making connections is, at best, rather weak in our data. This somewhat sporadic association between demographics, past real-life experience and television viewing history, and the cognitive impact of viewing selected programs was one of the chief surprising findings of the research overall.

Rather than making connections (with preexisting knowledge), creating *de novo* from current input may be a better way of conceptualising what is happening. In opposition to schema theory, recall and reconstruction that exhibits marked idiosyncratic characteristics across subjects has been accounted for by mental models. Mental models are mental representations of the message and are homomorphisms rather than isomorphisms of the program content. The power of this conception lies in the fact that it accepts and asserts that every definition of a message within a system of communication must be concerned with the message as received. That is, a chief concern is how a television program is perceived, interpreted, and categorized by a viewer. A full specification of mental models will have to account for the problems of comprehensibility, recallability, and the effects of messages on attitudes, beliefs, and opinions including as a nontrivial subset the affective outcomes of having received a message.

People cannot process the full complexity of informationally dense television programs. Thus, they must have some heuristic device to handle this density. The existence of such a heuristic is indisputable. What is less clear is the form of these heuristics and how to discover them. Are they schema, scripts, frames, scenarios (Sanford & Garrod, 1981), or mental models? And what differentiates mental models from the more familiar schemas, scripts, and frames?

Johnson-Laird (1983) argued that mental models do not appeal to stereotypic knowledge (schemas, scripts, and frames) or fixed storage systems (e.g., semantic memory). Thus, rather than retrieving pre-packed meaning structures when we meet a television program, Johnson-Laird argued that viewers use the input as "cues to build a familiar mental model." That is, meaning is computed, not retrieved. A mental model then is a representation in the form of an internal model of the state of affairs characterised by the program content. Readers, therefore, interpret input by constructing mental models in which the relevant events and entities are represented—but not necessarily in veridical form. Mental models result from the mind's innate ability to construct models of reality. These models, however, may differ from one individual to another. Mental models are capable of updating and radical change as a result of constant testing of the constructed model against the state of affairs described by the ever unfolding text. This notion of understanding via the construction and manipulation of mental models provides a useful metaphor for the way a piece of program content can be understood at different levels. It also allows for different "readings" of the same program content by different viewers.

The problem with mental models is that although proponents of this approach never describe understanding in terms of stereotypical elements found in "frames" or the set of characteristic events of a narrative "schema," they never really flesh-out the practical details of mental models. This gap in cognitive psychological research has also been discovered in mass media investigation (see Cappella & Street, 1989). Thus, the question remains: Are there practical, and hence important, differences between the several conceptions of the processing and products of processing of television programs represented by the terms *schema*, *frames*, *scripts*, *scenarios*, and *mental models*?

As Cappella and Street (1989) indicated, mental model generation, to be useful in explaining mass communication reception effects, requires a determination of how external messages are represented cognitively to the individual receiver and the rules describing the combination of message features with prior attitudes and/or beliefs to produce an outcome mental state. To the extent that Cappella and Street are correct in asserting that "implicitly or explicitly, mental models of messages are the sine qua non of effects theories" (p. 35), we felt the need to build such an approach into our model. Our data give some examples of the possible operation of this processing mechanism, especially in the reconstruction of story lines in our drama experiments, but we leave it up to other researchers to explore more adequately the potential of this concept.

In the light of all the information just presented then, the model of cognitive processing and television impact that emerges is presented in Figs. 8.1 and 8.2, where the model can be seen to involve both stages (Fig. 8.1) and structures and processes (Fig. 8.2).

The basic components of the this model are a series of stages concerned with either decision making or processing, invoked or applied either consciously or nonconsciously. The central processing is complex with various sources of knowledge interacting with one another, controlled by a processing structure called *working memory* (e.g., Baddeley, 1990). This working memory is regarded as an activated subset of long-term memory not short-term memory. Indeed, models of memory based on discrete short-term and long-term memory boxes seem to have little relevance to mass media processing models, and are in fact in the process of decline within structuralist memory researchers (e.g., Cowan, 1988) and have long

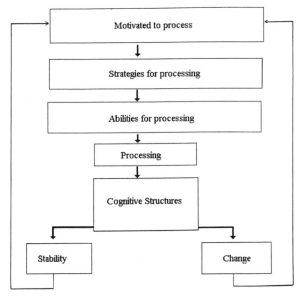

FIG. 8.1   Stage model.

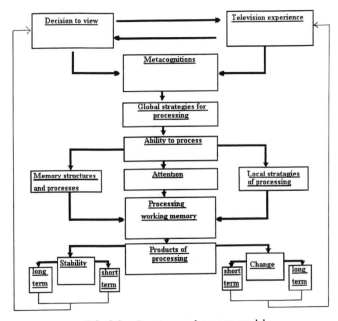

FIG. 8.2.   Structure and process model.

Key

Decision to view: This will involve current desires, thoughts, mood, emotion, motivation, and alternative means of gratification of these current needs. It will also involve perception of relevance and momentary issue involvement.

Television experience: This will involve an appraisal of the attributes and demands of television and the past history of different types of television serving different needs.

Metacognitions: This will involve decisions about "how" to view what has been selected to be attended to. A chief concept here is Salomon's (1983b) amount of invested mental effort (AIME). This high-level metadecision will precipitate different types of processing, depending on what has been chosen for viewing and the child's perceptions of the appropriate and optimal strategy for processing the selected program.

Global strategies for processing: Much television is for entertainment, some is for learning, some programs are for both, and some for neither. Each and all of these "types" of program will involve different degrees of mental engagement and effort on the part of the viewer. The viewer, however, will determine the "depth" to which any program will be processed, not the program itself. This is a key assumption.

Ability to process: The ability to process whatever program is selected for viewing requires the availability and employment of memory, attention, and relevant cognitive structures.

Memory structures and processes: This involves real-world knowledge of both social and physical reality. It also involves genre knowledge and story-grammar schema, in addition to episodic, semantic, and procedural knowledge. Memory is conceived of as both a passive storehouse of past experience and an active process of integrating incoming information from programs.

Attention: This can be shallow or deep; active or passive, being a function of local viewing conditions, internally generated thoughts and motivations concerning the particular program, and demand characteristics of that program.

Strategies: These comprise mainly of local comprehension and viewing strategies, based on past experience of how best to view a particular type of program.

Processing: The three components of ability are brought together and articulated by working memory. Working memory is involved in such tasks as searching, segmenting, interpreting, comprehending, monitoring, and criticizing. In terms of drama programs, the main function of working memory will be the creation of mental models of what the program is "really" about. With informational programs and quiz programs, working memory will be activating existing knowledge to interpret, embed, and consolidate structured facts, and to "tag" new, unstructured, essentially inarticulated, information as having been "learned."

Products of processing: The products of processing will vary with the type of program viewed, but in general the outcome of viewing will be knowledge structures that have been consolidated, refined, augmented, or changed. On line, there will be constructed meanings and mental models that will be constantly built and reformulated as the programme unfolds. Existing schema will be assimilated and accommodated in both a bottom-up and a top-down way.

Stability versus change: The end products of processing will be stored in either an enduring (long-term) or more transient (short-term) form. These stored products will include modified, refined, consolidated, or new attitudes, beliefs, values, behavioral dispositions, and knowledge structures. All these products will be available and accessible when the viewer next comes to decisions about what and whether to view, and for transaction with the nontelevision world.

been ignored by process-orientated researchers (e.g., Craik & Lockhart, 1972). Working memory is a useful concept in so far as it straddles the process-structure divide, being a mechanism that can be flexibly allocated to either processing or storage tasks (Baddeley & Hitch, 1974).

All the processing stages are dictated by particular parts of our data. Although we did not set out to advance theory and modeling in this field it would be remiss of us not to pull together the overall findings of our research and try to point out their relevance to systematization in the field of cognitive impact research.

Bryant and Rockwell (1991) finished their review of "Evolving Cognitive Models" by stressing that "whether all of the structures and processes posited (in models of mass communication reception) will ultimately prove to be valid and useful is (an) issue that will be resolved only via patient probing of empirical evidence" (p. 225). This research was primarily concerned with production of empirical evidence, as it related to children in the much neglected age range of 7 to 15 years of age, and their perceptions, evaluations, and comprehension of entertainment, drama, and informational programming. Hopefully, these empirical data will provide input to advances in modeling the processes that produce them. We have made a start on this process but it is only a start. Our major motivation was to begin to investigate the cognitive impact of several types of program within several types of television genre on older children and young adolescents. To this end, several ground-breaking strategies have been involved. For example, we always looked at more than one program in any study. Our findings serve to show that any study predicated upon one television program will suffer severe problems of generalizability and external validity. Over and above "going broad" we also "went deep." Thus, we have shown that within a specific program within a specific genre, different topics or parts are differentially easy to process and remember — and this can be a function of its content or formal features, the surrounding programme content, and the way its material is reinforced within and across modalities.

We have most strongly reinforced the idea that the general knowledge that a young viewer brings to the viewing situation is crucial in predicting what he or she will take away from it. We found this predictive relationship to be most strong with factual programs where structured knowledge is being addressed. It was also important, however, with entertainment programs (quizzes) that can be construed as addressing nonstructured knowledge. Background knowledge was least powerful in the social (drama) realm, where we found less clear predictions from knowledge and opinions about policemen and women to knowledge uptake from police drama. These variable findings again enter new data into the melting pot and, if replicated, will require modification of existing mass communication reception models.

The content of this book reflects our belief that a knowledge of the interactions among media components and content, viewer variables such as perception, evaluation and motivation, together with cognitive capabilities, and characteristics of different viewing and viewer backgrounds are essential components in the effort to understand the child's television experience and the impact of that experience upon them. To the extent that this research project has succeeded in providing sound data on at least some of these issues, then the effort will have proved worthwhile.

References

Alpert, W. S., & Leidy, T. R. (1970). The impact of information transmission through television. *Public Opinion Quarterly*, *33*, 556-562.

Anderson, D. R., & Collins, P. A. (1988). *The impact on children's education: Television's influence on cognitive development* (working paper No. 2). Washington, DC: U.S. Department of Education, Office of Educational Research and Improvement.

Anderson, D. R., & Lorch, E. (1983). Looking at television: Action or reaction? In J. Bryant & D. R. Anderson (Eds.), *Children's understanding of television: Research on attention and comprehension* (pp. 1-33). New York: Academic Press.

Anderson, J. (1976). *Language, memory and thought*. Hillsdale, NJ: Lawrence Erlbaum Associates.

Anderson, J. (1990). *Cognitive psychology*. Hillsdale, NJ: Lawrence Erlbaum Associates.

Archer, J. (1992). Gender stereo-typing of school subjects. *The Psychologist*, *5*(2), 66-69.

Atkin, C. (1983). Effects of realistic television violence vs. fictional violence on aggression. *Journalism Quarterly*, *60*, 615-621.

Atkin, C., & Gantz, W. (1978). Television news and political socialisation. *Public Opinion Quarterly*, *42*, 183-197.

Babrow, A. S., O'Keefe, B. J., Swanson, D. L., Meyers, R. A., & Murphy, M. A. (1988). Person perception and children's impressions of television and real peers. *Communication Research*, *15*, 680-698.

Baddeley, A. D. (1990). *Human memory: Theory and practice*. Hillsdale, NJ: Lawrence Erlbaum Associates.

Baddeley, A. D., & Hitch, G. (1974). Working memory. In G. A. Bower (Ed.), *Recent advances in learning and motivation* (Vol. 8, pp. 47-89). New York: Academic Press.

Ball, S., & Bogatz, G. A. (1970). *The first year of "Sesame Street": An evaluation*. Princeton, NJ: Educational Testing Service.

Ball, S., & Bogatz, G. A. (1973). *Reading with television: An evaluation of "The Electric Company"* (2 vols.). Princeton, NJ: Educational Testing Service.

Bargh, J. A. (1988). Automatic information processing: Implications for communication and affect. In L. Donohew, H. Sypher, & E. T. Higgins (Eds.), *Communication, social cognition, and affect* (pp. 9-32). Hillsdale, NJ: Lawrence Erlbaum Associates.

Bargh, J. A., & Pietromonaco, P. (1982). Automatic information processing and social perception: the influence of trait information presented outside of conscious awareness on impression formation. *Journal of Personality and Social Psychology, 43*, 437–449.

Benbow, C. P. (1988). Sex differences in mathematical reasoning ability. *Behavioural and Brain Sciences, 11*, 169–232.

Berkowitz, L. (1984). Some effects of thoughts on anti- and prosocial influences of media events: A cognitive-neoassociationist analysis. *Psychological Bulletin, 95*, 410–427.

Berry, C., & Clifford, B. R. (1985). *Learning from television news: Effects of presentation factors and knowledge on comprehension and memory* (unpublished manuscript). London: North East London Polytechnic.

Berry, C., Gunter, B., & Clifford, B. R. (1982). Research on television news. *Bulletin of the British Psychological Society, 35*, 301–304.

Blaxton, T. A. (1989). Investigating dissociations among memory measures: Support for a transfer-appropriate processing framework. *Journal of Experimental Psychology; Learning, Memory and Cognition, 15*, 657–668.

Blumler, J. (1979). The role of theory in uses and gratifications research. *Communication Research, 6*, 177–220.

Bogatz, G. A., & Ball, S. (1972). *The second year of "Sesame Street": A continuing evaluation.* Princeton, NJ: Educational Testing Service.

Boyanowsky, E. O. (1977). Film preference under conditions of threat: Whetting the appetite for violence, information or excitement? *Communication Research, 4*, 33–45.

Boyanowsky, E. O., Newtson, D., & Walster, E. (1974). Film preferences following a murder. *Communication Research, 1*, 32–43.

Brainerd, C. J., Reyna, V. F., Howe, M. L., & Kingma, J. (1990). The development of forgetting and reminiscence. *Monograph of the Society for Research in Child Development, 53* (3–4 Whole No. 222).

Brown, A. L., Bransford, J. D., Ferrara, R. A., & Campione, J. C. (1983). Learning, remembering and understanding. In J. H. Flavell & E. M. Markman (Eds.), *Handbook of child psychology* (Vol.3, pp.77–166). New York: Wiley.

Brown, M. H., Skeen, P., & Osborn, D. K. (1979). Young children's perception of the reality of television. *Contemporary Education, 50*(3), 129–133.

Bruner, J. (1957). On perceptual readiness. *Psychological Review, 64*, 123–152.

Bryant, J., & Anderson, D. R. (Eds.). (1983). *Children's understanding of television: Research on attention and comprehension.* New York: Academic Press.

Bryant, J., Alexander, A., & Brown, D. (1983). Learning from educational television programmes. In M. J. A. Howe (Ed.), *Learning from television: Psychological and educational research* (pp. 1–30). London: Academic Press.

Bryant, J., & Rockwell, S. C. (1991). Evolving cognitive models in mass communication reception processes. In J. Bryant & D. Zillmann (Eds.), *Responding to the screen: Reception and reaction processes* (pp. 217–226). Hillsdale, NJ: Lawrence Erlbaum Associates.

Bryant, J., & Zillmann, D. (Eds.). (1991). *Responding to the screen: Reception and reaction processes.* Hillsdale NJ: Lawrence Erlbaum Associates.

Burns, J. (1990). The generation effect: A test between single- and multifactor theories. *Journal of Experimental Psychology: Learning, Memory and Cognition, 16*, 1060–1067.

Cairns, E. (1984). Television news as a source of knowledge about the violence for children in Ireland. A test of the knowledge-gap hypothesis. *Current Psychological Research and Review, 3*, 32–38.

Cairns, E., Hunter, D., & Herring, L. (1980). Young children's awareness of violence in Northern Ireland. The influence of Northern Irish television in Scotland and Northern Ireland. *British Journal of Social and Clinical Psychology, 19*, 3–6.

Calvert, S., & Watkins, B. (1979). *Recall of television content as a function of content type and level of production features used.* Paper presented at the biennial meeting of the Society for Research in Child Development, San Francisco, CA.

Cantor, J., & Wilson, B. J. (1984). Modifying fear responses to mass media in preschool and elementary school children. *Journal of Broadcasting, 28,* 431–443.

Cappella, J. N., & Street, R. L. (1989). Message effects: Theory and research on mental models of messages. In J. J. Bradac (Ed.), *Message effects in communication science* (pp.24–51). London: Sage.

Carroll, M., & Nelson, T. O. (1993). Failure to obtain a generation effect during naturalistic learning. *Memory and Cognition, 21*(3), 361–366.

Cassata, M. B., Skill, T. D., & Boadu, S. O. (1979). In sickness and in health. *Journal of Communication, 29*(4), 73–80.

Chaffee, S., McLeod, J., & Wackman, D. (1973). Family communication patterns and adolescent political participation. In J. Dennis (Ed.), *Socialization in poliltics* (pp.32–51). New York: Wiley.

Christenson, P. G., & Roberts, D. F. (1983). The role of television in the formation of children's social attitudes. In M. J. A. Howe (Ed.), *Learning from television* (pp.79–99). New York: Academic Press.

Clifford, B. R., Franks, J., & Reed, T. (in press). An investigation into children's learning of science from television. *British Journal of Psychology.*

Collins, A. M., & Loftus, E. F. (1975). A spreading activation theory of semantic processing. *Psychological Review, 82,* 407–428.

Collins, W. A. (1970). Learning of media content: A developmental study. *Child Development, 41*(4), 1133–1142.

Collins, W. A. (1973). Effect of temporal separation between motivation, aggression and consequences: A developmental study. *Developmental Psychology, 8,* 215–221.

Collins, W. A. (1975). The developing child as viewer. *Journal of Communication, 25*(4), 35–44.

Collins, W. A. (1979). Children's comprehension of television content. In E. Wartella (Ed.), *Children communication: Media and development of thought, speech, and understanding* (pp.21–52). Beverly Hills, CA: Sage.

Collins, W. A. (1981). Schemata for understanding television. In H. Kelly & H. Gardner (Eds.), *Viewing children through television* (pp.31–45). San Francisco: Jossey-Bass.

Collins, W. A. (1982). Cognitive processing in television viewing. In D. Pearl, L. Bouthilet, & J. Lazar (Eds.), *Television and behavior: Ten years of scientific progress and implications for the eighties* (Vol.2, pp.9–23). Washington, DC: U.S. Government Printing Office.

Collins, W. A. (1983). Interpretation and inference in children's television viewing. In J. Bryant & D. R. Anderson (Eds.), *Children's understanding of television: Research on attention and comprehension* (pp.125–150). New York: Academic Press.

Collins, W. A. (1984). Inferences about the actions of others: Developmental and individual differences in using social knowledge. In J. C. Masters & K. Yarkin-Levin (Eds.), *Boundry areas in social and developmental psychology* (pp.221–239). New York: Academic Press.

Collins, W. A., & Wellman, H. M. (1982). Social scripts and developmental patterns in comprehension of television narratives. *Communication Research, 9,* 380–398.

Collins, W. A., Wellman, H., Keniston, A. H., & Westby, S. D. (1978). Age related aspects of comprehension and inference from a television dramatic narrative. *Child Development, 49,* 389–399.

Collins, W. A., & Westby, S. (1981, April). *Moral judgements of TV characters as a function of program comprehension.* Page presented at the Society for Research in Child Development Biennial Meeting, Boston, MA.

Collins, W. A., & Zimmermann, S.A. (1975). Convergent and divergent social cues: Effects of television aggression on children. *Communication Research, 2,* 331–346.

Comstock, G. (1989). *The evolution of American television.* Newbury Park, CA: Sage.

Comstock, G. A., Chaffee, S., Katzman, N., McCombs, M., & Roberts, D. (1978). *Television and human behavior*. New York: Columbia University Press.

Cook, T. D., & Conner, R. F. (1976). "Sesame Street" around the world: The educational impact. *Journal of Communication, 26*(2), 155-164.

Corder-Bolz, C. R. (1980). Mediation: The role of significant others. *Journal of Communication, 30*(3), 106-118.

Cowan, N. (1988). Evolving conceptions of memory storage, selective attention, and their mutual constraints within the human information-processing system. *Psychological Bulletin, 104*(2), 163-191.

Craik, F. I. M., & Lockhart, R. S. (1972). Levels of processing: a framework for memory research. *Journal of Verbal Learning and Verbal Behaviour, 11*, 671-684.

Crockett, W. (1988). Schemas, affect, and communication. In L. Donohew, H. Syphes, & E. T. Higgins (Eds.), *Communication, social cognition, and affect* (pp. 33-52). Hillsdale NJ: Lawrence Erlbaum Associates.

Cullingford, C. (1984). *Children and television*. England: Gower.

Davidson, E. S., Yasuna, A., & Tower, A. (1979). The effects of television cartoons on sex-role stereotyping in young girls. *Child Development, 50*(2), 597-600.

Davies, M. M. (1989). *Television is good for your kids*. London: Hilary Shipman.

Dervin, B. (1982). Mass media: Changing conceptions of the audience. In R. E. Rice & W. J. Paisley (Eds.), *Public communication campaigns* (pp. 71-88). Beverly Hills, CA: Sage.

Desmond, R. J. (1985). Metacognition: Thinking about thoughts in children's comprehension of television. *Critical Studies in Mass Communication, 2*, 338-351.

Dominick, J. R. (1972). Television and political socialization. *Educational Broadcasting Review, 6*, 48-56.

Dominick, J. R. (1973). Crime and law enforcement in prime-time television. *Public Opinion Quarterly, 37*, 243-250.

Dominick, J. R. (1987). *The dynamics of mass communication*. New York: Random House.

Dorr, A. (1980). When I was a child, I thought as a child. In S. B. Withey & R. P. Abeles (Eds.), *Television and social behavior: Beyond violence and children* (pp. 191-230). Hillsdale, NJ: Lawrence Erlbaum Associates.

Dorr, A. (1983). No shortcuts to judging reality. In J. Bryant & D. R. Anderson (Eds.), *Children's understanding of television* (pp. 199-220). New York: Academic Press.

Dorr, A., Graves, S., & Phelps, E. (1980). Television literacy for young children. *Journal of Communication, 30*(3), 71-83.

Dorr, A., Kovaric, P., Doubleday, C., Sims, D., & Seidner, L. B. (1985). *Beliefs about the realism of television programs featuring families*. Paper presented at the annual meeting of the American Psychological Association, Los Angeles, CA.

Drew, D., & Reeves, B. (1980). Learning from a television news story. *Communication Research, 7*, 121-135.

Durant, J. R., Evans, G. A., & Thomas, G. P. (1989). The public understanding of science. *Nature, 340*, 11-14.

Elliott, W., & Rosenberg, W. L. (1987). Media exposure and beliefs about science and technology. *Communication Research, 14*(2), 164-188.

Elliott, W. R., & Slater, D. (1980). Exposure, experience and perceived TV reality for adolescents. *Journalism Quarterly, 57*, 409-414.

Eron, L. D., Huesmann, L. R., Brice, P., Fischer, P., & Mermelstein, R. (1983). Age trends in the development of aggression, sex typing, and related television habits. *Developmental Psychology, 19*(1), 71-77.

Evans, G. A., & Durant, J. R. (1989). Understanding of science in Britain and the USA. In R. Jowell (Ed.) *British social attitudes: Special international reports*. Aldeshot: Gower Publishing.

Faber, R. J., Brown, J. D., & McLeod, J. M. (1986). Coming of age in the global village:

Television and adolescence. In G. Gumpert & R. Cathart (Eds.), *Inter/media. Interpersonal communication in a media world* (pp. 550–572). New York/Oxford: Oxford University Press.

Feshbach, S. (1976). The role of fantasy in the response to television. *Journal of Social Issues, 32*(4), 71–85.

Feshbach, S., & Singer, R. D. (1971). *Television and aggression*. San Francisco, CA: Jossey-Bass.

Fiedler, K., Lachnit, H., Fay, D., & Krug, C. (1992). Mobilization of Cognitive resources and the generation effect. *The Quarterly Journal of Experimental Psychology, 45A*(1) 149–171.

Findahl, O., & Hoijer, B. (1985). *Some characteristics of news memory and comprehension.* Unpublished manuscript.

Fiske, J. (1982). *Introduction to communication studies*. London: Methuen.

Fiske, S. T., & Taylor, S. E. (1984). *Social cognition*. Reading MA: Addison-Wesley.

Flin, R., Boon, J., Knox, A., & Bull, R. (1992). The effect of a five-month delay on children's and adults' eyewitness memory. *British Journal of Psychology, 83*, 323–336.

Fowles, J. (1992). *Why viewers watch: A reappraisal of television's effects*. Newbury Park, CA: Sage.

Freidlander, B., Wetstone, S., & Scott, L. (1974). Suburban preschool children's comprehension of an age-appropriate information television program. *Child Development, 45*, 561–565.

Furnham, A., & Gunter, B. (1983). Political knowledge and awareness in adolescents. *Journal of Adolescence, 6*, 373–385.

Garramone, G. M. (1992). A broader and "warmer" approach to Schema theory. In S. A. Deetz (Ed.), *Communication yearbook 15* (pp. 146–154). London: Sage.

Gaziano, C. (1983). The knowledge gap: An analytical review of media effects. *Communication Research, 10*(4), 447–486.

Gerbner, G. (1987). Science on television: How it affects public conceptions. *Issues in Science and Technology, 3*(3), 109–115.

Gerbner, G., & Gross, L. (1976). Living with television: The violence profile. *Journal of Communication, 26*, 173–199.

Gerbner, G., Gross, L., Eleey, M. F., Jackson-Beeck, M., Jeffries-Fox, S., & Signorielli, N. (1977). Television violence profile no.8: The highlights. *Journal of Communication, 27*, 171–180.

Gerbner, G., Gross, L., Jackson-Beeck, M., Jeffries-Fox, S., & Signorielli, N. (1978). Cultural indicators: Violence profile no.9. *Journal of Communication, 28*, 176–207.

Gerbner, G., Gross, L., Morgan, M., & Signorielli, N. (1980). The "mainstreaming" of America: Violence profile no.11. *Journal of Communication, 30*, 10–29.

Gerbner, G., Gross, L., Morgan, M. & Signorielli, N. (1982). Charting the main stream: Television's contribution to political orientation. *Journal of Communication, 32*(2), 100–127.

Gerbner, G., Gross, L., Morgan, M. & Signorielli, N. (1986). Living with television: The dynamics of the cultivation process. In J. Bryant & D. Zillmann (Eds.), *Perspectives in media effects* (pp. 17–40). Hillsdale, NJ: Lawrence Erlbaum Associates.

Gerbner, G., Gross, L., Signorielli, N., Morgan, M., & Jackson-Beeck, M. (1979). The demonstration of power: Violence profile no.10. *Journal of Communication, 29*, 177–196.

Gibson, E. J. (1969). *Principles of perceptual learning and development*. New York: Appleton-Century-Crofts.

Gibson, E. J., & Levin, H. (1975). *The psychology of reading*. Cambridge, MA: MIT Press.

Goodwin, A., & Whannel, G. (1990). *Understanding television*. London: Routledge.

Graf, P. (1980). Two consequences of generating: Increased inter and intra word organization. *Journal of Verbal Learning and Verbal Behaviour, 19*, 316–327.

Green, R. G. (1975). The meaning of observed violence: Real vs. fictional violence and consequent effects on aggression and emotional arousal. *Journal of Research in Personality*, *9*, 270–281.

Greenberg, B. S. (1974). Gratifications of television viewing and other correlates for British children. In J. G. Blumler & E. Katz (Eds.), *The uses of mass communications: Current perspectives on gratification research* (pp.71–92). Beverly Hills, CA: Sage.

Greenberg, B. (1976). Viewing and listening parameters among British youngsters. In R. Brown (Ed.), *Children and television* (pp.75–89). London: Collier Macmillan.

Greenberg, B. S., & Reeves, B. (1976). Children and the perceived reality of television. *Journal of Sociological Issues*, *32*, 86–97.

Greene, R. L. (1988). Generation effects in frequency judgments. *Journal of Experimental Psychology: Learning, Memory and Cognition*, *14*, 298–304.

Greene, R. L. (1989). On the relationship between categorical frequency estimation and cued recall. *Memory and Cognition*, *17*, 235–239.

Greene, R. L. (1992). *Human memory: Paradigms and paradoxes*. Hillsdale, NJ: Lawrence Erlbaum Associates.

Gunter, B. (1979). Recall of brief television news items: Effects of presentation mode, picture content and serial position. *Journal of Educational Television*, *5*, 57–61.

Gunter, B. (1980). Remembering television news: Effects of picture content. *Journal of General Psychology*, *102*, 127–133.

Gunter, B. (1985a). *Dimensions of television violence*. Aldershot: Gower.

Gunter, B. (1985b). News sources and news awareness: A British survey. *Journal of Broadcasting and Electronic media*, *29*(4), 397–406

Gunter, B. (1986). Come on down: A report on the popular appeal of TV quiz and game shows. *Airwaves: Quarterly Journal of the IBA*, p.5.

Gunter, B. (1987a). *Poor reception: Misunderstanding and forgetting broadcast news*. Hillsdale, NJ: Lawrence Erlbaum Associates.

Gunter, B. (1987b). *Television and the fear of crime*. London: John Libbey and IBA.

Gunter, B. (1988). *Viewers' opinions about science on television* (IBA Tech. Rep.). Unpublished manuscript.

Gunter, B., Berry, C., & Clifford, B. R. (1981). Release from proactive interference with television news items: Further evidence. *Journal of Experimental Psychology: Human Learning and Memory*, *7*, 480–487.

Gunter, B., Berry, C., & Clifford, B. R. (1982). Remembering broadcast news: The implications of experimental research for production techniques. *Human Learning, 1*, 13–29.

Gunter, B., Clifford, B. R., & Berry, C. (1980). Release from proactive interference with television news items: Evidence for encoding dimensions within television news. *Journal of Experimental Psychology: Human Learning and Memory*, *6*, 216–223.

Gunter, B., & McAleer, J. (1990). *Television and children: The one-eyed monster?* London: Routledge.

Gunter, B., McAleer, J., & Clifford, B. R. (1991). *Children's views about television*. England: Avebury.

Gunter; B., & Wober, M. (1982). Impressions of old people on TV and in real life. *British Journal of Social Psychology, 21*, 335–336.

Gunter, B., & Wober, M. (1983). Television viewing and public trust. *British Journal of Social Psychology*, *22*, 174–176.

Hagen, J. W. (1967). The effect of distraction on selective attention. *Child Development*, *38*, 685–694.

Haskell, R. E. (1987). Cognitive psychology and the problem of symbolic cognition. In R. Haskell (Ed.), *Cognition and symbolic structures: The psychology of metaphoric transformations* (pp. 85–102). Norwood, NJ: Ablex.

Hastie, R. (1981). Schematic principles in human memory. In E. T. Higgins, C. P. Herman,

& H. P. Zanna (Eds.), *Social cognition: The Ontario symposium* (Vol. 1, pp. 39–88). Hillsdale, NJ: Lawrence Erlbaum Associates.

Hawkins, R., & Pingree, S. (1982). Television's influence on social reality. In D. Pearl, L. Bouthilet, & J. Lazar (Eds.), *Television and behavior: Ten years of scientific progress and implications for the future* (DHSS Publication No. ADM 82–1196, Vol.2, pp. 224–247). Washington, DC: U.S. Government Printing Office.

Hawkins, R. P., & Pingree, S. (1986). Activity in the effects of television on children. In J. Bryant & D. Zillmann (Eds.), *Perspectives on media effects* (pp. 233–250). Hillsdale NJ: Lawrence Erlbaum Associates.

Hayes, D. S., & Kelly, S. B. (1984). Young children's processing of television: Modality differences in the retention of temporal relations. *Journal of Experimental Child Psychology, 38*, 505–514.

Hearold, S. (1986). A synthesis of 1043 effects of television on social behavior. In G. Comstock (Ed.), *Public communication and behavior* (Vol. 1, pp. 65–133). Orlando, FL: Academic Press.

Higgins, E. T., Bargh, J. A., & Lombardi, W. (1985). The nature of priming effects on categorization. *Journal of Experimental Psychology: Learning, Memory and Cognition, 11*, 59–69.

Higgins, E. T., & King, G. A. (1981). Accessibility of social constructs: information processing consequences of individual and contextual variability. In N. Cantor & J. F. Kihlstrom (Eds.), *Personality, cognition and social interaction* (pp. 69–122). Hillsdale, NJ: Lawrence Erlbaum Associates.

Himmelweit, H., Oppenheim, A., & Vince, P. (1958). *Television and the child: An empirical study of the effects of television on the young.* London: Oxford University Press.

Hirsch, P. (1980). The "scary world" of the nonviewer and other anomalies: A reanalysis of Gerbner et al.'s findings on cultivation analysis, Part 1. *Communication Research, 7*, 403–456.

Hirshman, E., & Bjork, R. A. (1988). The generation effect: Support for a two-factor theory. *Journal of Experimental Psychology: Learning, Memory and Cognition, 14*, 484–494.

Hodge, B., & Tripp, D. (1986). *Children and television.* Cambridge, UK: Polity Press.

Hoffner, C., & Cantor, C. (1985). Developmental differences in response to a television character appearance and behavior. *Developmental Psychology, 21*(6), 1065–1074.

Hoffner, C., & Cantor, J. (1991). Perceiving and responding to mass media characters. In J. Bryant & D. Zillmann (Eds.), *Responding to the screen: Reception and reaction processes* (pp. 63–101). Hillsdale, NJ: Lawrence Erlbaum Associates.

Hollenbeck, A. R., & Slaby, R. G. (1979). Infant visual and vocal responses to television. *Child Development, 50*, 41–45.

Houston, D., & Fazio, R. (1987). *Biased processing as a function of attitude accessibility.* Paper presented at the annual meeting of the Midwestern Psychological Association, Chicago, IL.

Hudson, J. A., Fivush, R., & Kuebli, J. (1992). Scripts and episodes: the development of event memory. *Applied Cognitive Psychology, 6*, 483–505.

Huesmann, L. R., Lagerspetz, K., & Eron, L. D. (1984). Intervening variables in the TV violence-aggression relation: Evidence from two countries. *Developmental Psychology, 20*(5), 746–775.

Hughes, M. (1980). The fruits of cultivation analysis: A reexamination of the effects of television watching on fear of victimization, alienation, and the approval of violence. *Public Opinion Quarterly, 44*, 287–302.

Husson, W. (1982). Theoretical issues in the study of children's attention to television. *Communication Research, 9*, 323–351.

Huston, A. C., & Wright, J. C. (1983). Children's processing of television. In J. Bryant & D. R. Anderson (Eds.), *Children's understanding of television* (pp. 35–68). New York: Academic Press.

IBA (1986) *Public attitudes towards science on television* (research report). London: Author.

James, K. (1986). Priming and social categorization factors: Impact on awareness of emergency situations. *Personality and Social Psychology Bulletin, 12,* 462–467.

Johnson-Laird, P. N. (1983). *Mental models.* Cambridge: Cambridge University Press.

Johnsson-Smaragdi, V. (1983). *TV use and social interaction in adolescence: A longitudinal study.* Stockholm: Almquist & Wiksell International.

Jones, G., Connell, I., & Meadows, I. (1971). *The presentation of science by the mass media.* Unpublished manuscript.

Katz, E., & Foulkes, D. (1962). On the use of the mass media as "escape": Clarification of a concept. *Public Opinion Quarterly, 26,* 377–388.

Katzman, N. (1972). Television soap operas: What's been going on anyway? *Public Opinion Quarterly, 36,* 200–212.

Kimura, D. (1992). Sex differences in the brain. *Scientific American, 267*(3), 80–87.

La Follette, M. (1982). Science on television: Influences and strategies. *Daedalus, 111,* 183–197.

Larsen, S. F. (1981). *Knowledge updating: Three papers on news memory, background knowledge and text processing.* Aurhus: University of Aurhus, Institute of Psychology.

Leary, A., Wright, J. C., & Huston, A. C. (1985). *Young children's judgment of the fictional/nonfictional status of television programming.* Paper presented at the biennial meeting of the Society for Research in Child Development, Toronto, Canada.

Leifer, A. D., & Roberts, D. F. (1972). Children's responses to television violence. In J. P. Murray, E. A. Rubenstein, & G. A. Comstock (Eds.), *Television as social behavior* (Vol. 2, pp. 48–180). Washington, DC: U.S. Government Printing Office.

Lesser, G. S. (1974). *Children and television: Lessons from "Sesame Street."* New York: Random House.

Levin, S. R., & Anderson, D. R. (1976). The development of attention. *Journal of Communication, 26,* 126–135.

Levy, M. R., & Windahl, S. (1984). Audience activity and gratification: A conceptual clarification and exploration. *Communication Research, 11,* 51–78.

Liebert, R. M. (1976). "Sesame Street" around the world: Evaluating the evaluators. *Journal of Communication, 26*(2), 165–171.

Liebert, R. M., Sprafkin, J. N., & Davidson, E. S. (1982). *The early window* (2nd ed.). New York: Pergamon Press.

Livingstone, S. M. (1987). The implicit representation of characters in "Dallas": A multi-dimensional scaling approach. *Human Communication Research, 13,* 399–420.

Livingstone, S. M. (1989). Interpretive viewers and structured programs. *Communication Research, 16,* 25–57.

Lucas, A. M. (1987). Public knowledge of radiation. *Biologist, 34*(3), 125–129.

Maccoby, E. E., & Hagen, J. W. (1965). Effects of distraction upon central versus incidental recall: developmental trends. *Journal of Experimental Child Psychology, 2,* 280–289.

McDaniel, M. A., Waddill, P. A., & Einstein, G. O. (1988). A contextual account of the generation effect: A three-factor theory. *Journal of Memory and Language, 27,* 521–536.

McElroy, L., & Slameka, N. J. (1982). Memorial consequences of generating nonwords: Implications for semantic-memory interpretations of the generation effect. *Journal of Verbal Learning and Verbal Behaviour, 21,* 249–259.

Mayes, S. L., & Valentine, K. B. (1976). Sex-role stereotyping in Saturday morning cartoon shows. *Journal of Broadcasting, 23*(1), 41–50.

Mead, M., & Metraux, R. (1957). Image of the scientist among high school students. *Science, 126,* 384–390.

Meyer, M. (Ed.). (1983). *Children and the formal features of television.* Munich: K. G. Saur.

Mielke, K. W., & Chen, M. (1980). Making contact: formative research in touch with children. In *CTW International Research Notes.* New York: Children's Television Workshop.

Mielke, K. W., & Chen, M. (1983). Formative research for 3-2-1: Methods and insights. In M.

J. A. Howe (Ed.), *Learning from television: Psychological and educational research* (pp. 31–55). London: Academic Press.

Miller, J. D., & Barrington, T. M. (1981). The acquisition and retention of scientific information. *Journal of Communication, 31*(2), 178–189.

Mitchell, D. B., & Hunt, R. R. (1989). How much "effort" should be devoted to memory? *Memory and Cognition, 17*, 337–348.

Moir, J., & Jessell, D. (1991). *Brain sex: The real difference between men and women.* London: Mandarin House.

Morison, P., McCarthy, M., & Gardner, H. (1979). Exploring the realities of television with children. *Journal of Broadcasting, 23*, 453–463.

Murray, J. (1988). Children's memory for auditory and visual information on television. *Child Development, 59*, 1015–1024.

Nairne, J. S., & Widner, R. L. (1987). Generation effects with nonwords: The role of test appropriateness. *Journal of Experimental Psychology: Learning, Memory and Cognition, 13*, 164–171.

Nelson, K. (Ed.). (1986). *Event knowledge: Structure and function in development.* Hillsdale, NJ: Lawrence Erlbaum Associates.

Newcomb, A. F., & Collins, W. A. (1979). Children's comprehension of family role portrayals in television drama: Effects of socioeconomic status, ethnicity and age. *Developmental Psychology, 15*, 417–423.

Palmer, E. L., & MacNeil, M. (1991). Children's comprehension process: From Piaget to public policy. In J. Bryant & D. Zillmann (Eds.), *Responding to the screen: Reception and reaction processes* (pp. 27–44). Hillsdale, NJ: Lawrence Erlbaum Associates.

Palmer, P. (1986). *The lively audience.* Sidney: Allen & Unwin.

Palmgreen, P., & Rayburn, J. D., II. (1985). An expectancy-value approach to media gratifications. In K. E. Rosengren, L. A. Wenner, & P. Palmgreen (Eds.), *Media gratification research: Current perspectives* (pp. 61–72). Newbury Park, CA: Sage

Pezdek, K. (1980). Life-span differences in semantic integration of pictures and sentences in memory. *Child Development, 51*, 720–729.

Piaget, J. (1970). *Genetic epistemology.* New York: Columbia University Press.

Pingree, S. (1983). Children's cognitive processing in constructing social reality. *Journalism Quarterly, 60*, 415–422.

Pingree, S. (1986). Children's activity and television comprehensibility. *Communication Research, 13*, 239–256.

Pingree, S., Hawkins, R. P., Rouner, D., Burns, J., Gikonyo, W., & Neuwirth, C. (1984). Children's reconstruction of a television narrative. *Communication Research, 11*, 477–496.

Potter, W. (1986). Perceived reality and the cultivation hypothesis. *Journal of Broadcasting and Electronic Media, 30*, 159–174.

Quarforth, J. M. (1979). Children's understanding of the nature of TV characters. *Journal of Communication, 29*(3), 210–218.

Rarick, D., Townsend, J., & Boyd, D. (1973). Adolescent perceptions of police: Actual and as depicted in TV drama. *Journalism Quarterly, 50*, 438–446.

Reeves, B., & Greenberg, B. S. (1977). Children's perceptions of television characters. *Human Communication, 3*, 113–127.

Reeves, B., & Lometti, G. E. (1979). The dimensional structure of children's perceptions of television characters: A replication. *Human Communication Research, 5*, 247–256.

Reeves, B., & Miller, M. M. (1978). A multidimensional measure of children's identification with television characters. *Journal of Broadcasting, 22*, 71–85.

Rice, M. L., Huston, A. C., & Wright, J. C. (1986). Replays as repetition: young children's interpretation of television forms. *Journal of Applied Developmental Psychology, 7*(1) 61–76.

Robinson, J. P., & Levy, M. (1986). *The main source: Learning from television news.* Beverly Hills, CA: Sage.

Robinson, J. P., & Sahin, H. (1984). *Audience comprehension of television news: Results from some exploratory research.* London: British Broadcasting Corporation Research Department.

Ross, D. F., & Condry, J. C. (1985). *The effects of perceived reality on adults' responses to filmed and televised events.* Paper presented at the annual meeting of the American Psychological Association, Los Angeles, CA.

Royal Society. (1985). *The public understanding of science.* London: Author.

Rubin, A. M. (1977). Television usage, attitudes and viewing behaviour of children and adolescents. *Journal of Broadcasting, 21,* 355–369.

Rubin, A. M. (1979). Television use by children and adolescents. *Human Communication Research, 5,* 109–120.

Rubin, A. M. (1985). Media gratification through the life cycle. In K. E. Rosengren, L. A. Wenner, & P. Palmgreen (Eds.), *Media gratification research: Current perspectives* (pp. 195–208). Beverly Hills, CA: Sage.

Rubin, A. M. (1986). Uses, gratifications, and media effects research. In J. Bryant & D. Zillmann (Eds.), *Perspectives on media effects* (pp. 281–301). Hillsdale, NJ: Lawrence Erlbaum Associates.

Rubin, A. M., Perse, E. M., & Taylor, D. S. (1988). A methodological examination of cultivation. *Journal of Communication, 15*(2), 107–134.

Rumelhart, D. E., & Norman, D. A. (1978). Accretion, tuning and restructuring: three models of learning. In J. W. Cotton & R. Klatzky (Eds.), *Semantic factors in cognition* (pp. 37–53). Hillsdale, NJ: Lawrence Erlbaum Associates.

Ryder, N. (1982). *Science, television and the adolescent.* Report presented to the IBA, London.

Salomon, G. (1977). Effects of encouraging Israeli mothers to co-observe "Sesame Street" with their five-year-olds. *Child Development, 48,* 1146–1151.

Salomon, G. (1979). *Interaction of media, cognition and learning.* San Francisco: Jossey-Bass.

Salomon, G. (1981). Introducing AIME: The assessmnet of children's mental involvement with television. In H. Kelly & H. Gardner (Eds.), *Viewing children through television* (pp. 89–102). San Francisco: Jossey-Bass.

Salomon, G. (1983a). Beyond the formats of television: The effects of student preconceptions on the experience of televiewing. In M. Meyer (Ed.), *Children and the formal features of television* (pp. 89–102). Munich: K. G. Saur.

Salomon, G. (1983b). Television watching and mental effort: A social psychological view. In J. Bryant & D. R. Anderson (Eds.), *Children's understanding of television: Research on attention and comprehension* (pp. 181–198). New York: Academic Press.

Sanford, A. J., & Garrod, S. C. (1981). *Understanding written language.* Chichester: Wiley.

Sawin, D. (1981). The fantasy-reality distinction in TV violence. *Journal of Research in Personality, 15,* 323–330.

Schramm, W., Lyle, J., & Parker, E. B. (1961). *Television in the lives of our children.* Stanford, CA: Stanford University Press.

Sanbonmatsu, D. M., & Fazio, R. H. (1991). Construct accessibility: Determinants, consequences, and implications for the media. In J. Bryant & D. Zillmann (Eds.), *Responding to the screen: Reception and reaction processes.* Hillsdale, NJ: Lawrence Erlbaum Associates.

Siegler, R. S. (1983) *Children's thinking: An information processing approach.* Englewood Cliffs, NJ: Prentice-Hall.

Siegler, R. S. (1991). *Children's thinking.* Englewood Cliffs, NJ: Prentice-Hall.

Silverstone, R. (1985). *Framing science: The making of a TV documentary.* London: British Film Books.

Singer, J. (1980). The power and limitations of television: A cognitive-affective analysis. In P. Tannenbaum (Ed.), *The entertainment function of television* (pp. 31–65). Hillsdale, NJ: Lawrence Erlbaum Associates.

Sheppard, A. (1990). *Children, television and morality* (research working paper I). London: Broadcasting Standards Council.

Skeen, P., Brown, M. H., & Osborn, D. K. (1982). Young children's perception of "real" and "pretend" on television. *Perceptual and Motor Skills, 54,* 883–887.

Slamecka, N. J., & Fevreiski, J. (1983). The generation effect when generation fails. *Journal of Verbal Learning and Verbal Behaviour, 22,* 153–163.

Slamecka, N. J., & Graf, P. (1978). The generation effect: Delineation of a phenomenon. *Journal of Experimental Psychology: Human Learning and Memory, 4,* 592–604.

Slamecka, N. J., & Katsaiti, L. T. (1987). The generation effect as an artifact of selective displaced rehearsal. *Journal of Memory and Language, 26,* 589–607.

Slater, D., & Elliott, W. R. (1982). Television's influence on social reality. *Quarterly Journal of Speech, 68,* 69–79.

Smith, R., Anderson, D. R., & Fischer, C. (1985). Young children's comprehension of montage. *Child Development, 56*(4), 962–971.

Snow, R. P. (1974). How children interpret TV violence in play context. *Journalism Quarterly, 51*(1), 13–21.

Sparks, G. C., & Cantor, J. (1986). Developmental differences in fright responses to a television program depicting a character transformation. *Journal of Broadcasting and Electronic Media, 30,* 309–323.

Sprafkin, J. N., & Liebert, R. M. (1978). Sex-typing and children's television preferences. In G. Tuchman, A. K. Daniels, & J. Benet (Eds.), *Heart and home: Images of women in the mass media* (pp. 228–239). New York: Oxford University Press.

Sproull, N. L., Ward, E. F., & Ward, M. D. (1976). *Reading behaviors of young children who viewed the "Electric Company."* New York: Children's Television Workshop.

Srull, T. K., & Wyer, R. S., Jr. (1979). The role of category accessibility in the interpretation of information about persons: some determinants and implications. *Journal of Personality and Social Psychology, 37,* 1660–1672.

Sutherland, J. C., & Siniawsky, S. J. (1982). The treatment and resolution of moral violation in soap operas. *Journal of Communication, 32,* 67–74.

Svennevig, M. (1988, September). *Television science and its audience.* Background paper presented to the IBA Consultation on Science, London, UK.

Svennevig, M. (1989). *Attitudes to television in 1988.* London: Independent Broadcasting Authority.

Tamborini, R., Zillmann, D., & Bryant, J. (1984). Fear and victimization: Exposure to television and perceptions of crime and fear. In R. N. Bostrum (Ed.), *Communication yearbook 8* (pp. 492–513). Beverly Hills, CA: Sage.

Tannenbaum, P. (1954). Effects of serial position on recall of radio news stories. *Journalism Quarterly, 31,* 319–323.

Tannenbaum, P. (1979). TV images of the police: Docu-drama production. In *Annual Review of Audience Research Findings* (pp. 16–24). London: British Broadcasting Corporation.

Taylor, S. E., & Crocker, J. (1981). Schematic bases of social information processing. In E. T. Higgins, C. P. Herman, & M. P. Zanna (Eds.), *Social cognition: The Ontario Symposium* (Vol. 1, pp. 89–134). Hillsdale, NJ: Lawrence Erlbaum Associates.

Teevan, J., & Hartnagel, T. (1976). The effect of television violence on the perception of crime by adolescents. *Sociology and Social Research, 60,* 337–348.

Tulving, E. (1985). How many memory systems are there? *American Psychologist, 40,* 385–398.

Tulving, E., & Thompson, D. M. (1973). Encoding specificity and retrieval processes in episodic memory. *Psychological Review, 80,* 352–373.

Tyler, T., & Cook, F. (1984). The mass media and judgments of risk: Distinguishing impact on personal and societal level judgments. *Journal of Personality and Social Psychology, 47*(4), 693–708.

Tyler, T. R. (1980). The impact of directly and indirectly experienced events: The origin of crime-related judgements and behaviours. *Journal of Personality and Social Psychology, 39*, 13–28.

Tyler, T. R. (1984). Assessing the risk of crime victimization and socially-transmitted information. *Journal of Social Issues, 40*, 27–38.

Van der Voort, T. (1986). *Television violence: A child's eye view.* Amsterdam: Elsevier Science.

Vernon, M. D. (1955). The functions of schemata in perceiving. *Psychological Review, 62*, 180–192.

Wartella, E., & Anderson, A. (1977). *Children's organization of impressions of television characters.* Paper presented at the annual meeting of the International Communication Association, Chicago, IL.

Watkins, M. J., & Sechler, E. S. (1988). Generation effects with an incidental memorization procedure. *Journal of Memory and Language, 27*, 537–544.

Weaver, J., & Wakshlag, J. (1986). Perceived vulnerability to crime, criminal victimisation experience, and television viewing. *Journal of Broadcasting and Electronic Media, 30*, 147–158.

Wicks, R. H. (1992). Schema theory and measurement in mass communication research: Theoretical and methodological issues in news information processing. In S. A. Deetz (Ed.), *Communication yearbook 15.* London: Sage.

Williams, T. (1986). *The impact of television: A national experiment in three communities.* New York.: Academic Press.

Wilson, B. J., Hoffner, C., & Cantor, J. (1987). Children's perception of the effectiveness of techniques to reduce fear from mass media. *Journal of Applied Developmental Psychology, 8*, 39–52.

Winn, M. (1985). *The plug-in-drug.* New York: Penguin. (Original work published 1977)

Winn, M. (1987). *Unplugging the plug-in-drug.* New York: Penguin.

Wirth, T. E. (1988). The television environment: Cultivating the wasteland. In S. Oskamp (Ed.), *Television as a social issue* (pp. 69–78). Newbury Park, CA: Sage.

Wober, M. & Gunter, B. (1988) *Television and social control.* Aldershot, UK: Avebury.

Wright, C. R. (1986). *Mass communication: A sociological perspective* (3rd ed.). New York: Random House.

Wright, J. C., & Huston, A. (1983). *The information processing demands of television and "media literacy" in young viewers.* Paper presented at the annual meeting of the American Educational Research Association, New York.

Wright, J. C., Kunkel, D., Pinon, M., & Huston, A. C. (1987). *Children's affective and cognitive reactions to television coverage of the space shuttle disaster.* Paper presented to the biennial meeting of the Society for Research in Child Development, Baltimore, MD.

Wyer, R. S., Jr., & Srull, T. K. (1981). Category accessibility: Some theoretical and empirical issues concerning the processing of social stimulus information. In E. T. Higgins, C. P. Herman, & M. P. Zanna (Eds.), *Social cognition: The Ontario Symposium* (Vol. 1, pp. 161–197). Hillsdale, NJ.: Lawrence Erlbaum Associates.

Wyer, R. S., Jr., & Srull, T. K. (1986). Human cognition in its social context. *Psychological Review, 93*, 322–359.

Zillmann, D. (1974). *Hostility and aggression.* Hillsdale, NJ: Lawrence Erlbaum Associates.

Zillmann, D. (1980). Anatomy of suspense. In P. H. Tannenbaum (Ed.), *The entertainment function of television* (pp. 133–163). Hillsdale, NJ: Lawrence Erlbaum Associates.

Author Index

Page numbers in *italics* denote pages with complete bibliographic information

A

Ables, R. P., *231*
Alexander, A., 92, 93, *229*
Alpert, W. S., 17, *228*
Anderson, A., 39, *239*
Anderson, D. R., 1, 2, 40, 117, 166, 218, 220, 221, *228, 229, 230, 231, 234, 235, 238*
Anderson, J., 9, 117, 125, 208, *228*
Archer, J., 126, 212, *228*
Atkin, C., 18, 45, *228*

B

Babrow, A. S., 39, *228*
Baddelely, A. D., 223, 226, *228*
Ball, S., 92, 93, *228, 229*
Bargh, J. A., 4, 208, 209, *228, 229, 234*
Barrington, T. M., 96, *236*
Benbow, C. P., 126, *229*
Benet, J., *238*
Berkowitz, L., 3, *229*
Berry, C., 18, 156, 204, *229, 233*
Bjork, R. A., 198, *234*
Blaxton, T. A., 197, *229*
Blumler, J., 220, *229, 233*
Boadu, S. O., 11, *230*
Bogatz, G. A., 92, 93, *228, 229*
Boon, J., 125, *232*

Bostrum, R. N., *238*
Bouthilet, L., *230, 234*
Bower, G. A., *228*
Boyanowsky, E. O., 61, *229*
Boyd, D., 12, 57, 62, *236*
Bradae, J. J., *230*
Brainerd, C. J., 125, *229*
Bransford, J. D., 200, *229*
Brice, P., 43, *231*
Brown, A. L., 200, *229*
Brown, D., 92, 93, *229*
Brown, J. D., 4, *231–232*
Brown, M. H., 56, *229, 238*
Brown, R., *233*
Bruner, J., 3, *229*
Bryant, J., 2, 3, 13, 20, 89, 92, 93, 211, 226, *228, 229, 230, 231, 232, 234, 236, 237, 238*
Bull, R., 125, *232*
Burns, J., 198, 218, *229, 236*

C

Cairns, E., 19, *229*
Calvert, S., 8, *229–230*
Campione, J. C., 200, *229*
Cantor, C., 45, *234*
Cantor, J., 5, 45, 200, *230, 234, 238, 239*
Cantor, N., *234*
Cappella, J. N., 223, *230*

Carroll, M., 197, *230*
Cassata, M. B., 11, *230*
Cathart, R., *232*
Chaffee, S., 2, 17, 18, *230, 231*
Chen, M., 93–94, *235*
Christenson, P. G., 9, 40, *230*
Clifford, B. R., 17, 18, 26, 126, 127, 156, 160, 166, 167, 169, 204, 205, 219, *229, 230, 233*
Collins, A. M., 208, *230*
Collins, P. A., 40, *228*
Collins, W. A., 3, 5, 8, 9, 15, 39, 40, 57, 63, 88, 201, 214, 220, *230, 236*
Comstock, G., 2, 16, 17, *230, 231, 234, 235*
Condry, J. C., 45, *237*
Connell, I., 94, *235*
Conner, R. F., 92, *231*
Cook, F., 13, 63, *238*
Cook, T. D., 92, *231*
Corder-Bolz, C. R., 3, *231*
Cotton, W., *237*
Cowan, N., 223, *231*
Craik, F. I. M., 226, *231*
Crocker, J., 4, 211, *238*
Crockett, W., 4, *231*
Cullingford, C., 5, 8, 38, 40, 57, *231*

D

Daniels, A. K., *238*
Davidson, E. S., 7, 87, *231, 235*
Davies, M. M., 2, *231*
Deetz, S. A., *232, 239*
Dennis, J., *230*
Dervin, B., 220, *231*
Desmond, R. J., 117, *231*
Dominick, J. R., 4, 11, 18, 212, *231*
Donohew, L., *228, 231*
Dorr, A., 3, 5, 41, 46, 56, *231*
Doubleday, C., 56, *231*
Drew, D., 19, *231*
Durant, J. R., 96, 124, *231*

E

Einstein, G. O., 198, *235*
Eleey, M. F., 11, 60, 61, 88, 212, *232*
Elliott, W. R., 12, 64, 95, *231, 238*
Eron, L. D., 43, 56, *231, 234*
Evans, G.A., 96, 124, *231*

F

Faber, R. J., 4, *231–232*
Fay, D., 198, 199, *232*
Fazio, R., 6, 11, 12, 64, 86, 87, 214, *234, 237*
Ferrara, R. A., 200, *229*
Fesbach, S., 43, 45, *232*
Fevreiski, J., 196, *238*
Fiedler, K., 198, 199, *232*
Findahl, O., 106, 129, *232*
Fischer, C., 218, 221, *238*
Fischer, P., 43, *231*
Fiske, J., 4, 217, *232*
Fivush, R., 218, *234*
Flavell, J. H., *229*
Flin, R., 125, *232*
Foulkes, D., 18, *235*
Fowles, J., *232*
Franks, J., 127, *230*
Freidlander, B., 7, 8, *232*
Furnham, A., 18, 212, *232*

G

Gantz, W., 18, 212, *228*
Gardner, H., 45, 56, *230, 236, 237*
Garramone, G. M., 218, *232*
Garrod, S. C., 222, *237*
Gazlano, C., 217, *232*
Gerbner, G., 5, 10, 11, 60, 61, 88, 95, 209, 212, *232, 234*
Gibson, E. J., 3, *232*
Gikonyo, W., 218, *236*
Goodwin, A., 182, *232*
Graf, P., 196, 198, *232, 238*
Graves, S., 5, *231*
Green, R. G., 45, *232–233*
Greenberg, B. S., 18, 43, 49, 56, 87, 172, *233, 236*
Greene, R. L., 196, 197, 198, *232*
Gross, L., 5, 10, 11, 60, 88, 209, 212, *232*
Gumpert, G., *232*
Gunter, B., 2, 5, 6, 12, 13, 15, 17, 18, 25, 26, 38, 41, 43, 61, 62, 63, 88, 89, 96, 106, 126, 129, 130, 144, 156, 160, 165, 166, 167, 201, 204, 205, 212, 213, 219, *229, 232, 233, 239*

H

Hagen, J. W., 5, 8, 39, *233, 235*
Hartnagel, T., 13, 14, 62, *238*

Haskell, R. E., 4, *233*
Hastie, R., 218, *233-234*
Hawkins, R., 64, 220, 221-222, 218, *234, 236*
Hayes, D. S., 8, *234*
Hearold, S., 43, *234*
Herman, C. P., *233, 238, 239*
Herring, L., 18, *229*
Higgins, E. T., 6, 86, 208, *228, 231, 233-234, 234, 239*
Himmelweit, H., 16, *234*
Hirsch, P., 88, *234*
Hirshman, E., 198, *234*
Hitch, G., 226, *228*
Hodge, B., 12, 43, *234*
Hoffner, C., 5, 45, 200, *234, 239*
Hoijer, B., 106, 129, *232*
Hollenbeck, A. R., 1, *234*
Houston, D., 12, *234*
Howe, M. J. A., *229, 230, 235-236*
Howe, M. L., 125, *229*
Hudson, J. A., 218, *234*
Huesmann, A. R., 43, 56, *231, 234*
Hughes, M., 88, *234*
Hunt, R. R., 197, *236*
Hunter, D., 19, *229*
Husson, W., 211, *234*
Huston, A. C., 1, 8, 40, 56, *234, 235, 236, 239*

J

Jackson-Beeck, M., 11, 60, 61, 88, 209, 212, *232*
James, K., 209, *235*
Jeffries-Fox, S., 11, 60, 61, 88, 212, *232*
Jessell, D., 126, *236*
Johnson-Laird, P. N., 222, *235*
Johnsson-Smaragdi, V., 90, *235*
Jones, G., 94, *235*
Jowell, R., *231*

K

Katsaiti, L. T., 198, *238*
Katz, E., 18, *233, 235*
Katzman, N., 2, 11, 17, *231, 235*
Kelly, H., *230, 237*
Kelly, S. B., 8, *234*
Keniston, A. H., 39, 57, *230*
Kihlstrom, J. F., *234*

Kimura, D., 125, *235*
King, G. A., 6, 86, 208, *234*
Kingma, J., 125, *229*
Klatzky, R., *237*
Knox, A., 125, *232*
Kovaric, P., 56, *231*
Krug, C., 198, 199, *232*
Kuebli, J., 218, *234*
Kunkel, D., 56, *239*

L

La Follette, M., 94, *235*
Lachnit, H., 198, 199, *232*
Lagerspetz, K., 56, *234*
Larsen, S. F., 129, *235*
Lazar, J., *230, 234*
Leary, A., 56, *235*
Leidy, T. R., 17, *228*
Leifer, A. D., 39, *235*
Lesser, G. S., 92, *235*
Levin, H., 3, *232*
Levin, S. R., 1, *235*
Levy, M. R., 201, 212, 220, *235, 236*
Liebert, R. M., 7, 49, 92, *235, 238*
Livingstone, S. M., 214, *235*
Lockhart, R. S., 226, *231*
Loftus, E. F., 208, *230*
Lombardi, W., 204, *234*
Lometti, G. E., 43, *236*
Lorch, E., 117, 166, 220, *228*
Lucas, A. M., 94, *235*
Lyle, J., 1, 16, *237*

M

Maccoby, E. E., 39, *235*
MacNeil, M., 4, 5, 7, *236*
Markman, E. M., *229*
Masters, J. C., *230*
Mayes, S. L., 87, *235*
McAleer, J., 2, 17, 25, 26, 38, 126, 160, 166, 167, 169, 205, 219, *233*
McCarthy, M., 46, 56, *236*
McCombs, M., 2, 17, *231*
McDaniel, M. A., 198, *235*
McElroy, L., 198, *235*
McLeod, J., 4, 18, *230, 231-232*
Mead, M., 94, *235*
Meadows, I., 94, *235*
Mermelstein, R., 43, *231*

Metraux, R., 94, *235*
Meyer, M., 2, *235, 237*
Meyers, R. A., 39, *228*
Mielke, K. W., 93–94, *235–236*
Miller, J. D., 96, *236*
Miller, M. M., 49, 87, *236*
Mitchell, D. B., 197, *236*
Moir, J., 126, *236*
Morgan, M., 5, 10, 11, 209, *232*
Morison, P., 46, 56, *236*
Murphy, M. A., 39, *228*
Murray, J., 124–125, *235, 236*

N

Nairne, J. S., 198, *236*
Nelson, K., 218, *236*
Nelson, T. O., 197, *230*
Neuwirth, C., 218, *236*
Newcomb, A. F., 39, 201, 214, *236*
Newtson, D., 61, *229*
Norman, D. A., 220, *237*

O

Oppenheim, A., 16, *234*
O'Keefe, B. J., 39, *228*
Osborn, D. K., 56, *229, 238*
Oskamp, S., *239*

P

Paisley, W. J., *231*
Palmer, E. L., 4, 5, 7, *236*
Palmer, P., 12, *236*
Palmgreen, P., 4, *236, 237*
Parker, E. B., 1, 16, *237*
Pearl, D., *230, 234*
Perse, E. M., 43, *237*
Pezdek, K., 125, *236*
Phelps, E., 5, *231*
Piaget, J., 125, *236*
Pietromonaco, P., 209, *229*
Pingree, S., 13, 15, 62, 63, 64, 86, 88, 209, 214–215, 218, 220, 221–222, *234, 236*
Pinon, M., 56, *239*
Potter, W., 13, 14–15, 62, *236*

Q

Quarforth, J. M., 56, *236*

R

Rarick, D., 12, 58, 62, *236*
Rayburn, J. D., 4, *236*
Reed, T., 127, *230*
Reeves, B., 19, 43, 49, 56, 87, *231, 233, 236*
Reyna, V. F., 125, *229*
Rice, M. L., 40, *236*
Rice, R. E., *231*
Roberts, D. F., 2, 9, 17, 39, 40, *230, 231, 235*
Robinson, J. P., 106, 201, 212, *236, 237*
Rockwell, S. C., 3, 211, 226, *229*
Rosenberg, W. L., 95, *231*
Rosengren, K. E., *236, 237*
Ross, D. F., 45, *237*
Rouner, D., 218, *236*
Rubenstein, E. A., *235*
Rubin, A. M., 4, 5, 9, 18, 40, 43, 90, *237*
Rumelhart, D. E., 220, *237*
Ryder, N., 94, *237*

S

Sahin, H., 106, *237*
Salomon, G., 18, 19–20, 38, 39, 91, 103, 144, 162, 211, 220, 225, *237*
Sanbonmatsu, D. M., 6, 11, 64, 86, 87, 214, *237*
Sanford, A. J., 222, *237*
Sawin, D., 45, *237*
Schramm, W., 1, 16, *237*
Scott, L., 7, 8, *232*
Sechler, E. S., 198, *239*
Seidner, L. B., 56, *231*
Sheppard, A., 57, 202, *238*
Siegler, R. S., 125, *237*
Signorielli, N., 5, 10, 11, 60, 61, 88, 209, 212, *232*
Silverstone, R., 94, *237*
Sims, D., 56, *231*
Singer, J., 20, *237*
Singer, R. D., 43, 91, *232*
Siniawsky, S. J., 11, *238*
Skeen, P., 56, *229, 238*
Skill, T. D., 11, *230*
Slaby, R. G., 1, *234*
Slamecka, N. J., 196, 198, *235, 238*
Slater, D., 12, 64, *231, 238*
Smith, R., 218, 221, *238*
Snow, R. P., 45, *238*

Sparks, G. C., 45, *238*
Sprafkin, J. N., 7, 49, *235, 238*
Sproull, N. L., 93, *238*
Srull, T. K., 208, 209, *238, 239*
Street, R. L., 223, *230*
Sutherland, J. C., 11, *238*
Svennevig, M., 25, 96, *238*
Swanson, D. L., 39, *228*
Sypher, H., *228, 231*

T

Tamborini, R., 13, 63, 89, *238*
Tannenbaum, P., 12, 204, *237, 238, 239*
Taylor, D. S., 43, *237*
Taylor, S. E., 4, 211, 217, *232, 238*
Teevan, J., 13, 14, 62, *238*
Thomas, G. P., 96, 124, *231*
Thompson, D. M., 198, *238*
Tower, A., 87, *231*
Townsend, J., 12, 57, 62, *236*
Tripp, D., 12, 43, *234*
Tuchman, G., *238*
Tulving, E., 198, 217, *238*
Tyler, T., 13, 63, 89, *238, 239*

V

Valentine, K. B., 87, *235*
Van der Voort, T., 12, 13, 14, 43, 62, *239*
Vernon, M. D., 3, *239*
Vince, P., 16, *234*

W

Wackman, D., 18, *230*
Waddill, P. A., 198, *235*

Wakshlag, J., 13, 62, 63, 89, *239*
Walster, E., 61, *229*
Ward, E. F., 93, *238*
Ward, M. D., 93, *238*
Wartella, E., 39, *230, 239*
Watkins, B., 8, *229–230*
Watkins, M. J., 198, *239*
Weaver, J., 13, 62, 63, 89, *239*
Wellman, H., 39, 57, 201, 214, *230*
Wenner, L. A., *236, 237*
Westby, S. D., 8, 39, 57, *230*
Wetstone, S., 7, 8, *232*
Whannel, G., 182, *232*
Wicks, R. H., 217, 218, *239*
Widner, R. L., 198, *236*
Williams, T., 20, *239*
Wilson, B. J., 45, *230, 239*
Windahl, S., 220, *235*
Winn, M., 126, *239*
Withey, S. B., *231*
Wober, M., 5, 6, 12, 61, 88, 213, *233, 239*
Wright, C. R., 10, *239*
Wright, J. C., 1, 8, 40, 56, *234, 235, 236, 239*
Wyer, R. S., Jr., 208, 209, *238, 239*

Y

Yarkin-Levin, K., *230*
Yasuna, A., 87, *231*

Z

Zanna, M. P., *233–234, 238, 239*
Zillmann, D., 13, 20, 61, 64, 89, *229, 232, 234, 236, 237, 238, 239*
Zimmermann, S. A., 201, *230*

Subject Index

A

Adult audiences, 6, 10, 30, 41, 61, 94, 96–97
Age differences, 4–5, 8–9, 14–15, 23, 40–41, 43, 44–45, 46–47, 51–52, 56, 57, 66–67, 69, 79, 80, 83, 84, 88–89, 99, 100, 102–103, 106–108, 113, 124–125, 132–133, 133–134, 134–135, 136, 137, 142–143, 148–149, 161, 169–170, 170–171, 171–172, 173, 175, 178, 179, 180–182, 187, 188–189, 193–194, 211–212
Analysis of variance tests (ANOVAs), 107, 112, 117, 124–125, 148, 151, 154
Annenberg School of Communications, 60, 61
Appreciation of programs, 25–26
  police drama, 43–45
  quiz and games shows, 169–170, 191, 193
  science programs, 98–100, 100–101, 124, 159–160
Attitudes to programs, 22–23, 25–26
  police drama, 29, 43–45, 45–50
  quiz and games shows, 37, 170–173, 174–175, 175–178, 193–194
  science programs, 33, 98–100, 101–105, 131–133, 133–137, 137–138, 139–141, 151–152

Audiences,

  adults, 6, 10, 30, 41, 61, 94, 96–97
  children, see Children
  ethnic minorities, 5–6
  families, 6, 27, 193

B

BARB, see Broadcasters' Audience Research Board
Ball, Johnny, 33
Behavioral effects of television, 2, 3, 5, 14–15, 166–167
Beliefs, 7, 9–10, 22, 33, 38–39, 41, 60, 61–62, 79–82, 85, 89, 206–210
Bias, perceptions of, 5
"The Bill," 26–30, 41–42, 45–59, 66–72, 207–209, 214
"Blockbusters," 35–37, 168, 169, 174–195, 205–206, 210
"Blue Peter," 91
"Body Matters," 31–33, 97–98, 101–128
Broadcasters' Audience Research Board, 24, 35

C

CBS National Citizenship Tests, 17
Cartoons, 19, 93

"Charlie's Angels," 14, 64
Children,
  "active" viewers, 3–7, 165–167, 172–173,
    176, 221
  age differences, 4–5, 8–9, 14–15, 23,
    40–41, 43, 44–45, 46–47, 51–52, 56,
    57, 66–67, 69, 79, 80, 83, 84, 88–89,
    99–100, 102–103, 106–108, 113,
    124–125, 132–133, 133–134, 134–135,
    136, 137, 142–143, 148–149, 161,
    169–170, 170–171, 171–172, 173, 175,
    178, 179, 180–182, 187, 188–189,
    193–194, 211–212
  age of viewing, 1, 7–9
  appreciation of programs, 25–26, 43–45,
    98–100, 100–101, 124, 159–160,
    169–170, 191, 193
  attitudes to programs, 22–23, 25–26, 29,
    33, 37, 43–45, 45–50, 98–100,
    101–105, 131–133, 133–137, 137–138,
    139–141, 151–152, 170–173, 174–175,
    175–178, 193–194
  beliefs, 7, 9–10, 22, 29, 33, 38–39, 41, 60,
    61–62, 79–82, 85, 89, 206–210
  class differences, 28, 41
  cognitive processes, 3, 4–5, 7–9, 14–16,
    16–21, 40–41, 65, 86, 125–126,
    201–202, 202–206, 217–227
  comprehension, 7–9, 29, 32, 38–41,
    42, 51–55, 57–59, 62, 62–63, 66,
    68–69, 98, 105–111, 113–124,
    141–147, 160–161, 169, 178, 187–188,
    201–206
  early life experiences, 1, 3
  effects of television on behavior, 2, 3, 5,
    14–15, 166–167
  empathy with characters portrayed, 5, 15,
    39, 44–45, 49–50, 55–56
  ethnic differences, 41, 97, 168
  gender differences, 23, 41, 46, 49–50, 52,
    58, 67, 69, 79–82, 99, 103–104, 107,
    108, 125–126, 132–133, 133–134, 135,
    143–144, 149, 169–170, 171, 172,
    184, 187, 189, 212
  hours of viewing, 1, 25, 29
  knowledge before viewing, 3, 9, 22–23,
    29, 31, 35, 38, 39, 41–42, 53–54,
    63–64, 65–66, 66–67, 69, 70, 71, 72,
    86, 98, 113–114, 129, 142–143,
    146–147, 148, 149, 168, 188–191,
    195, 213–214
  knowledge growth after viewing, 7, 9,
    16–21, 32–33, 36–37, 42, 66–67,
    67–68, 68–73, 76–82, 86, 94–97,
    111–113, 130, 141–142, 142–147,
    147–151, 154, 162, 168, 178–182,
    187–191, 191–193, 195, 201, 207,
    209–210, 216
  language fluency differences, 28, 33, 34,
    41, 52, 58, 65, 67, 69, 97, 99, 104–105,
    107, 108, 131, 136, 144, 149–150, 168,
    184–186, 187, 190, 195, 212
  learning at school, 126, 163–164, 215–216
  learning from television, 1–3, 7–9, 9–13,
    15, 16–21, 22–23, 33, 38, 62–63,
    90–91, 91–93, 94–97, 111–113,
    124–128, 129–130, 142–144, 146–147,
    147–151, 151–152, 159–164, 166–167,
    188–191, 195, 196–199, 200–227
  opinions, 18, 37, 44, 73, 76–82, 82–83,
    87–89, 98–100, 131–133, 168,
    170–173, 175, 193, 194, 206
  perceptions, 1, 3, 8, 9–13, 14–16, 20–21,
    43, 45–49, 56, 60, 61–65, 67, 68,
    69–73, 73–76, 76–82, 87, 202,
    203–204, 207
  political knowledge, 17–19
  reading ability and habits, 17–18, 19–20,
    33, 94, 114–117, 127, 132, 146–148,
    154–156, 162
  recall of information, 8, 15, 19, 23, 29,
    33, 36–37, 39, 40, 42, 57–59, 63, 98,
    105–111, 113–124, 124–125, 130–131,
    141–144, 144–146, 147, 151–159,
    160–161, 178–182, 182–186, 194–195,
    204
  samples, 9, 23–24, 28–29, 31–32, 34, 36,
    42, 97, 131, 167–168
  understanding of program formats and
    presentation, 4–5, 9, 14–16, 17, 29,
    33, 37, 50, 51, 56, 98–100, 131,
    135–137, 170–173
  use of television in the home, 25
  viewing amounts and levels, 1, 5–6, 10,
    11, 25, 29, 68, 71, 110–111, 126, 137,
    144–146, 213
  viewing experience before tests, 3, 4–5, 8,
    12, 23, 25–26, 29, 33, 37, 58, 68,
    108–111, 126–127, 137–138, 139–141,
    144–146, 150–151, 160, 161–162, 186,
    195, 212–213
  vocabulary increase, 16

Children's programs, 33–34, 97–98, 131,
    133–137, 137–141, 143–146, 146–147,
    147–151, 151–159, 159–164
Children's Television Workshop, 91–93
Class differences, 28, 41
Cognitive processes, 3, 4–5, 7–9, 14–16,
    16–21, 40–41, 65, 86, 125–126,
    201–202, 202–206, 217–227
Comprehension of program content, 7–9,
    38–41, 62, 62–63, 105, 201
  police drama, 29, 42, 51–55, 57–59, 66,
    68–69, 202–203
  quiz and games shows, 36, 169, 178–179,
    205–206
  science programs, 32, 98, 106–111,
    113–124, 141–147, 160–161, 203–205
Control groups, 30, 77, 79
Crime,
  belief in the prevalence of, 10, 13, 29,
    61–62, 207
  fear of, 14, 61
  on television, 10–13, 13–16, 61–65
  perceptions of, 10–11, 12, 13, 14–16, 48,
    60, 61–65, 76–82, 87
  personal experience of, 11, 13, 48–49, 52,
    58, 63–65, 67–68, 70, 85, 89, 214
  types of, 11, 76–82
  victims of, 11, 13, 48–49, 52, 53, 58,
    67–68, 70, 214
Cultivation theory, 5–6, 10–12, 42

D

Daniels, Paul, 35, 175
Declarative memory, 217–218
"Dick Turpin," 14
Drama programs, 2, 5, 8, 9–16, 24, 26,
    38–59, 60–89, 202–203, 206–209
  police series, 2, 9, 10–15, 26, 26–30,
    38–39, 41–59, 202, 206–209, 213–214
  situation comedies, 24, 56
  soap operas, 11, 24

E

Educational programs, 17, 30–33, 33–34,
    91, 91–93, 93–94
  science programs, 2, 16, 23, 24, 26,
    30–33, 33–34

Educational television, 91–93
Effects and influences, 2–3, 3–7, 14–16,
    16–21, 85–86
  accessibility, 6, 11
  behavioral, 2, 3, 14–15, 166–167
  cognitive, 2, 3–4, 6–7, 14–16, 16–21
  defining viewer's identity, 4, 14–15
  generation effect, 196–199
  informational influences, 2
  mainstreaming, 5–6
  on children's development, 20
  priming, 6–7, 11–12, 65, 207–209
  resonance, 5–6
  socializing, 3, 6, 14–15
  vocabulary increase, 16
"The Electric Company," 92–93, 228, 238
Empathy with characters portrayed, 5, 15,
    39, 44–45, 49–50, 55–56
Enrichment theory, 3
Entertainment programs, 2, 5, 24, 26,
    165–199, 201–202, 205
  drama, 2, 5, 8, 9–16, 24, 26, 38–59,
    60–89, 202–203, 206–209
  quiz and games shows, 2, 24, 26, 35–37,
    165–199, 205, 210
  situation comedies, 24, 56
"Erasmus Microman," 31–33, 97–98,
    101–128
Ethnic minorities,
  audiences, 5–6, 41, 168
  differences, 41, 97, 168
"Every Second Counts," 35–37, 168, 169,
    174–195, 205–206, 216

F

Factor analysis, 73–76, 100–101, 151–152,
    162–163
Factual programs, 2, 16–19, 24, 26, 90–128,
    129–164, 203–205, 209–210
  informational, 2, 26
  news, 17–19, 24, 94, 130
  science programs, 2, 16, 23, 24, 26,
    30–33, 33–34, 90–128, 129–164,
    203–205, 209–210
  sports, 24
Family audiences, 6, 27, 193
Family viewing time, 27
"Feeling Good," 92, 93

G

Games shows, *see* Quiz and games shows
Gender differences, 23, 41, 46, 49–50, 52,
  58, 67, 69, 79–82, 99, 103–104, 107,
  108, 125–126, 132–133, 133–134, 135,
  143–144, 149, 169–170, 171, 172,
  184, 187, 189, 212
Generation effect, 196–199

H

"Hawaii Five-O,", 64
Health education, 92, 93
"Horizon," 94
Hours of viewing, 1, 25, 29

I

IBA, *see* Independent Broadcasting
  Authority
"The Incredible Hulk," 14
Independent Broadcasting Authority, 23,
  24, 96

J

"Juliet Bravo," 27–30, 41–42, 45–59, 66–72,
  202, 207–209, 214, 215

K

"Knock, Knock," 35–37, 168, 169, 174–195,
  205–206, 210, 213, 216
"Know How," 33–34, 131, 132–164, 204,
  215–216
Knowledge before viewing, 3, 9, 22–23, 29,
  31, 35, 38, 39, 41–42, 53–54, 63–64,
  65–66, 66–67, 69, 70, 71, 72, 86, 98,
  113–114, 129, 142–143, 146–147, 148,
  149, 168, 188–191, 195, 200–201,
  213–214
Knowledge growth after viewing tests, 7, 9,
  16–21, 32–33, 36–37, 42, 66–67,
  67–68, 68–73, 76–82, 86, 94–97,
  111–113, 130, 141–142, 142–147,
  147–151, 154–156, 162, 168, 178–182,
  187–191, 191–193, 195, 201, 207,
  209–210, 216

L

Language fluency differences, 28, 33, 34,
  41, 52, 58, 65, 67, 69, 97, 99,
  104–105, 107, 108, 131, 136, 144,
  149–150, 168, 184–186, 187, 190,
  195, 212
Learning,
  at school, 126, 163–164, 215–216
  from television, 1–3, 7–9, 9–13, 15,
    16–21, 22–23, 33, 38, 62–63, 90–91,
    91–93, 94–97, 111–113, 124–128,
    129–130, 142–144, 146–147, 147–151,
    151–152, 159–164, 166–167, 188–191,
    195, 196–199, 200–227

M

Mainstreaming, 5–6
Memory processes and structures, 196–199,
  217–218, 222–226
Mental models, 13, 222–227

N

"The Natural World," 94
News programs, 17–19, 24, 94, 130
Newspapers, 17, 19–20, 33, 94, 114–118,
  127, 146–148, 154–156, 162
Northern Ireland, programs about, 19

O

Opinions, 18, 37, 73
  entertainment programs, 168
  police, 76–82, 82–83, 87–89, 208
  police drama, 44, 206–209
  presenters, 175, 194
  quiz and games shows, 170–173, 175,
    193, 206
  science programs, 98–100, 131–133
"Owl TV," 33–34, 131, 132–164, 204

P

Perceptions, 9–13
  bias, 5
  content of programs, 13, 20–21, 163
  crime, 10–11, 12, 13, 14–16, 48, 60,
    61–65, 76–82, 87

police drama, 14–16, 29, 49–50
police roles, 47–49, 49–50, 51, 55–56, 60,
   61–65, 66–67, 68, 69–73, 73–76,
   76–82, 87, 207
reality, 1, 3, 5, 10, 14–15, 20–21, 29, 43,
   45–49, 55–56, 60, 85, 202
science programs, 100–101, 163, 203–204
social problems, 5, 10
stereotypes, 5, 9–10, 49–50, 51, 87, 126
"Play Bus," 91
"Play School," 91
Police,
   attitudes to, 29, 82–83, 83–86
   beliefs about, 13, 29, 30, 41–42, 46–48,
      89, 207
   characteristics of, 74, 75
   contact with, 41, 48, 58, 63–65, 65–66,
      67–68, 70, 85, 89, 209, 214
   knowledge of, 29, 41, 53–54, 59, 66–67,
      86, 207, 213
   opinions of, 76–82, 82–83, 87–89, 208
   perceptions of, 12, 47–49, 49–50, 51,
      55–56, 60, 61–62, 66–67, 69–73,
      73–76, 76–82, 85–86, 87, 207–209
   portrayal of, 12, 27, 49–50, 51, 209
   stereotypes, 49–50, 51, 87
Police drama, 2, 9, 10–15, 23, 26, 26–30,
   38–39, 41–59, 202, 206–209,
   213–214
   attitudes to, 29, 30, 43–45, 45–50
   opinions of, 44, 206–209
   perceptions of, 11–13, 38–39, 45–50, 58,
      62–63
Political knowledge, 17–19
Portrayal of,
   age, 10
   crime, 10–13, 14–16, 56, 61–65, 76–82
   gender, 10
   police, 12, 14, 27, 49–50, 51, 209
   professions, 10
   race, 10
   reality, 5
   science, 95
   sex, 28
   violence, 10, 14, 28, 47, 48, 56, 62
Presenters, 33, 134–135, 139–140, 169–170,
   173, 175, 194
Priming process, 6–7, 11–12, 65, 207–209
Print media, 17–18, 19–20, 33, 94, 114–117,
   127, 132, 146–148, 154–156, 162
Prizes in quiz and games shows, 35, 165,
   169–170, 170–171, 182–183

Program types,
   children's programs, 33–34, 97–98, 131,
      133–137, 137–141, 143–146, 146–147,
      147–151, 151–159, 159–164
   drama, 2, 5, 8, 9–16, 24, 26, 38–59,
      60–89, 202–203, 206
   educational programs, 17, 30–31, 33–34,
      91–93, 93–94
   entertainment programs, 2, 5, 24, 26,
      165–199, 201–202, 205
   factual programs, 2, 16–19, 24, 26,
      90–128, 129–164, 203–205, 209–210
   see also individual program titles
Programs,
   content, 2, 13, 22–23, 24–25, 26–28, 29,
      33, 35, 41–42, 62–63, 97–98, 98–100,
      171–172, 178, 181, 182–184, 185,
      187, 201
   formats, 2, 24–25, 33, 35–36, 41–42, 50,
      56, 92–93, 98–100, 127, 135–136,
      139–141, 156–159
   presentation style, 31, 33, 34, 45, 50, 51,
      100, 119–124, 135–136, 139–141, 159,
      178
   presenters, 31, 33, 34–35, 134–135,
      139–140, 173, 175, 194
   samples, 2, 24–25, 26–27, 30–31, 33, 35,
      41–42, 97–98, 131, 168
   special effects, 93, 136–137

Q

Qualitative research, 17, 23–26, 161, 163
Quantitative research, 23, 26
Questionnaires, 26, 28–30, 31–33, 34,
   36–37, 41, 42, 45, 65–66, 98,
   130–131, 136, 168–169
Quiz and games shows, 2, 23, 24, 26,
   35–37, 165–199, 205–206, 210
   attitudes to, 170–171, 205–206
   opinions of, 170–173, 175, 193, 206

R

Reading ability and habits, 17–18, 19–20,
   33, 94, 114–117, 127, 132, 146–148,
   154–156, 162
Reality,
   images of, 5
   perceptions of, 1, 3, 5, 9, 10, 14–15, 20–21,
      29, 43, 45–49, 55–56, 60, 85, 202

Recall of information, 8, 15, 19, 23, 29, 33, 36–37, 39, 40, 42, 57–59, 63, 98, 105–111, 113–124, 124–125, 130–131, 141–144, 144–146, 147, 151–159, 160–161, 178–182, 182–186, 194–195, 204

Regression analysis, 113–118, 155–156, 162, 204

Research experiments,
design, 22–23
Experiment 1, 26–30, 38–59, 60–89, 202–203, 206–209
Experiment 2, 30–33, 90–128, 203–205, 209–210
Experiment 3, 33–34, 129–164, 203–205, 209–210
Experiment 4, 35–37, 165–199, 205–206, 210
funding body, 23

Research methodology, 16–18, 23, 26–30, 30–33, 33–34, 35–37, 41–42, 65–66, 97–98, 130–131, 167–169
analysis of variance tests (ANOVAs), 107, 112, 117, 124–125, 148, 151, 154, 180
control groups, 30, 77, 79
design, 22–23
factor analysis, 73–76, 100–101, 151–152, 162–163
group discussions, 25–26
interviews, 25
laboratory procedures, 196
qualitative research, 17, 23–26, 161, 163
quantitative research, 23, 26
questionnaires, 26, 28–30, 31–33, 34, 36–37, 41, 42, 45, 65–66, 98, 130–131, 136, 168–169
regression analysis, 113–118, 155–156, 162, 204
sample children, 9, 23–24, 28–29, 31–32, 34, 36, 42, 97, 131, 167–168
sample programs, 2, 24–25, 26–27, 30–31, 33, 41–42, 97–98, 131, 168
uses and gratifications, 4, 220

Research objectives, 1–3, 22–23, 26–30, 30–33, 33–34, 35–37

Research theory, 1–3, 3–7, 7–9, 9–13, 196–199, 217–227
cultivation theory, 5–6, 10–12, 42
effort hypothesis, 197
enrichment theory, 3
generation effect, 196–199
media dependency theory approach, 95

mental models, 13, 222–227
schema theory, 3–4, 217–218

Resonance, 5–6

"Rockford Files," 64

S

Samples,
children, 9, 23–24, 28–29, 31–32, 34, 36, 42, 97, 131, 167–168
programs, 2, 24–25, 26–27, 30–31, 33, 35, 41–42, 97–98, 131, 168

Schema theory, 3–4, 217–218

School learning, 126, 163–164, 215–216

Science on television, 93–94, 94–97, 124

Science programs, 2, 16, 23, 24, 26, 30–33, 33–34, 90–128, 129–164, 203–205, 209–210
attitudes to, 98–100, 100–101, 131–133, 133–137, 137–138
perceptions of, 100–101, 163, 203–204

Semantic memory, 217

"Sesame Street," 92, 119, 228, 229, 231, 235, 237

Situation comedies, 24, 26

"The Sky at Night," 94

Soap operas, 11, 24

Socializing effects of television, 3, 6, 14–15

Sports programs, 24

"Starsky and Hutch," 14

Stereotypes, 5, 9–10, 49–50, 51, 87, 126

T

Television,
audiences, see Audiences
influence of, 3, 6, 10, 14–15, 20
literacy, 5
programs, see Program types; Programs
as source of information, 2, 10, 16, 17, 90–91, 95–96
as source of learning, 2–3, 5, 8–9, 9–10, 39, 215–216
use in the home, 25
viewing amounts and levels, 25, 29, 68, 71, 110–111, 126, 137, 144–146, 213

"3-2-1," 93–94

"Tomorrow's World," 33–34, 94, 131, 132–164, 204, 213, 215–216

U

Understanding of program formats and presentation, 4–5, 14–16, 17, 45–46
 police drama, 29, 50, 51, 56
 quiz and games shows, 37, 170–173
 science programs, 33, 98–100, 131–133, 135
Uses and gratifications research, 4, 220

V

Videocassette recorders, 25
Viewing,
 amounts and levels, 1, 5–6, 10, 11, 25, 29, 68, 71, 110–111, 126, 137, 144–146, 213
 experience before viewing tests, 3, 4–5, 8, 12, 23, 25–26, 29, 33, 37, 58, 68, 108–111, 126–127, 137–138, 139–141, 144–146, 150–151, 160, 161–162, 186, 195, 212–213
Violence on television, 10–15, 28, 43, 47, 48, 56, 62
Vocabulary increase, 16

W

Watershed (television scheduling time for adult programs), 27